**Praise for *Nightmare in Wichita:*
*The Hunt for the BTK Strangler***

"A very detailed accounting of the individual known BTK murders that began with the Otero family in 1974. From interviews with police, victim family members and associates, and journalists, Beattie has gleaned quite a bit of detail that never got into the newspapers."
—Crimelibrary.com

"Rich in detail and explanation . . . riveting reading."
—*The Wichita Eagle*

"This is a must-have. *Nightmare in Wichita* has set the bar pretty high for any future efforts from other writers." —Huff's Crime Blog

"It's an ugly story, but one that is well worth telling, and Beattie tells it well. The first thing one notices about the book is its respectful treatment of the victims and their families . . . [and] a great deal of respect for the dedication and personal feelings of the officers assigned to the hunt. He shows us the emotional and psychological strain the detectives work under. The book is an excellent analysis of the crimes and investigation. . . . Out of all the true crime books I have in my library, this is one of the, if not *the*, best I have. You will be fascinated."
—David Webb, Media Director for
Unsolved Crimes International

LANGUAGE
OF EVIL

ROBERT BEATTIE

A SIGNET BOOK

SIGNET
Published by New American Library, a division of
Penguin Group (USA) Inc., 375 Hudson Street,
New York, New York 10014, USA
Penguin Group (Canada), 90 Eglinton Avenue East, Suite 700, Toronto,
Ontario M4P 2Y3, Canada (a division of Pearson Penguin Canada Inc.)
Penguin Books Ltd., 80 Strand, London WC2R 0RL, England
Penguin Ireland, 25 St. Stephen's Green, Dublin 2,
Ireland (a division of Penguin Books Ltd.)
Penguin Group (Australia), 250 Camberwell Road, Camberwell, Victoria 3124,
Australia (a division of Pearson Australia Group Pty. Ltd.)
Penguin Books India Pvt. Ltd., 11 Community Centre, Panchsheel Park,
New Delhi - 110 017, India
Penguin Group (NZ), 67 Apollo Drive, Rosedale, North Shore 0632,
New Zealand (a division of Pearson New Zealand Ltd.)
Penguin Books (South Africa) (Pty.) Ltd., 24 Sturdee Avenue,
Rosebank, Johannesburg 2196, South Africa

Penguin Books Ltd., Registered Offices:
80 Strand, London WC2R 0RL, England

First published by Signet, an imprint of New American Library,
a division of Penguin Group (USA) Inc.

First Printing, January 2009
10 9 8 7 6 5 4 3 2 1

Ⓟ REGISTERED TRADEMARK—MARCA REGISTRADA

Printed in the United States of America

PUBLISHER'S NOTE
The publisher does not have any control over and does not assume any
responsibility for author or third-party Web sites or their content.

If you purchased this book without a cover you should be aware that this
book is stolen property. It was reported as "unsold and destroyed" to the
publisher and neither the author nor the publisher has received any payment
for this "stripped book."

The scanning, uploading, and distribution of this book via the Internet or via
any other means without the permission of the publisher is illegal and punish-
able by law. Please purchase only authorized electronic editions, and do not
participate in or encourage electronic piracy of copyrighted materials. Your
support of the author's rights is appreciated.

For
Bruce Cowdrey
and
Katie McGroarty

*Up from Earth's Centre, through the Seventh Gate
I rose, and on the Throne of Saturn sate,
And many a Knot unravell'd by the Road;
But not the Master-knot of Human Fate.*

—*The Rubáiyát of Omar Khayyám*

LANGUAGE
OF EVIL

Author's Note

This book is about a brutal murder. It occurred in a quiet rural area outside a small town in Kansas. The ex-husband murdered his ex-wife during their child custody battle. That part of the story is tragic but commonplace. The family and friends grieve for the victim. The investigators and prosecutors are proud of their work. Is anyone else interested?

Yes.

This case is so interesting that it has drawn nationwide attention. The CBS *48 Hours Mystery* program devoted an hour to the story. Court TV's *The Investigators* devoted an hour to the story. The National Geographic Channel featured this case in a March 2008 program titled "The Science of Interrogation."

What is so interesting?

For one thing, this case may include the greatest recorded linguistic battle between a homicide detective and a homicide suspect in police history. That story comprises much of this book.

In an earlier case the lead detective, son of a renowned homicide detective, was so skilled in interrogation that he had obtained a confession in a case in which the evidence was so thin that without a confession there would not have been a prosecution. In this case he had a team of trained detectives, including one

who knew how to read body language—the science
of kinesics—to monitor the interrogation over closed-
circuit television. The team provided the lead detective with feedback and advice during the interview.

The suspect was a brilliant and arrogant professor of
linguistics. He declined to hire an attorney. He talked,
bantered, soliloquized, dialogued, and debated with
the detectives for ten hours. His ex-wife had just been
murdered, he was the suspect, yet during his interrogation he said he was having fun with this from a *CSI*
perspective.

The detectives were convinced he was the murderer,
but they did not have the direct evidence needed to
arrest him. A year passed. They still had not obtained
evidence that tied him directly to the murder. But,
convinced of his guilt, they arrested him.

The case against Tom Murray was circumstantial. It
was a hard case, not an easy case. There was no smoking gun. The evidence of his guilt was vague, ambiguous, and indirect. The evidence was like the famous
illusion that looks like a young woman or an old
woman depending on perspective. Or an M. C. Escher
drawing in which one sees what one looks for. Even
the hard scientific evidence was controversial. Whether
or not the suspect's DNA was at the crime scene was
a question debated before the Kansas Supreme Court.

The stakes were high. Legal observers were skepti-
cal of a conviction without direct proof. Nevertheless,
the jury voted for conviction. There was no proof that
he'd done it, but there was no doubt that he'd done it.

When the case ended, the state supreme court affirmed the jury's verdict. The brilliant, arrogant university professor Tom Murray had murdered his
beautiful ex-wife, attorney Carmin Ross. Murray's
sentence was life imprisonment.

Dr. Thomas Edward Murray, Ph.D., was the author
or coauthor of nine books, an internationally known

linguist, and a tenured professor of English at Kansas State University. He gave the police permission to search his computer only hours after they found his ex-wife's body. He told the police that they would find he had researched murder. He said he was not researching how he could murder, but was working on a crime script. A year later, in his trial, his attorneys made the same argument.

On October 8, 2003, the month before his ex-wife was murdered, at 3:11 P.M., using the Yahoo search engine, Professor Murray entered the query "How to murder someone and not get caught." A host of similar Internet inquiries continued until the murder occurred on November 13, 2003. Then they stopped.

Tom Murray said that he thought he could write and sell crime stories to Hollywood, including to the number one crime fiction television program *CSI*. That was why he was researching murder, he claimed. That was why he searched a *CSI* script Web site, he claimed. Murray's defense attorney, in closing argument, declared, "Those Web searches are the demonstration [defense attorney points to his head] of a mind, looking at real interesting strange twists, like odorless gases and poisoned fish and things that related to a *CSI* episode, not this crime."

Is such a claim plausible?

Yes.

Famous fictional stories exist that describe in brilliant detail exactly how such a thing could happen. Patricia Highsmith's 1965 novel *The Story-Teller* focuses on an author who is writing a fictional story for a television crime program about a man who murders his wife. The author writes many notes about this murder. Then his wife disappears. He becomes a murder suspect. From the author's notebook, it appears he kept a detailed handwritten journal of the crime. Later, his wife's body is found. The police and public interpret his actions as those of a killer. However, the reader knows the author's wife left him for another man and then, in remorse, threw herself off a cliff. The author was writing a novel, not preparing for murder. In that fictional story, the husband who looked guilty was innocent.

In the real world, is this what happened in the Tom Murray case?

The police, prosecution, judge, jury, and state supreme court said, "No."

In March 2005, in lead prosecutor Angela Wilson's closing argument to Murray's jury, she shouted, "The only *CSI* script Murray had anything to do with is this real one."

The prosecution's argument is not Highsmith's *The Story-Teller*; it is closer to Dostoyevsky's classic novel *Crime and Punishment*. In *Crime and Punishment*, a brilliant, arrogant writer murders an inconvenient woman he believes should be dead. He believes that he is the best judge of whether the woman should live or die. He believes that he knows how to escape conviction, but he is wrong. In the end, he confesses his guilt.

The evidence in Murray's real-world case was well preserved and well presented. The trial court judge, Robert Fairchild, is not only as respected as any judge in Kansas but has taught every other judge in Kansas a program titled "Not in My Court." It emphasizes legal safeguards and practices to help judges avoid wrongful and mistaken criminal convictions in hard cases, like this one. Murray's jury included three people with earned Ph.D.s. All were literate and intelligent. "He [Murray] had as close to a jury of his peers as it is possible to have," the judge told the author.

A note on accuracy: Helen is not the name of the child born to Tom Murray and Carmin Ross. Although her true name and image were repeatedly broadcast on the CBS *48 Hours* program (with the apparent approval of her family), and her real first and last names were used in news reports, she is a little girl, a victim, who has been adopted because of a hideous tragedy, and I just didn't feel right about using her real name in this book.

The report of Tom Murray's interrogation in Riley County Police Department interview room #2 is based on the transcript provided by the Douglas County court clerk's office and the author's viewing of video of that interrogation with Detective Brad Schlerf. Some portions of the interview were omitted from this book—some because they were repetitive, some for other reasons (for example, Tom Murray's Social Security number was omitted). A very few portions were redacted. For example, in one place for clarity I provide a proper name instead of a descriptive term.

This book is also based on interviews with friends, family, and colleagues of Carmin Ross and Tom Murray; comments and conclusions by various witnesses, investigators, analysts, and the judge; the jury verdict; news media reports (sometimes competing news media outlets reported different facts of the same event); research via the Internet and books; an audio recording of prosecutor Angela Wilson's closing argument; and the author's personal observations, which included driving the routes the prosecution claimed the professor drove between Manhattan, Kansas, and Lawrence, Kansas, personally watching the oral arguments in the professor's case in the Kansas Supreme Court, and later reading the court's written decision, and interviews conducted by phone, by mail, by e-mail, and in person. Several people promised interviews but then broke their promises. Others, including Tom Murray, never replied to my messages.

I write in chapter 8 that in their first meeting Detective Doug Woods squeezed Tom Murray's hand as hard as he could to see if Murray would wince in pain. My source is my September 4, 2007, in-person interview with Doug Woods in the Expresso Café located in the Borders bookstore, 700 New Hampshire Street, Lawrence, Kansas. I wrote notes and the interview was audio-recorded. Murder victim Carmin Ross had thirty wounds, either blunt-trauma or stab wounds, to her head, neck, and torso, and defensive bruises on her forearms and wrist. Woods told me that he squeezed Murray's hand as hard as he could because he thought that if Murray had hit Carmin Ross more than thirty times the day before, Murray's hands might still be hurting. Woods explained what he did, his motive and intent, his state of mind, what happened afterward, and how he interpreted it.

On June 1, 2006, Pittsburg, Kansas, psychologist Dr. Julie Allison, coauthor of *Rape: The Misunderstood Crime* and an expert on research into after-death communication, was the first person to tell me I should write this book. During a telephone call Dr. Allison summarized for me the events related in this book and persuaded me to look into this story. She knew I was looking for something to write after *Nightmare in Wichita: The Hunt for the BTK Strangler*.

Minutes after Dr. Allison told me I should write about this case, I spoke by phone with James Preston Girard, prizewinning author of true crime (*Adams Road*) and crime fiction (*The Late Man*). Although Jim Girard lives near Lawrence, Kansas, where the murder related in this book took place, when I asked him if he had any ideas about what I should write next, he suggested that I write this book. That was generous of him. Thanks, Jim. I hope someday to return the favor.

Then I called lead detective Doug Woods and prosecutor Angela Wilson. After brief in-person interviews I started writing a book proposal.

Michael Hauge teaches that there are five turning points in a traditional fiction story. When I outlined this nonfiction story I was astonished to see that, although the key characters come into the story at different points and have different time lines, they all have these same five turning points, a case of life imitating art.

As are all true crime stories, this story is a tragedy. It ends with the hope that everyone involved can cope with their scars and live with their ghosts and that the reader will never have to contend with the challenges that these people faced.

Whatever the cosmic truth, the legal truth is that Professor Murray was convicted of murdering his ex-wife. He was sentenced to spend the rest of his life in prison. Most people who consented to talk with the author said that they think that Murray brutally murdered his ex-wife and that he used his great intellect and every rhetorical tool in his vast linguistic repertoire to persuade people otherwise.

The jury has rendered its verdict, as have the courts. You, the reader, will reach your own verdict.

ACT I

How did he succeed in creating the illusion that he did not kill? It is the task of the detective to strip away the "fake reality" created by the murderer.

—Carolyn Wheat, *How to Write Killer Fiction*

1

Joslyn had prepared the meeting rooms for Carmin's visit with joy. It was Thursday afternoon, November 13, 2003.

The small consultation conversation room was comfortable and inviting. A soft, folded towel was on the table. Carmin would rest both of her wrists on it. Joslyn would palpate and interpret Carmin's wrist pulses. She would observe Carmin's tongue. Then, she would listen to all Carmin had to say about how she was feeling and what was going on in her life.

There were four chairs: two straight-back chairs for the time they sat across from each other at the intake table with the towel and two comfortable chairs. There they would sit, sip tea, and talk for a while before going into the treatment room. Each room had been professionally composed, painted and decorated. The temperature, gentle lighting, soft music and inspiring aromas were correct. They would be altered when and as appropriate. The needles were arranged. The treatment table and towels were warm and ready. Joslyn was ready. Joslyn Dugas, in Kansas City, Missouri, was a licensed acupuncturist and practitioner of Chinese medicine.

Carmin and Joslyn had met when Carmin had sought one of Joslyn's regionally famous shiatsu sessions. Their rapport was instant. Joslyn now also provided acupuncture for both Carmin and Carmin's ex-husband, Tom Murray. Tom continued treatment with Joslyn because of the stress and tension he had felt during and after the divorce.

Joslyn practices what in the USA is considered an alternative healing practice, though in China a billion people consider Western medicine the alternative medical practice. Over thousands of years, Chinese medicine's philosophy and effectiveness have built a devoted following.

Joslyn was looking forward to seeing Carmin. She kept looking out her office's third-floor windows for Carmin's green SUV. Carmin was late for her appointment, and Joslyn began to wonder why. Carmin's tardiness was becoming conspicuous because it was so unlike her. She had never been late without a call, nor had she ever missed an appointment. According to Joslyn, Carmin Ross was considerate, kind, and thoughtful.

Joslyn Dugas looked out her office window again. She listened for Carmin's footsteps. The Kansas City weather was cold, a bit blustery but clear at two in the afternoon. The weather should not impede traffic. But there was still no sign of Carmin.

Joslyn and Carmin had met almost eight years earlier through a professional relationship. Carmin was still Joslyn's business client, but now they were more than that—they were also good friends. They had regular meetings to socialize over coffee or a meal. Whenever Carmin had to fly through Kansas City's international airport for her frequent trips to and from San Diego, she often spent the night at Joslyn's home. This trip to the Kansas City airport was so common that Carmin had discussed becoming Joslyn's roommate. Because of their friendship, they shared many of the intimate details of their lives. For example, Joslyn was the first person to know that Carmin was pregnant. Only after her talk with Joslyn did Carmin tell her husband.

Since they were friends, Joslyn was willing to wait for Carmin, but she was expecting another client after Carmin. If Carmin was too late, there would be a conflict. Perhaps Carmin was stuck in traffic. Or, Joslyn thought, maybe a last-minute custody meeting had come up.

Joslyn hoped that Carmin would arrive soon. She hoped that whatever caused the delay would be reason for a laugh, a smile, and a funny story from Carmin. Joslyn trusted that Carmin must have run into a situation that needed her immediate attention.

Time passed. Joslyn sat. She stood. She reviewed Carmin's file. She was reminded that they had met on April 4, 1996, introduced by Joslyn's client Angela Hayes, another of Carmin's close friends. Joslyn reheated the tea in the pot. She paced a little. Again, she looked out the windows. She wondered what could have happened to Carmin. Two fifteen came. Carmin still did not arrive.

Carmin had three telephones. She had a cell phone with a San Diego, California, area code because she spent so much time there with her fiancé. She had a cell phone with a northeast Kansas area code. She also had a home phone landline at her residence in Douglas County, outside of Lawrence.

Reasoning that Carmin had started to drive to Kansas City, Joslyn first called Carmin's Kansas cell phone and left a message. Then, thinking that perhaps there was a problem with that phone and therefore Carmin was using her California cell phone, Joslyn called and left a message on that phone as well.

Finally, thinking that there could be reasons she

would not answer or check messages on either cell phone, Joslyn called Carmin's home number. There was no answer, but Joslyn did not leave a message.

Joslyn waited thirty minutes, becoming more concerned as to what could be causing Carmin's delay. At one point, she thought that maybe the doorbell wasn't working. She checked it. It was fine, but still no Carmin.

At 2:45 P.M., Joslyn again called Carmin.

At 2:53 P.M. Joslyn called Carmin's home number and left a message.

Joslyn was concerned about Carmin and wanted to know what had happened, but she persuaded herself that Carmin had merely been detained. She concluded that a phone call explaining her tardiness was imminent. She busied herself with the next client's arrival and looked forward to hearing Carmin's apologetic voice.

2

After their recent decision to have their wedding on Thursday, November 27, 2003, Larry Lima and his fiancée, Carmin Ross, spoke by phone a couple of hours each day. They had a lot to discuss. Plus, their love was in full bloom. Their frequent conversations made the impossible seventeen-hundred-mile distance between them bearable. They hated being apart. Larry, a social worker, lived in San Diego, California.

San Diego was the eighth most populous city in America, an urban, twenty-four-hour Southern California metropolis that was home to the largest military naval fleet in the world, to the famous SeaWorld, and to the sometimes Super Bowl contender NFL football team the San Diego Chargers. The Pacific Ocean's calmest region was San Diego's western border. Its Mediterranean climate was temperate and mild year-round. It almost never stormed there. Larry Lima loved it. On their visits, so did Carmin and her almost five-year-old daughter, Helen.

Lawrence, Kansas, in contrast, was a small town in the center of the nation. It was about as far away from an ocean as it is possible to be in America. The Google Earth online map of the world located Lawrence at its center. In Lawrence, known for the University of Kansas and its NCAA champion or championship-contender basketball, football, and track teams, during the academic year the university students outnumbered the natives. Here, the flat Great Plains had stormy extremes of heat and cold. It was baking hot in the summer, sometimes punctuated by oppressively high humidity when soaking storms rose up from the Gulf of Mexico. In the winter, the cold winds swept directly down from the arctic and brought paralyzing blizzards. Each spring, ravaging tornadoes sent folks fleeing to their basements for shelter.

Though they lived in places that could scarcely have been more different, Larry and Carmin were so much alike that they had determined to live the rest of their lives together whatever the weather. They were the enviable epitome of a happy couple in love. It was a joy to see them together. Carmin's family and friends said she was just glowing, absolutely glowing. They were so happy for her.

Larry planned to move to Lawrence after the wedding, at least until Carmin's child custody situation with her ex-husband, Tom Murray, was resolved. Carmin and Larry expected that it would not be long before Carmin and Helen would move to San Diego. They all loved San Diego and were excited about becoming a family and living there together.

Larry was busy all morning on November 13 with a medical procedure. He knew Carmin was going to her appointment with Joslyn (who did not yet know the wedding date had been set—Carmin was to tell her today), but he called at 12:40 P.M., a time when he thought Carmin would be home before she left for Kansas City. She did not answer. Maybe she had left early to run some errands on the way. He left a message on her answering machine.

He called her on her cell phone. She did not answer. He left a message.

He made several phone calls to Carmin on Thursday. None of his calls were answered or returned. At 6:57 P.M. he left another message on her home phone.

Larry wondered what could have happened. Could Carmin be having second thoughts about the marriage? Could she have had an accident? Where could she be?

Carmin's friend Angela Hayes lived in Manhattan, Kansas, an hour and a half from Lawrence, but she still spoke with Carmin almost daily. Angela called Carmin and was surprised to hear the answering machine. Angela left a message in the evening. She left several messages. None of her calls were returned.

Early Thursday evening Carmin's mother called from Lapel, Indiana. She had been expecting Carmin to call her. She thought Carmin must be busy with wedding and travel plans and might have forgotten to call. She left a message on Carmin's answering machine.

Late Thursday, Joslyn left another message on Carmin's home phone. Joslyn did not know what happened to Carmin and the uncertainty was distressing, but for now there was nothing to do.

Larry Lima continued to call Carmin until after midnight on Thursday. Then he called again on Friday morning. She did not answer her phone or return his many calls.

On Friday morning Larry called the only hospital in Lawrence, Lawrence Memorial Hospital, to see whether she was there. She was not. Larry was becoming frantic worrying about Carmin's welfare.

At noon on Friday he called Joslyn. Had Carmin

arrived for her Thursday appointment? When Larry learned she had not, he told Joslyn, "I'm going to call the police."

Joslyn and Angela Hayes spoke with each other by phone. Neither had heard from Carmin. Angela left another message on Carmin's home phone.

At 12:56 P.M., Larry called the Lawrence police.

3

Larry Lima called the Douglas County sheriff's office, explained the situation, and asked that an officer go to Carmin's home to check on her. Because of their upcoming wedding, he told the dispatcher, they spoke often and at length. He emphasized that Carmin's failure to answer her phone or call for the past twenty-four hours, and the fact that she never arrived at her appointment with Joslyn the previous day in Kansas City were dramatic and worrisome changes in Carmin's routine. (Investigators would later determine that Carmin and Larry had last spoken by phone from 10:02 P.M. Wednesday, November 12, until 12:30 A.M. on Thursday, November 13.)

At this point it was still reasonable to believe that there might be some conventional explanation for Carmin's absence. Sometimes as the wedding approached, prospective brides became overburdened. Maybe Carmin was simply too busy or just wanted a break from talking. But he worried that she might have had an accident at home. Lima was assured that an officer would go to her home to check on her welfare.

The address Lima gave was in a picturesque rural area northwest of Lawrence, outside the city limits in

Douglas County, near one of the few private resorts in the Great Plains.

Most of Kansas is flat as a table and there is no "scenery." However, in the nineteenth century, the settlement that became the city of Lawrence was built in a hilly region on an uncommonly great hill, a mountain by Kansas standards. In August 1854, abolitionists from Massachusetts built a settlement on this hill so they could see approaching proslavery raiders. They named the hill Mount Oread, and the city was named Lawrence for Amos Lawrence, the principal Boston financier for "the New England Emigrant Aid Company," which had paid for and organized the abolitionists' expedition.

The Lawrence immigrants' stated goal was political: to vote for Kansas to be a free state rather than a slave state when it entered the Union. (One of Lawrence's two high schools is named Free State High School.) The siege of Lawrence by proslavery forces from Missouri started December 1, 1855. John Brown and his antislavery sons then came to defend Lawrence. There was no peace in Lawrence for ten years. This was the era of "Bleeding Kansas." Lawrence was first sacked in the spring of 1856. Proslavery ruffians harassed all antislavery immigrants and killed some. In August 1860 most of Lawrence was burned and destroyed by Quantrill's Raiders. When the Civil War officially started in April 1861 with the Confederate attack on Fort Sumter, South Carolina, Lawrence had already been in combat for more than five years.

Geologists say this scenic, hilly region exists because 600,000 years ago a five-hundred-foot glacier from the north stopped in northeast Kansas and deposited these foothills. The deposits also changed the flow of the Kansas River, moving the river northeast and leaving a natural lake, Lake View Lake, just northwest of Carmin's home. Surrounded by hills and crisscrossed with rows of trees for windbreaks, here was a beautiful farmed valley with soil as rich as chocolate cake.

Carmin lived in a rented farmhouse in an isolated spot in this valley. It was beige and solid—a home. A green and white government sign identified the road on which Carmin lived on as a SCENIC DRIVE—a rarity in Kansas.

Checking on a citizen's welfare was a routine assignment, and there seemed to be no urgency. The law enforcement dispatcher sent a message to two patrol officers of the Douglas County Sheriff's Department. They were to go to this peaceful, pastoral setting to check on forty-year-old Carmin Ross at 1860 East 1150 Road. Two patrol officers in separate cars, Sergeant Steve Grammer and Deputy Rita Fulton-Mays, completed their existing assignments and arrived at Carmin's about one o'clock.

It would not be long before Larry Lima had his tragic answer.

In the early afternoon of Friday, November 14, 2003, Douglas County deputy sheriff Doug Woods was having a bad day at the end of a bad week. It had been filled with minor but constant irritations and setbacks. A pile of tedious paperwork remained on his desk. He had a headache. Detective Woods decided that he was going to tell his supervisor he was going home a little early. He was looking forward to a nap, which he expected would clear his headache. Tomorrow he would go deer hunting with fellow detective Scott Bonham. They had been friends since high school. Woods started packing his briefcase. His workweek was over, he thought.

Just then, Deputy Woods's immediate supervisor, Lieutenant Ken Massey, ordered him to investigate a report of a dead body found at a "check the welfare" call. That stopped him cold. He closed his eyes. He sighed. Even if this was a death by natural causes, it meant an incredible number of thankless hours investigating, then more hours filling out mountains of paperwork. In addition, he might have to tell a family member of the death. He had done that twenty times before. It was a dreadful duty. He paused to collect himself. His head was throbbing. Woods would go to the crime scene with Detective Jay Armbrister. Armbrister would drive.

Woods walked out of his second-floor office and went downstairs to the employee exit near the parking lot south of the building. He put his briefcase in the trunk of an unmarked green Ford Crown Victoria sedan. There was a police radio in the car, but he used his cell phone to advise the dispatcher that he was en route to the call on East 1150 Road. There would be citizens and news media listening to calls on a police scanner, and until he had control of the scene and an understanding of the cause of death, he did not want a crowd to gather. They could obliterate tire marks or otherwise disturb evidence.

Although some streets had names, many streets in Lawrence and in Douglas County retained the numerical designations that they had been given when surveyors plotted the roads. Most of Lawrence and Douglas County had been developed in a grid, with arterial roads development on the mile or half-mile square.

Detectives Woods and Armbrister drove from downtown, in eastern Lawrence, a short distance north, and then west on Sixth Street, which was also Kansas Highway 40. When they arrived in western Lawrence, they turned north on Kasold Street. Sixth and Kasold was a busy intersection with a strip mall on the southwest corner and Lawrence's only twenty-four-hour pharmacy, a Walgreens, on the southeast corner.

Once they turned north on Kasold from that intersection, they drove into a residential neighborhood
road lined with trees and wooden fences. The transition from a residential area to a rural, sparsely popu-
lated area was sudden.

They drove north for two miles, crossing a bridge
over the Kansas Turnpike, then turned west on North
1800 Road, which is also known as West Lakeview
Road, but known to locals as the "Trucker's Turnpike." A heavy industrial area to the east drew a
steady stream of truckers hauling various food prod-
ucts to the Del Monte complex and grains to the railroad exchange. Then they drove a half mile to East
1150 Road, which runs north-south. As they turned
north, they saw that a single farmhouse was on the
west side of the road near the intersection. A big yellow dog ran into the road and barked at them. The
1860 address was half a mile farther north, on the east
side of the road.

Woods knew the area from his hunting. The nearest
neighbor to 1860 was a couple of football fields distant, off the road and behind another row of trees,
and the next nearest neighbors were about half a mile
to the north and south. To the west there were no
neighbors for more than a mile and for a half mile to
the east.

It was a wonderful home for seclusion and privacy,
but its isolation meant that if there had been foul play
no one would have been nearby to hear it. And,
Woods thought, this being the autumn hunting season,
if a gunshot were heard, it would not be memorable.

The drive from the Douglas County Law Enforcement Center, located downtown, in the most urban
area of Lawrence, to this isolated rural farmhouse was
only six miles. It did not take long to arrive anywhere
in or near Lawrence.

As Woods approached the address, he saw that wal-

nut and oak trees surrounded it. Almost all their
leaves had fallen. The wheat had been cut, and the
stubble fields that surrounded the house were bor-
dered by the perfect rows of trees, planted by careful
design. Few trees are native to Kansas. When the Eu-
ropean settlers arrived, they discovered that the fertile
prairies of native grasses were ripe for tilling and
planting, but strong winds or wildfires destroyed most
nascent trees. Rows of strong trees were planted and
protected as they grew to form windbreaks around
crops and farmsteads. The trees around Carmin Ross's
home were not here by accident of nature, and they
were not ornamental; they were purposeful, func-
tional, and premeditated.

Woods saw two marked Douglas County patrol cars
in the gravel drive and two officers standing outside
the old farmhouse. They parked behind the cars, following their tracks. If there were tire tracks or footprints to be examined, they would not add to them.

Woods looked at the house. It was a big, sturdy,
nine-room farmhouse with a basement and living
space in a third-floor attic. Many people in the community knew this particular house because it had a
well-known architectural history. It was a nearly one-
hundred-year-old model, slightly modified and up-
dated, of a Sears Roebuck kit home. Ordered from
the Sears catalog, from 1908 to 1940, 100,000 of these
kit homes, in 447 different styles, were shipped all
over the country. The exterior of this home, called an
American Foursquare, was very similar to the old 1908
Chelsea 111 model, but its interior was different. This
"Honor-bilt" home, of the finest materials then available, arrived via railroad car, precut and with plenty
of nails. It was hauled by horse-drawn wagon to the
site and built as if it was a barn-raising party. It was
a lovely, strong home, built to withstand Kansas
weather, with a big front porch, in a beautiful location.

Woods saw that the backyard, southeast of the house, had a children's swing set with a slide.

Detective Woods asked Sergeant Steve Grammer for a report.

"There's a dead woman inside. She looks like she was beaten and stabbed to death in a furious fight. There is evidence of a struggle in the living room. There is blood everywhere," Grammer said.

Grammer had arrived about one o'clock and knocked on the front door. There was no answer. He looked in the window. Because it was dark inside the house it was hard to see, but once his eyes adjusted he saw on the floor what he believed was a person's knee in blue jeans sticking around a corner.

"I thought that it could be someone with a medical problem," he said.

At that time, Sergeant Grammer identified himself by shouting, but there was no movement. He put on elastic gloves. He did not want to leave fingerprints if this was a crime scene. He started trying the doors and windows. The back door was unlocked and he gained entry. He continued to shout to identify himself as "sheriff's department" as he walked through the house. He found the knee—it belonged to a dead woman. He checked for vital signs—breathing and heartbeat—but there were none. Rigor mortis had already started.

"Take me in the way you went in," Woods said.

They entered through the back door. They passed through a "mudroom"—commonplace in rural Kansas homes—then the kitchen, dining room, and then arrived in the living room.

Woods, an experienced detective, took in the scene. The woman was lying on her back, faceup, eyes closed. She had been beaten and stabbed. The front of her throat was slashed open and mutilated. She had been dead for maybe a day. In chemical terms, a human

body is naturally base, salty, and has a slightly salty
smell. But at death a body starts becoming acidic. The
classic smell of death is that of vinegar. At the end of
three days the body begins to putrefy. This body did
not have the stink of decay, but only the odor of
death.

This was a homicide. The fight had been all over
the living room. Potted plants were knocked over. The
coffee table was overturned. A candleholder was broken, the candle near the body. Blood was on the walls.
Blood was spattered on a Spiegel catalog lying on the
floor. The woman had tried to escape, but near the
front door she had stopped moving. Her blood had
pooled there, indicating that she was motionless and
bleeding. A blood smear trail showed that her killer
had then dragged her away from the door and around
a corner, where it would be difficult to see her from
the front door or window.

The woman was barefoot. She was wearing blue
jeans and a casual sweater. Her shirt and sweater had
been pulled up so that her abdomen was exposed. A
basket of folded laundry was near her. It appeared to
Woods that the basket had been set down, not thrown.

Detective Woods's first impression was that this was
a case of a residential burglary gone bad. He surmised
that near the front door the woman had interrupted
a burglar and they had struggled. She had fought hard
for her life, and her killer had a hard time subduing
her. It appeared that the woman was hit on the head
with a blunt instrument and went down. There was a
struggle around the living room as she tried to scramble away on her hands and knees. The potted plants
and the coffee table were knocked over, picture
frames were knocked off the wall, and fragile items
were broken. Blood was on the walls, carpet, and
ceiling.

Woods thought that the burglar had panicked and

killed her. The killer may have been a young man looking for money or other valuables to buy drugs. They might find the killer's fingerprints, DNA, or other identifying evidence.

They would have to check records and photos to create an inventory of her valuables, then conduct a careful search to see what the burglar had stolen that was worth this woman's life. If it was unique jewelry, or somehow identifiable, and the killer had immediately sold or pawned it, they might be able to quickly trace it back to the killer, or at least obtain the killer's description.

On the other hand, the many blows, the furious fight, the cut throat suggested that this could be a crime of passion. Woods thought she might have been murdered by someone angry at her.

Detective Woods telephoned the dispatcher, declared the site a crime scene, and called for the M-Squad. Woods was thinking that they would need a warrant when he looked carefully around the room. Although most of the furniture and decorations were in rich wood and earth tones, the carpet and couch were robin's-egg blue. Near the entrance was a rectangular woven throw rug of Native American design with horizontal lines in dramatic brown and red colors. The plants were green. The fireplace was made of red brick. Quality lace drapes hung at the windows. Here and there, the speckled blood trails formed a dark pattern on the off-white walls. Woods later told the author that at first he'd thought the blood spatter pattern on the wall was part of its design.

Then he saw the framed photos of a woman and child, a little girl. He thought the woman pictured was the dead woman. The mother and child in the photos were heartbreakingly beautiful. He surmised that the girl was her daughter and, because of the swing set in the yard, that she probably lived here.

Woods's next thought was alarming. "Where is the little girl?" he asked.

They would need a court-ordered search warrant to seek evidence. But they could do a rapid search because they believed the little girl might be in need of emergency assistance. Had she hidden from her mother's attacker and become trapped somewhere?

Woods learned that Grammer had already done the search. They had found the little girl's room in the third-floor attic. It was decorated for fun and filled with stuffed animals, toys, and children's books. The girl was not found on the premises.

They were still alarmed. Had the little girl been abducted? What had happened to her?

4

Because none of the small communities in the area have the resources necessary to handle major cases, when a major crime, such as murder, does occur, the law enforcement entities combine their resources to form a major case squad, or M-Squad. Together, they can handle most any criminal investigation. If they need even more help, they can call on the assistance of the Kansas Bureau of Investigation. After the search warrant was obtained, the M-Squad team would begin working.

After a couple of hours of paperwork, a detective arrived at the house with a search warrant signed by a judge. Douglas County coroner Dr. Erik Mitchell arrived to work the crime scene. At about the same time the CSI squad from the Lawrence Police Department arrived. They would be at the crime scene through Sunday, then would depart but would return for continued forensic testing for two weeks.

Undersheriff Major Ken McGovern, Lieutenant Ken Massey, and Detective Scott Bonham arrived. Other investigating officers soon followed. The patrol officers blocked the driveway entrance with a marked car so that only authorized persons could enter. The entire house was circled by bright yellow police tape

that warned in bold black letters SHERIFF LINE—DO
NOT CROSS.

Detective Doug Woods was a big, rugged man, a
cop from a family of cops, but when he graduated
high school he did not want work in law enforcement.
At age eighteen he went to work milking cows. After
tiring of the early hours, he applied to the fire department. He became a jail deputy, then a deputy sheriff,
and then a detective. Now thirty-five, with gray showing in his crew-cut hair, somewhere along the way he
had become what his father, brothers, uncle, and closest friends had also become: a cop, heart and soul.

He felt the normal human emotions after seeing the
body of a beautiful woman, apparently a mother, who
had been brutally murdered. He was angry. He was
sad. He knew that soon it would be his duty to tell
several of her family and friends about her death.
After delivering the bad news, he would have to wait
until they overcame their initial grief so that he could
question them for his investigation. He did not yet
know the whereabouts or condition of the little girl,
and he was very concerned about her. He was human,
and in his coming interactions with the woman's family and friends, he would behave professionally, so-
berly, and humanely.

However, as a cop, he was invigorated. He was
charged. He was alive. His brain's endorphins had
killed the pain of his headache. He didn't expect others who were not cops to understand, but he was now
a hunter. The hunt was his entire focus. The killer was
his prey. His primary motivation, his feeling, what
made his heart pound now, was the chase.

He had planned to go hunting this weekend, and he
would. But he would not be hunting deer. He would
be hunting a killer.

*   *   *

Detective Woods conferred with the other members of his team. Information came rapidly.

They had run the tag on the vehicle in the driveway. It was registered to Carmin Ross.

The mail in the mailbox was addressed to Carmin Ross.

The photos in the home, and the woman's driver's license found in her purse, appeared to be of the woman found on the floor—Carmin Ross.

Searching through the home, they found documents bearing the name of Carmin Ross and her daughter.

They had listened to telephone messages on the answering machine in the home. The messages were for Carmin.

The coroner's office would later have to do a positive identification, but the officers on the scene believed that the woman was Carmin Ross.

Sheriff Rick Trapp, a former FBI agent, arrived. He explained that the call to check the welfare of Carmin Ross had come from a Mr. Larry Lima of San Diego, California. Lima had told the dispatcher that he and Carmin Ross were to be married after Thanksgiving and then he was coming to live in Lawrence. Lima had become worried because Ross had not answered her phone for more than a day. They had been speaking several times a day. The dispatcher had verified that the calls had indeed come from San Diego.

Sheriff Trapp would make the call to Lima from his car, using a speakerphone. Woods sat in the passenger seat and started his recorder. The sheriff called Lima's number in San Diego. Their conversation was short. Sheriff Trapp told Lima that he regretted to inform him that Carmin Ross had died.

Lima made a sound, and then expressed grief. He sounded genuine.

He asked, "What happened?"

The sheriff said that they would have to get back to him later with details, but they had a question. They had seen photos in the home of Miss Ross with a little girl. Who was that?

Lima explained that the girl was Carmin's almost five-year-old daughter, Helen. Carmin shared custody of Helen with her ex-husband, Thomas Murray. Murray was an English professor at Kansas State University. Helen should be in Manhattan, Kansas, with Tom.

If Carmin had been murdered, Lima said, they should look at Tom.

The sheriff did not respond to that, but said that he had to make other notifications and terminated the call.

The sheriff and Detective Woods looked at each other.

Detectives quickly verified by phone that Lima had been at work in San Diego all week, except for a medical appointment on Thursday morning. They could find no evidence that Lima had traveled to Lawrence that week. Sheriff Trapp and Detective Woods believed that Lima would not have had time to travel from San Diego to Lawrence and back. He was not a good suspect in Carmin's death.

Lima had said they should look at Tom as a suspect.

As Woods went back into the house, he heard Angela Hayes calling again. Earlier the officers had heard her voice when they listened to Carmin's answering machine messages. Hayes had left several messages for Carmin. They inferred from the phone messages, and the information in Carmin's address book and appointment book, that Angela was a friend who babysat for Helen.

It was Doug Woods's case, and he had to make the hard decisions. He made a judgment call and decided to answer the telephone and speak with Angela.

Woods said, "Hello."

Angela paused, and then said, "I want to speak with Carmin."

Woods asked, "Who is this?"

Angela answered, "This is Angela . . . Angela Hayes. Who is *this*?"

"This is Detective Doug Woods, Douglas County Sheriff's Department," Woods answered.

"I want to talk with Carmin," Angela demanded.

Woods and Angela Hayes had a go-round while Woods tried not to give any information and Angela became increasingly insistent. She demanded that she be allowed to speak with Carmin. She had been calling since yesterday and was unsuccessful in reaching Carmin. She was in Manhattan, Kansas, about ninety miles away. The route between their homes would later prove important.

Woods decided that he should tell Angela that Carmin was dead. Angela might be able to throw more light on the situation if she would cooperate, but it was clear that she was not going to cooperate until she was allowed to speak with Carmin, which was impossible.

Woods told her to prepare herself for bad news. They had found Carmin dead.

For several minutes, Angela Hayes wept.

Then Woods told her that it looked to be a homicide. Carmin had been murdered.

Angela broke down. She was devastated. This was horror piled upon heartbreak.

A few minutes later, when Detective Woods judged that Mrs. Hayes could handle the question, he asked, "Who do you think we should look at?"

Angela Hayes shouted, "Tom!"

Angela explained that Tom Murray had been furious about the recent divorce (June 23, 2003), and he was even more enraged that five months later Carmin was already getting married. Murray was an English professor at Kansas State University in Manhattan, where he and Carmin had lived during their marriage. Carmin had moved to Lawrence to be away from Tom but still close enough to share custody of Helen with him. They were in a bitter custody fight over Helen.

Two conversations and two of the people closest to the victim—her fiancé and a close girlfriend—said Carmin's ex-husband, Tom Murray, should be looked at as a suspect.

Angela explained about Helen's custody situation and said that at this time Tom should be at work in his Manhattan office in the English department at Kansas State University. Helen should be at her Friday afternoon preschool. Angela babysat Helen Tuesday and Thursday mornings.

Woods asked Angela if she could babysit for Helen this afternoon or evening. He would like to talk with Tom Murray without Helen being present. Angela immediately agreed. She was adamant: Tom should be their prime suspect.

There was another message on Carmin's answering machine. Her mother had left a message reminding her to call her dad for his birthday. From the time stamp, this message would have been left after Carmin was murdered. Her mother's voice would have resonated loudly in the silent house, as Carmin's body lay on the floor. "Hi, Sweetie, it's Mom. Just wanted to remind you to call your dad for his birthday."

Carmin was murdered on her father's birthday.

Woods checked Carmin's address book for numbers. He called Carmin's attorney, Anne Miller, and gave her the news that Carmin had been murdered. She was shocked. When Woods asked if she had any idea as to who they should look at as a suspect, she said, "Tom Murray," because they were involved in a child custody battle.

At that point, after three consecutive people said the police should consider the victim's ex-husband a suspect, Woods decided that this might not have been a residential burglary gone bad. This might have been a murder by the ex-husband. Almost half of all women murdered in America are murdered by their men at some stage when the women try to end their relationships. The ex-husband is a logical suspect.

Woods decided to contact the police in Manhattan, Kansas.

5

In 1974, Riley County, containing Manhattan, Kansas, eliminated its sheriff's office in an effort to become more efficient. Most of the crime in Riley County came from the adjacent U.S. Army base at Fort Riley, and the community wanted a single, larger police entity. The Kansas State University Police Department retained its autonomy, but the other agencies were combined into one body—the Riley County Police Department. This was roughly the equivalent of creating a permanent M-Squad, such as was used in Douglas County. Detective Woods called the Riley County Police Department to explain the developing situation in Douglas County. He asked the officers not to approach Thomas Murray but to try to locate him and place him under loose surveillance.

Woods wondered if they would find Murray maintaining his usual schedule or if he had taken his daughter and become a fugitive.

The Riley County officer assigned as liaison was Brad Schlerf, a senior detective and the highest-ranking Riley County officer who would work directly on the case. Schlerf told the author that his understanding at that time was that "the wife's dead and the husband is the first suspect." Schlerf thought that when it rained it poured. Like Douglas County, Riley County did not have many homicides, but at the time Schlerf was deeply involved in a homicide investigation of his own. This Douglas County homicide would be only work for him, no credit, no glory, because it would be Douglas County's case, a Douglas County investigation. Still, he would help as best he could. He might have a murderer in his jurisdiction. His work would be limited, he thought, to the roles of resource officer and official liaison.

Schlerf explained the situation to a Riley County officer and then sent him to drive by Murray's home and report.

Schlerf then contacted Don Stubbings of the Kansas State University Police Department and explained the situation. Schlerf asked Stubbings to try to locate Murray, quietly.

The officer sent to Murray's home reported a vehicle in the driveway, a black Nissan pickup. The vehicle's tag was registered not to Murray but to a Kansas State University student named Peiwen Wang. It was soon learned she was one of Helen's babysitters.

Stubbings told Schlerf that Murray was in his office on campus, in room 122F, Denison Hall, where the English department was located.

When Murray left his office, an officer followed him in what Schlerf called "a loose tail." Murray went home. Peiwen appeared to be a babysitter. She departed sometime after Murray arrived. A girl, apparently Helen, was there. Murray lived in a cul-de-sac in one of the nicer neighborhoods, only a couple of miles from the police station.

Schlerf assigned two surveillance teams. They stayed in Murray's neighborhood and kept his home in sight, but switched off at intervals.

Schlerf also activated the Riley County ERU (emergency response unit) team, in some communities called the SWAT team, and reported the situation to Detective Woods.

Woods arranged to meet with their tactical team when they arrived. Four detectives set out from Lawrence on the ninety-minute drive to Manhattan. Armbrister and Woods rode together. Armbrister drove because Woods was constantly on the telephone.

While Woods was en route to Manhattan, the Riley County police called again. Surveillance reported that after dinner, in the dark, Murray had walked out into his yard and looked around and up and down the street, as if he was suspicious. He had put his hands on his hips and stared down the street as if he was expecting someone and they were late. "He looks like he's waiting for us," the Riley County officer said.

6

When approaching Manhattan, Kansas, from I-70 on the only four-lane road to town, one immediately sees a huge billboard with a big apple. The billboard text reads, MANHATTAN, THE LITTLE APPLE. Manhattan in New York is known as the Big Apple. Since the late 1970s, Manhattan, Kansas, has tried to capitalize on a little of that renown. This is reasonable because the town was named for Manhattan, New York, by the investors who founded the Kansas town—who were from Manhattan, New York.

Manhattan, Kansas—surrounded by prairie, farms, and cattle ranches—has its own rich history and famous natives. Damon Runyon, one of the most celebrated writers in America from the 1920s to the 1940s, who for a time was called "America's premier journalist," was from Manhattan, Kansas. Runyon became world famous for writing about both real people and fictional characters, many of whom were in or around Manhattan, New York. Runyon's influence in his time is difficult to describe with brevity, but it was pervasive. He had a habit of giving people slang nicknames, such as "the Lemon Drop Kid" or "Harry the Horse," and in the 1930s this practice became an American fad. As a result, even President Franklin Roosevelt gave many of his inner circle Runyonesque nicknames, such as "Tommy the Cork" for Thomas Corcoran, his chief political operative. A score of Runyon's reports and stories inspired successful stage plays and films, including *Guys and Dolls*, *Double Indemnity*, and *The Lemon Drop Kid*. Two of his young assistants, Walter Winchell and Ed Sullivan, went on to have high-profile careers. When Runyon died in 1946, World War I flying ace Eddie Rickenbacker scattered his ashes over Broadway.

Earl Woods, the father of golfer Tiger Woods, was born and raised in Manhattan, Kansas.

Cassandra Peterson, known as the entertainer Elvira, Mistress of the Dark, inspirer of the "Goth" look among a segment of young people, is a Manhattan, Kansas, native.

Erin Brockovich attended Kansas State University in Manhattan, though she was born in Lawrence, Kansas (the eponymous film said she was from Wichita).

Directly east of Manhattan, on Kansas Highway 24, only a few minutes' drive, is the city of Wamego, home to the celebrated Oz Museum, which has a rich collection of *Wizard of Oz* memorabilia. People associated with the *Oz* books and the movie, including L. Frank Baum's grandson, periodically make appearances there, and the *Oz* play is performed at the nearby recently restored theater. Next door one may dine at Toto's Tacos.

Like Lawrence, Manhattan is located in an area of interesting geography. This area was once the bottom of an ocean and has miles of rich wheat fields and open ranges. Carmin and Tom used to walk and talk in the Konza Prairie, a beautiful region of nine thousand acres of preserved wild grassland.

Kansas State University was the first land-grant college. It was founded as an agricultural college and still does first-rate agricultural research. It has a nationally known veterinary school and teaching hospital where doctors of veterinary medicine may take a two- or three-year residency in exotic, wildlife and zoo animal medicine.

Not everyone is enamored of the town's heritage of ranching and farming. Many young people, visitors, and some natives refer to Manhattan as "Moohattan."

Kansas State University is also known for its football team, which was identified by *Playboy* magazine in the 1980s as "the worst major college football program in America." When Coach Bill Snyder came in, however, the program turned around and for a few years KSU was ranked among the best teams in America. Win or lose, the Kansas State University Wildcats have incredibly devoted fans. Anywhere one travels in Kansas, one may see a purple Powercat symbol, representing KSU.

Where one doesn't see a Powercat, one sees a big-beaked red-and-blue Jayhawk, a mythical bird that early settlers claimed to see and the mascot of KSU's rival, KU (Lawrence). It's easy to tell K-State fans because they're wearing purple. One may journey to Manhattan, Kansas, and see a crowd in which everyone is wearing purple. There is a great intrastate rivalry between Kansas State University Wildcat fans and the University of Kansas Jayhawk fans. One may see signs in Manhattan proclaiming I BRAKE FOR ALL ANIMALS EXCEPT JAYHAWKS and signs in Lawrence that read I BRAKE FOR ALL ANIMALS EXCEPT WILDCATS.

Seen on a large-scale map, Manhattan, Paxico, Topeka, and Lawrence are on a straight horizontal east-west line on I-70. Manhattan is about sixty miles from Topeka, with Paxico being almost exactly halfway between them. Lawrence is thirty miles to the east of Topeka. Kansas Highway 24 runs east-west about ten miles north of I-70 between Manhattan and Topeka, and Kansas Highway 40 runs parallel to I-70 between Topeka and Lawrence.

According to Brenda Williams, a KSU graduate, Manhattan resident, and a former Kansas Investigative Reporter of the Year, in 1994 the best-selling author Stephen King, a brilliant writer known for his macabre stories, once was riding his motorcycle around the country, and as he approached Manhattan, Kansas, on a Saturday afternoon, he had an eerie feeling, as if he were in a *Twilight Zone* episode or a Stephen King novel. He saw no people. He continued driving, but the streets were empty, deserted. There was no other traffic. But there was a loud sound that he could not identify, animalistic and threatening. As he sped closer to the heart of the city, the sound became louder and more frightening until it became a roar. He realized it sounded like a growl, as if a giant monster was growling, and he was getting closer to it.

And so it was.

At Saturday afternoon Kansas State University football games, virtually the entire town converges on the stadium, especially when they play rival Kansas University. At some point during the game fifty thousand people will give a long "Wildcat growl." That is what Stephen King heard—fifty thousand crazed Kansas State University Wildcat fans growling in unison.

7

While still on the drive to Manhattan, Woods reached Carmin and Thomas's child custody mediator, Nancy Hughes. The moment she understood that Carmin had been murdered, she told the investigators, "You need to look at Tom Murray." She said that Murray's reaction to the news that Carmin wanted to take Helen and move to California had been negative.

Woods wanted to be careful. He had not in his own judgment determined that Tom Murray was the only suspect. None of the people who suspected Tom seemed to like him. Being disliked was not enough to make one a legitimate homicide suspect. If it was, every disliked eccentric in the community would become a suspect. Still, Woods was going to be careful in his interview of Tom Murray.

Woods thought that if Murray was the killer he might pretend to be an ally and agree to talk to "help the police solve the case." If so, Woods thought he might obtain Murray's confession.

In the meantime someone needed to notify Carmin Ross's parents in Indianapolis, Indiana, of her murder.

Telling a family that a loved one has been murdered is a part of the training of every police chaplain. The thirty-third annual training seminar for police chaplains in Indianapolis even featured a seminar session on "death notification." It is part of a police chaplain's job to inform the family when a loved one has unexpectedly died from accident, suicide, or homicide.

Some police departments are much better at such notification than others. Some do not use chaplains.

In *Helter Skelter*, the best-selling true-crime book of all time, Vince Bugliosi and Curt Gentry relate how in 1969 Steven Parent's father was notified about the murder of his teenaged son by the Manson family.

Wilfred Parent was at home when a police officer knocked on his door. He handed Mr. Parent a card with a number on it and told him to call it. He left without saying anything else.

Mr. Parent called the number and a man answered by saying, "County Coroner's Office."

That confused Mr. Parent. He explained why he had called. His call was transferred to a deputy county coroner. The deputy coroner described a body's physical characteristics and Mr. Parent realized that was his son.

When Mr. Parent hung up the phone, he started sobbing. "All I can say is that it was a hell of a way to tell somebody that their boy was dead."

The Los Angeles police might have been expected to improve death-notification procedures after a quarter century, but that had not happened. On Sunday, June 12, 1994, Fred Goldman received a call from the Los Angeles County coroner's office. Mr. Goldman was asked, "Did you hear today that Nicole Brown Simpson has been murdered?"

Mr. Goldman answered, "Yes."

Goldman was then told, "Your son was the other person."

Goldman wrote: "The instant I heard those words I fell into shock, stunned by a blast of disbelief and pain so great that the only thing I could do was push it down and bury it somewhere deep inside. I could not face this reality."

Big-city police departments might handle death notifications in a perfunctory, impersonal way, such as happened in Los Angeles to Mr. Parent and Mr. Goldman, but small towns like Lawrence, Kansas, insist on a more humane and personal method of death notification.

With the help of the Indiana State Police, Carmin's parents were located. They lived near Indianapolis, in Lapel, Indiana. The officers had heard the message that Carmin's mother had left—"Hi, Sweetie, it's Mom. Just wanted to remind you to call your dad for his birthday." No one wanted to be the bearer of bad news, but it had to be done.

The Douglas County sheriff's department arranged for a police chaplain and an Indiana state trooper to go to Carmin's parents' home. The chaplain and trooper told the Rosses that their daughter had been murdered. The Rosses became distraught, as one would expect, but the family immediately made plans to go to Kansas to help Tom care for Helen and to hold a memorial for Carmin.

8

Four Douglas County officers—Woods, Armbrister, and two others—arrived in Manhattan, Kansas, to confer with the local police. According to testimony in the transcript of the preliminary hearing and interviews with Detectives Doug Woods and Brad Schlerf, they made a "strategic plan" to make contact with Thomas Murray. The Riley County ERU was assembled and stationed out of sight a block away from Murray's home. The sniper and spotter from the ERU were positioned to target Murray if he came to the door. The rest of the ERU made ready to enter the home by force. Everyone was concerned that if Murray was the killer he might hold the girl as a shield and turn this into a hostage situation. If so, the negotiators and the ERU would take over.

At 7:45 P.M., Douglas County detective Doug Woods and Riley County detective Brad Schlerf went to Murray's door. Detective Armbrister stood in the driveway. Two uniformed officers were at a marked Riley County police car that was parked where it would be visible when Murray came to the door. Detectives Schlerf and Woods saw Murray and Helen through glass at the door. Murray was seated and Helen was playing on the floor in the hallway. At

Schlerf's knock, Murray started to the door, but when he saw the officers, he retreated down the hallway, backward, picking up Helen. When Woods saw that, he prepared to break the door in and chase Murray.

But Murray came to the door, holding Helen tightly with both of his arms. Detective Woods thought that Murray was using Helen as a shield, exactly as they had feared might happen. This could get ugly.

Schlerf told the author later that if Murray had raised a weapon that threatened the officers or the girl and the sniper had decided to shoot, Schlerf would have been told which way to move (left-right-down) to avoid the shot.

When Murray opened the door, Detective Schlerf, as the senior officer, introduced himself and the others as law enforcement officers and detectives. He strove to be calm, polite, and respectful, but firm. Schlerf's main interest was in keeping Murray calm and in separating Murray from the child. When they stepped inside, Woods told Murray that he needed to speak with him immediately.

Murray asked if this was something they could talk about tomorrow.

Woods insisted that he needed to speak with him right now. Murray let the officers into his home but kept Helen in his arms. Murray backed up, and Woods and the others advanced. Schlerf asked if Murray could put the child down. After Murray did so, Woods asked if she could be put in another room. Murray wanted to know if that was necessary.

Woods said it was. The officers kept Murray in sight as he reluctantly put Helen in another room to play. An officer stayed between Helen and her father.

When Murray was alone with the officers, Woods reached out to shake hands. Having seen the crime scene, Woods thought that if Murray was the killer, he might have a sore hand from striking Carmin. Woods shook Murray's hand as hard as he could. He anticipated that Murray might flinch.

Woods was disappointed. Murray was strong. He had an equally firm grip, and he did not flinch. The two were evenly matched.

Woods then delivered the news. He said, "Your wife has died and I need to talk with you."

At that news, Murray gasped, grasped a table, and then took a few steps to a chair and sat down. In the preliminary hearing Detective Schlerf, who had made many death notifications, and also was experienced and educated in reading body language, testified that the man's reaction was what he expected. But Murray's next reaction was not typical. The apparent grief was momentary. Murray's demeanor quickly turned cold, and he asked, "Do we really have to talk about this tonight?"

Woods and the other officers exchanged looks. What was up with this guy? He did not react as Larry Lima had and ask, "What happened?" Instead, he wanted to put off talking. The officers insisted that they did need to talk now.

Meanwhile, they surveyed the house. The floor of the foyer, dinette, hallways, and kitchen had gray stone or tiles that looked like stone. Some walls were painted off-white, while others were robin's-egg blue. The closet door and the stairway banister in the foyer were of blond wood. To the left of the foyer were a closet and a short hallway that led to the kitchen and dinette. A board game and a box of Kleenex were on the kitchen table. To the right was a stairway. Straight ahead was a hallway to the living room. In the living room, which had a Western theme, was a large gray stone wood-burning fireplace. Above the mantel was a shotgun.

The officers continued to wait for Murray to ask

what they expected to be his next question, but he did not ask how his ex-wife had died. Each of the twenty previous times that Doug Woods had told a person that someone close to him or her had died, the first question had always been, "What happened?" Murray would talk with Woods until six the next morning, for ten hours. The entire conversation was recorded. Murray never asked how his ex-wife had died, and no one told him.

Ten minutes after meeting Murray, Doug Woods thought he was the person responsible for his ex-wife's murder. He thought Murray's actions were those of a guilty man with a guilty mind who was trying to deceive others to avoid arrest. Woods expected that any minute he would receive a call advising him of some evidence directly tying Thomas Murray to his ex-wife's murder or that Murray would say or do something linking himself to Carmin Ross's murder. Woods wanted to separate Murray from Helen and get Murray into an environment where Woods had more control.

Would Tom Murray agree to go to the police station?

Woods and Schlerf convinced Murray that they needed to talk with him at the police station. Murray called Angela Hayes. She and her husband, Rob, came to Murray's home to watch Helen while Murray was with the police.

The officers wanted Murray to remain calm. Schlerf offered to provide a ride for him, but Murray preferred to drive himself to the police station. After the Hayeses arrived and Murray said goodbye to Helen, they drove the two and a half miles to the Riley County police station, at 1001 Seth Child Road, a busy intersection. Schlerf led the convoy, Murray followed, and Woods and the rest of the officers tailed them.

At the police station, Murray parked near the front door in the visitors' parking on the west side. Schlerf drove around to the south side and entered adjacent to the room where Murray would soon be interviewed.

In the interview Murray confirmed that his presence was voluntary; he explicitly said that he did not want a lawyer and signed a waiver of his Miranda rights. The questioning in the Riley County police station went on from 8:23 P.M. Friday evening to about 6:00 A.M. Saturday morning and was audio- and video-recorded. Murray reviewed for the detectives each place he had been and everything he had done on the dates of November 11, 12, 13, and 14 and gave a written statement. He wrote that on Thursday he had left Helen at the sitter's at 8:45 A.M. and Carmin had e-mailed him in the afternoon. When he was asked about things Carmin's murderer might have done, such as leave evidence of planning the murder, Murray dryly replied, "No intelligent man would do that." The implication was always that *he*, as an intelligent man, would never do *that*, whatever it was, and that the cops were being stupid if they thought he would.

Murray's alibi for the time when Carmin Ross was murdered was unequivocal and clear. He said that after leaving Helen at the sitter's, "I drove home and graded my midterms." He emphasized that he graded papers all morning. He gave permission to search his computer and said they'd find he had researched ho-micide for a commercial crime story he was writing.

Murray had an answer for everything. He was never rattled. He appeared as comfortable as the casual clothes he wore. His purple-pink sweatshirt depicted a determined wolf pack running through snow-covered woods. Detective Woods later thought that sweatshirt was apt, because he considered Murray to be a wolf in sheep's clothing. Woods was confident that before they parted company he would have Murray's confession.

In 2005 Murray's defense attorneys argued at trial that Murray was an innocent man who was writing a fictional crime story but that the circumstantial evidence, when looked at with suspicion, had made an innocent man look guilty.

The prosecution argued that a guilty storyteller planned and executed a murder, artfully composing a lens through which the evidence, when viewed sympathetically, could create the illusion that it could not be proved that he had committed murder.

One story must be true, and the other false. In this case, that is the fundamental controversy.

9

*Dialogue is a form of action, a potent technique
for expressing conflict. It is the mightiest power
tool on the writer's workbench for making characters come alive.*
—Chris Roerden, *Don't Murder Your Mystery*, 2006

At a trial, an attorney asks questions of a witness, the
witness has a lawyer present as an advocate, and the
judge is the referee. The judge and the lawyers know
the rules and practices, and the text of their verbal
exchanges is recorded in the trial transcript. The dialogue recorded between Murray and Woods in Riley
County Police Department's interview room #2 is far
from a trial transcript. It is an unrefereed war of language. A career linguist who describes himself as
being "at the top of his profession" is battling with a
commonsense small-town detective who learned the
techniques of interviewing homicide suspects from his
homicide detective father. The subtext of the transcript and the body language of the suspect speak
volumes.

After entering the Riley County police station, Detective Schlerf went to the main entrance on the west
side of the building. He led Murray and Woods down

a long hallway to interview room #2. Labeled above
the door as ROOM 259, it is a nine-by-nine-foot space
with cream-white walls and gray-brown carpet. The
only door into the room is in the northeast corner.

On the other side of the room's south wall, unseen
by the people inside the room, is a VHS recorder.
The microphone to the recorder is near the southwest
corner, close to the chair where the interview subject
sits. The camera is on the east wall, near the south
side, opposite the interview subject. The chair for the
interview subject is a cushioned straight chair that has
its back flush against the west wall, so that the interview subject is facing east, toward the camera. The
person being interviewed may easily turn the chair,
but Murray never does so. He does, however, torque
his body into unusual postures.

A sturdy, heavy, gray metal table sits flush with the
west wall. The detective primarily conducting the interview sits at that table with the chair directly north
of the table. The person seated in the chair faces
south. To be closer to the interview subject, sometimes
the detective will move the chair to the east side of
the table.

Schlerf provided Murray some water in a white Sty-
rofoam cup, then left him alone in the interview room.
He walked back north up the hallway, turned to the
east, used his magnetic key, and led the other detectives into a secure area. In room 236, the detectives
assembled to watch and listen to the interview over
a closed-circuit setup. The entire interview would be
recorded on a VHS tape and later transferred to
DVD. By pressing an icon, photos would be taken
and printed out. The detective team who watched as
the drama unfolded would function as both witnesses
and participants. It was as if they were player-coaches
up in the press box watching a high-stakes football
game and analyzing the plays as the game progressed.

At intervals, Detective Schlerf would provide Woods feedback on what he was seeing, and this would help guide the interview.

Detective Woods did not pretend to be other than what he was—an earthy man, a man's man, a folksy person—and in their interview, he talked with the urbane professor as a man. He was direct with Tom Murray. He sometimes shared the troubles that American men have in the early twenty-first century.

The detective began the interview in an easy, practical manner, asking simple questions that anyone, innocent or guilty, could answer. How do you spell your name? How tall are you?

Then the questions became more difficult.

Interview Room #2

While the team was assembled in room 236, they watched Murray as they discussed their game plan. At 8:23:16 P.M., Friday, November 14, 2003, the tape begins. Murray has his head down as if to trying to sleep, but he is breathing deeply. His chair is facing east with the chair back flush with the west wall. His knees are facing northeast. The chair where Doug Woods will sit is facing south, directly toward Murray.

Schlerf, Woods, and Armbrister reenter interview room #2. At exactly 8:25 P.M. Schlerf reintroduces Detectives Woods and Armbrister. Woods sits down north of Murray and places his yellow notepad on the table. Armbrister sits in the chair at the east wall. When they are seated, only Murray is visible to the camera, though Woods's yellow pad on the table is visible. When Woods leans forward to write notes on the pad he becomes visible. Schlerf, watching the monitor in room 236, noted that Murray's posture is hunched over. Murray looks at the floor, mostly down and to his right. Although the officers try to make eye contact with him, at this time Murray does not make eye contact with any of the officers.

In the video, Murray is seen to have a "buzz-cut" haircut. His head was practically shaved. His scalp was visible. Detective Schlerf told the author that he thought that Murray had recently cut his hair off to avoid having any hair for Carmin to pull if she was able to fight back.

As Detective Schlerf left the room, he said, "I am going to step out. These folks from Douglas County are going to take care of everything, all right? If you need something, just let us know. Doing all right?"

Thomas Murray said, "I don't know. Do her mom and dad know yet?"

Douglas County detective Doug Woods said, "We are working on that right now too. I need to get some basic information from you first off. Is it Tom or Thomas? What is your legal name, sir?" (Woods begins simply. Murray continues to look down and to the right, not making eye contact.)

"Thomas."

"What is your middle initial?"

"E."

"And your last name? Ross?"

"No. Murray. M-U-R-R-A-Y."

Detective Woods knew the professor's last name was Murray, but he wanted to provide the subject with the opportunity to correct him. It already seemed to Woods that the professor thought the police were inferior. Why not give the subject the opportunity to inwardly smirk and verify that the police did not even know basic information, such as their interview subject's name. Also, using the victim's name might provoke a reaction in the subject.

"And your date of birth, sir?"

"June 27, 1956."

"And your height, sir?"

(In the beginning of the interview, always "sir." Always respectful and deferential, like the famous fictional detective Lieutenant Columbo.)

"About six foot two." (Murray's driver's license said six foot three, which would have been what he told the examiner at the driver's license office.)

"How much do you weigh, sir?"

"Around one hundred eighty, I guess."

"Brown hair? Let's not talk about gray, though." (Woods was becoming prematurely gray.)

"Yes."

(Success. Murray has a somewhat warm response to Woods's question.)

"Eye color, sir?"

"Blue."

"Scars? Marks? Tattoos?"

"No." (Somewhat coldly, again.)

"Your current address, sir?"

"3668 Everett. E-V-E-R-E-T-T."

(3668 Everett in Manhattan, Kansas, was 2.5 miles from the Riley County police station, 1001 S. Seth Child Road. Murray did not live far away.)

"Your home phone number, sir?"

(Murray provides his home phone number.)

"Do you have a cell phone?"

"No."

"Social Security number?"

(Murray provides his Social Security number.)

"Year of your vehicle?"

"2003."

"What kind of car is that?"

"Saturn. Ion Three."

"Is it maroon?"

"They call it cranberry. That [maroon] is close enough." (One of the detectives would later tell the author, "Real men don't say a car is 'cranberry.'")

"And you're employed by who?" (Woods already knows the answers to many of his questions, but he wants to get Murray in the habit of answering his questions. It is a great beginning technique to pose nonthreatening questions that the subject feels comfortable answering.)

"The University of Kansas State."

"And what department do you work for?" (Again, Woods already knows the answer.)

"English."

"You're a professor?"

"Yes."

"You're currently divorced?"

"Yes."

"And what is your degree of education?"

"Ph.D." [A doctor of philosophy in English.]

(Detective Schlerf notices that Murray's left hand is covering his face and forehead, his head is facing down, and his right hand is concealed under his blue sweatpants. He is sitting on his right hand. Five minutes into the interview, Murray has still not made eye contact with the officers.)

"Do you have any medical problems or anything like that?"

"Well, I think the answer is 'no,' unless you are talking about hay fever."

"Do you take any medications for that?"

"No."

"Any mental problems or anything like that?"

"No. Well . . . I mean, who knows?"

"You're of sound mind, I assume?"

"Well, I hope so." (Murray continues looking at the floor. He has not yet made eye contact with Detective Woods.)

"Have you ingested any alcohol or drugs in the last four to six hours?"

"No."

"You are not taking any prescription medications?"

"No." (Woods wants to know whether Murray might later claim he was impaired by drugs and his statement should be suspect on that basis.)

"We always have to ask: Do you have any kind of criminal history?"

"No. Not so much as a ticket." (At this, Murray shifts his gaze from the floor to the ceiling. His eyes are wide open. Detective Schlerf commented to the author: "He stares at the ceiling as if the answers were up there." But then Murray again closes his eyes.)

"Um, kind of tell me about your relationship with Carmin, and how long ago you guys met. When did you guys get married, and so on?" (Concluding an inquiry or statement with "and so on" is a typical Kansas phrase. It implies a broad question and invites an open response. The person being spoken to may politely answer more than what was asked.)

"We met in Columbus, Ohio. I was teaching at Ohio State University and she took one of my classes. We met in 1984, early January, and we were married in June of 1985, June 15th."

"You were married in 1985?"

"Eighty-five. Then we moved to Manhattan in 1988 and I have been here ever since. Well, I mean, she [Carmin] moved to Lawrence about August the 1st." (2003.)

"What is your child's name, sir?"

"Helen. H-E-L-E-N." (Murray opens his eyes before answering.)

"What is her last name? She uses Murray as her last name?"

"She uses Ross-Murray. That's the name on the birth certificate."

"She is how old?"

"She will be five next month."

"So she was born in 1999?"

"Ninety-eight. December 19th. My father's birthday."

"Is that the only child you guys have?" ("You guys" is another commonly used term. It is not as folksy as "Y'all" or "You-all.")

"Yeah."

"When did you guys start having problems?" (Murray again starts looking at the floor. His eyes are again open.)

"We had a summer home in Wisconsin. We came back from that at the end of August 2002 and I thought everything was fine. I mean, we did the things that we always do. We checked in with our financial advisor. We talked about goals and where we might retire. Then, Carmin is involved in a New Age movement, New Age ideology, philosophy. She is deep into that. And she has been studying energy medicine for a few years and—"

Doug Woods interrupted Murray with a new question. "What kind of work did she do when she was out here?"

"She was trained as an attorney. She worked as an attorney in town for a year or two."

"Here in Manhattan?"

"Yes. She worked for Morrison, Frost and Olsen."

"What was her specialty?"

"She didn't have a specialty. She was the prosecutor for the city and she did one or two other cases of divorce or something. But then she got tired of it. She went to work for FACTS."

(It is 8:33 P.M. In one of the most dramatic changes of his body position, Murray has turned completely toward the wall, looking down, facing south, facing 180 degrees away from Woods, who is north of him. Murray has his back to Woods, yet is speaking to

Woods. Woods seems clearly puzzled by Murray's body posture. Woods is seen writing notes on his yellow pad, leaning forward, leaning around, trying to make eye contact with Murray, which Murray's body position makes impossible. He's talking to Murray's back.)

Murray said, "FACTS was an acronym for Farmer Assistance Counseling and Training Service. It was like a hotline thing where people would call in and get advice. She worked there for a couple of years full-time and then a couple of years part-time. Then she got tired of that and she became an expert in mediation. She tried to work on her own for a while but wasn't too successful. So she eventually took a job at the university. She was the director of employee relations about 1993 to 1997. I think she left in December of 1997 and started to work for her dad. He has his own business."

"What kind of business is that?"

(Detective Schlerf noted that the level of detail Murray is providing on collateral matters is abnormal. In Schlerf's education and experience, an interview subject, in the hours after having been told about the death of someone close, is able to function only on immediate matters. The answers to collateral questions will be short. It is more likely that the interview subject will repeatedly want to ask questions of the police, will want to know what happened, how the person died. Murray does not ask how Carmin died. He provides far too much detail in his answers. And, of course, his body posture says that he does not want to discuss this, regardless of the text of his words.)

(Murray gradually torques his body back around. He is no longer facing the wall, but his knees are still facing southeast while his torso is facing east and his head is facing east-northeast. He still does not make eye contact.)

"He gives training on quality systems control—how to be more efficient. She worked for him for a while," Murray said.

"So this is while you guys are still married?"

"Oh, yeah. But then we got pregnant."

"Was that a planned thing?"

"No."

Murray paused for several seconds before speaking again.

"No, we got pregnant in March or April and Helen was born in December. And from then on she would do one or two things like mediation training, but mostly she was at home with Helen. But then she started to get into this New Age business and into this energy medicine, which is the most bizarre thing. This is going to make her sound like a crackpot, but I don't want to do that. About how much detail do you want?" (Here, at 8:35 P.M., for the first time, Murray momentarily glances toward Woods, though they do not make eye contact.)

"That's fine," Woods said. "I mean, so did you guys start having problems in 2002?"

"Oh, no. We got back from Wisconsin and we did all of the things we normally did, but it was the third week in September she went away to a one-week-long training seminar in energy medicine and she came back."

"Where was the seminar at?"

"It was in Wichita. And she came back and it was like—"

"This was in 2002, right?"

"Uh-huh. I thought, I was telling friends that she was going through a midlife crisis, but honestly, it was like the same body with a different person in it. All of her values and beliefs had changed. She had started questioning everything, including our relationship. Then I discovered that she had begun having an intimate"—Murray suddenly sticks his hand in his eye and rubs hard, as if he is gouging his eye out—"relationship with another man while she was in Wichita. She said that after just sitting in the same room with the man, like we are, just for one or two hours, she knew that she loved him more deeply and on every level than she ever loved anybody."

"What's this man's name? Do you know this man?" (Detective Woods had been on the phone with the man not long before, but Murray does not know that.)

"No," Murray answered.

"What's his name?" Woods asked.

"Larry. Larry. So, I think she spent the fall trying to decide what she was going to do. I was trying to convince her to stay and I think he was trying to convince her not to."

"Is this Larry guy in Wichita?"

"He was there for the training, but I think he was from San Francisco. That's where he was living. But originally from New Jersey, I think. But I'm not sure. I think he was from San Francisco. He had a business in San Francisco. Then, right after the new year—"

"2003?" Woods asked.

"This year. I told her that I thought we were in limbo long enough. That I wanted to know what was going to happen. I couldn't go on like that. She said, well . . ."

During the pause Woods asked, "Did she continue seeing this other man or did it end?"

"No, it was . . ."

"When you talk about being in limbo, did you guys separate?" Woods asked.

"No. She did see him. She took—against my wishes—she took Helen to San Diego to visit her sister and brother-in-law. He was in the Marines out there. This guy Larry drove down from San Francisco. His brother lives in San Diego, and he and Carmin got together. I begged her not to go. If she was going to go I begged her to leave Helen back with me. But she said no."

Murray continued. "She wanted to take her. And then after the first of the year, when I said, 'Well, you know we've been living like this and I think I deserve to know what is going to happen.' She said, 'Well, I don't think our relationship has a future.' She moved out over spring break in March. She took an apartment downtown. It was a little two-room bedroom flat above the theater building."

"Downtown in Manhattan?"

"Yes. We sold the cabin."

"The cabin in Wisconsin?"

"Yes, the cabin in Wisconsin. In April or May we went up there and moved all of the stuff out."

"You said in April or May you sold the cabin?"

"Yes."

"Okay."

"And her mom was there," Murray added.

"So, once you moved out did you guys remain civil?"

"Oh, yeah. We were friendly. Very friendly."

"So, after you sold the cabin, what happened?"

"She continued to live here in Manhattan until the end of July or till the lease ran out. (8:40 P.M. Murray looks toward Armbrister. This is his first eye contact with a detective since the interview started.) She moved to Lawrence. I said, 'Why!?' (Murray puts great emphasis on "Why!?" virtually shouting the word.) I mean, the divorce was final on June 23rd (a little more than four months ago). It was right before, like two days before we appeared in court, three days before that, she said she intended to move to San Diego. Larry had a house there or something. And she was going to be a healer or they were going to start a healing foundation or something."

"She was going to move to what city in California?"

"San Diego."

"Okay."

"And she had visited him through the spring. A couple of times, I think, although every time I tried to ask her where she was going she was, she had grown very secretive. I cannot believe this. Throughout this period, for the last year or so, she had gotten more into this New Age business where she, um, (shaking his head) started communicating with spirit guides and angels and deceased relatives and, I mean, it was just bizarre. She believed that she could heal anybody of any ailment, anything structural or psychological, even if you had MS or cancer, from any distance away. She could heal, so she said that she was going to be a healer in San Diego. And then she moved to Wichita, I mean Lawrence, in about August. August the first. She found an old house on the west side of town and from August first until now, well, the divorce decree stipulates shared custody . . ." (Murray's voice trails off into silence. His head is facing the floor, his left hand is over his face, covering his face, and his right hand is concealed between his legs.)

"How did the custody order work out?"

"Well (8:43 P.M., more than eighteen minutes after the recorded interview started, Murray briefly makes eye contact with Detective Doug Woods for the first time), I don't know if you know how this works, but as I understand it, in this state there is only two options. You can have full custody of a child or you can have shared custody. If you have shared custody, the parents work it out. It is supposed to be fifty-fifty. But the parents work it out however they want to as long as it is agreeable among them. So when she said she was going to move to Wichita—I mean when she said she was going to move to San Diego—I said, 'What does this do to the concept of shared custody?' And she said, 'We will just have to get on an airplane every couple of weeks and fly Helen back and forth.' I said, 'No, we can't do that. There is no stability for Helen.' But, anyway, as the fall has progressed she continued to want to be friends and I said, 'It is real hard for me to be a friend after all you have put me through.' Here, I would like just to make it a business relationship. By this point, I was pretty much over the divorce, but I was focused on Helen because I didn't want to turn into the kind of father that sees his kid every other holiday and a couple of weeks in the summer.''

"I can understand that.''

"The divorce documents that we have stipulates that before you go back into court and try to modify the existing arrangement you have to go through mediation.''

"Is this other guy still in the picture, or is he out at this point now?'' (Woods continues to pretend to know less than he does.)

"Oh, yeah! They married about two weeks after the divorce was final, I think.''

"How do you know they're married?''

"Helen told me one day that when she was staying with Mommy in San Diego she would try to go to Mommy's bedroom at night and Larry would walk her back to her own bed. So, I said, 'Larry and Mommy are sleeping in the same bed with you there?' And she said, 'Yeah.'

"So, I told Carmin I don't want Helen exposed to this. I wrote her an e-mail and said I don't want Helen exposed to this, so I went on for a long time [and] at the very bottom I said, sort of facetiously I thought, I said, 'If you and Larry are married disregard the whole preceding paragraph.'

"So, we were out walking one day in July in the middle of the Konza Prairie [just south of Manhattan,

on the route to Interstate 70], where we did most of
our talking, and we were talking about this. And she
said, well, to disregard it if we were married and I
looked right at her because it was only two or three
weeks after we had divorced and I said, 'You married
the guy already?' She said, 'We're married.'

"But the reason I am not sure whether it is a legal
marriage is her aunt Betty and I e-mail back and forth
once in a while. Betty lives in Ohio and she told me
that Carmin had told her parents that she and Larry
had married but not in front of a minister or anything
because it was too much of this world. So that made
me think that it was sort of common law, but I guess
I don't know."

"So they got married, not in front of a minister or
something like that?" Woods asked.

"Well, that's what Betty said. But I don't know. I
really don't. I made notes of all of this because I
thought if we would ever have to go back to court,
you know, it would be—I have notes at home; that
was in July."

"Then in August is when she moved and it became
clearer and clearer."

"I said [to Carmin], 'When do you intend to go to
San Diego?'

"And she said, 'I don't know, but I'm going to live
here through this year.'

"I asked, 'Is that through 2003 or through the academic year?'

"And she said, 'Through the academic year, but I
would like to be in San Diego sometime in the summer before Helen starts school.'

"So, when I looked at the divorce document it said
before you go back to court. My thought was before
you go back to court I'll try to find, I'll try to get the
judge to award me full custody, because Carmin said
if I ever had full custody she would go, she would stay

here. So the divorce document says before you can go back and have the judge modify an existing order, you have to go through mediation. So the attorney that I consulted, one of them in town here—"

Woods interrupted, "Which attorney was that?"

"Oh, God," Murray said. "Well, I talked to Jim Morrison, which was the senior partner at the firm that Carmin worked at."

"Did you help her get a job there? Did you know him personally?" Woods asked.

"No. We did not relate. I talked to him once. Then I talked to a woman once in town. Her name was, um, I only talked to her once, um, Jacobson, Sue Jacobson. I talked to her."

"Was she here in Manhattan, too?" Woods asked.

"Yes. And of course Sue was all for being litigious. 'No, we've got to go to court,' [she said]. And I said, 'No, we are going to give mediation a try.' And I said, 'Frankly, I don't want full custody of Helen. I would be a basket case if I had to do this by myself.' But I said, 'What I want to do is try to keep Carmin in Manhattan. Can the judge do that?' And she said, 'No. She can go and live wherever she wants to. That is what the Supreme Court says.' So my only option was to get full custody. But Sue recommended a mediator in Lawrence named Nancy Hughes, who is wonderful. She works at the psych clinic in Fraser Hall at KU. Carmin and I have gone to her now for probably three or four times and talk anywhere from two to three and a half hours at a pop. We were there this Tuesday. Yeah, we were there Tuesday, and I had a proposal on the table—"

Doug Woods asked, "That was Tuesday . . . ?"

Murray said, "This week."

Doug said, "Tuesday being the eleventh?"

Murray said, "Whatever Tuesday was. I know it was Tuesday because I don't have classes on Tuesday. We had the mediation and afterwards, and it was the mediation before that when Sue said, 'Hey, you guys are doing good. You're going to reach an accord here. But then after this last mediation . . .''

"What time was your appointment on Tuesday?" Woods asked.

Murray closes his eyes and turns toward the ceiling. He keeps his eyes closed and looks to the ceiling while talking about Tuesday.

"Two o'clock."

"Two o'clock?" Woods asked.

"And we went into a little bit after four o'clock because the babysitter that Carmin had secured for Helen was a college student who had another job or class to go to at four thirty."

"Who was the college student watching your child?" Detective Woods asked.

"I don't know her name. I never met her. I think this was the first time Carmin ever used her."

"Okay," Woods said.

Murray continued, "So, after the mediation we drove back to Carmin's house. I was a little bit late because I had stayed to talk to Nancy. I had said to Nancy, 'How do you think we are doing?' I mean, as you know, she said, 'I don't know. In situations like this it becomes sort of a struggle for power.' A struggle for . . . she didn't say power, I forget what she said, but you know, control of the situation."

"So, was it a good meeting on Tuesday? Was it standoffish?" Woods asked.

"It was a good meeting. Although Carmin and I both said some things. We accused one another of lying. I had caught her doing something," Murray said.

"What was that?" Woods asked.

"She went to New Mexico the beginning of August—the first, the first couple weeks in August of this year—for some, I don't know, one of her New

Age things. Some healing thing. I think Larry was there with her too. And she had arranged with Helen, I guess we call about every night or every other night, she was sending some mail to Helen before that, right after August the first. The post office sent a letter to Helen at my address saying, 'You have requested that your address be changed to this address,' and it was the Lawrence house.''

"So she was doing Helen's address change?"

"And this was to confirm this. Well, that's what pissed me off. And I mean, I don't get mad often. But I was pissed off that she had done this behind my back. I figured she had done this behind my back and I figured it was to try to gain something in court if we went back for a custody hearing.''

"And this was when you got the address change?"

"It was like the first week in August when the confirmation letter came.''

"Did you talk to her about it?'' Woods asked.

"No. I didn't say anything about it. But I called the post office and I canceled it. I didn't want to say anything about it, but when she was in New Mexico, she sent letters to Helen, but they always came in care of me. Well, I knew the reason was because she told the order that she wanted the mail to come to my address and not be forwarded to hers. But one of the times I answered the phone when she was gone, I said, 'Carmin, you keep sending me things to Helen but in care of me. Why are you doing that?' And I wanted to see what she would say.

"She said, 'I didn't know if you could address a letter to a child, so I thought I should do it in care of you.'

"So, this is the way I told it at the mediation on Tuesday. I said, 'Any fourth grader knows that the post office doesn't deliver mail by names, they use addresses. You can send a letter to your dog, your

parakeet, Santa Claus, or anything. It doesn't matter.'
And I said, 'Tell me again, why did you send it in
care of me?'

"And she said, 'Well, maybe I'm just stupid. Maybe
I didn't know that.'

"I said, 'Carmin, you are not stupid. You attempted
to change Helen's legal address.'

"And she said, 'I didn't attempt to change her
address.'

"And I said, 'Carmin, that is a lie.' And she got
all huffy.

"And she said, 'I don't lie. I have never lied. I have
done some deceptive things.'

"So, that was the tone of the part of the mediation.
But, you know, even when we talk to one another like
that, we always ended on a good note. We got back
to her house and—"

Doug Woods interrupted. "You went back to her
house. So, did you get the mail issue resolved in the
mediation?"

"No," Murray answered.

"So, did it just kind of hang there?" Woods asked.

"Yes. Unresolved."

Woods decided to move on. "So, about four o'clock
you got done with the mediation?"

"Yes, it was a little after four. Carmin had to dash
back to get to the student by four thirty."

"Was Helen at her house or at the student's
house?"

"She was at Carmin's house. The student had to
come to Carmin's house. I talked to Nancy about re-
working relationships for about five minutes."

Woods said, "Hold on just a second. In your first
thing you told me, what did she accuse you of lying
about?"

"She didn't get specific. But what she was alluding
to was this summer when she was in New Mexico. I

had a preset appointment at the eye doctor [for Helen]. Helen had to go to the eye doctor off and on for the last couple of years. Now you might have noticed that she wears glasses. The appointment that we had in July, I had to leave a little bit early, and when I left I said, 'Don't forget, I have to have a receipt for reimbursement.' The doctor said she wants to see Helen in about a month. I got a call a couple of weeks later (8:57 P.M., Murray's right hand remains hidden, tucked between his legs. He has kept it concealed for more than thirty minutes. He here gestures wildly with his left hand), or three weeks later, from the eye doctor's office and they said, 'We don't have another appointment for Helen on our books. When did you want to bring her in?' I said, 'Carmin was going to make the appointment.' Carmin didn't do it." (Murray is again facing the south wall. He is turned completely away from Doug in what Schlerf calls "closed, protected body language.")

"Is that your eye doctor here in Manhattan or Lawrence?"

"Here. I made the appointment and it happened to be for when Carmin was out of town. I thought I had told her about it and she thought she had told me that she did not want me to take Helen to any kind of doctor without her, Carmin, also being there. So when she got back and she was moving things out of the house on Everett, her mom was there. We got into it a little bit, although for us getting into it was never what you would think of getting into it." (Murray has squirmed around in his chair, but when he finishes speaking he is again facing the south wall.)

"What is your definition of 'getting into it'?" Woods asked.

"We never argued (Murray turns and looks at Doug, making eye contact again, then immediately looks back at the floor) when we were married. We

never raised voices. We never yelled. She was raised
in a house where her mom and dad yelled a lot. She
let me know early on that we couldn't do that. Plus,
she was a mediator, so we resolved our conflicts
peacefully."

10

The most glorious exploits do not always furnish us with the clearest discoveries of virtue or vice in men; sometimes a matter of less moment, an expression or a jest, informs us better of their characters and inclinations, than the most famous sieges, the greatest armaments, or the bloodiest battles whatsoever.
—Plutarch, *Lives*, "Alexander," A.D. 79

The first portion of the interview confirmed for Detective Doug Woods basic profile information about suspect Thomas Murray and his relationship with the murder victim. Woods knew that Murray had earned a doctorate in English and met Carmin Ross when she was his student at Ohio State University. Professors are not supposed to date their students, but Murray apparently did not believe that rule applied to him. It was a bit of a stretch, but that disregard for the rules could indicate that he did not believe that other rules, such as the law against homicide, applied to him either.

Woods understood from his phone calls with Angela Hayes and others that Murray became furious with Carmin when she became pregnant. Before they married, when Carmin turned twenty-one, Murray had told Carmin and her family he wanted to have lots of children. After they were married, he told Carmin he never wanted to have children. After Carmin became pregnant, Murray would no longer have intercourse with her.

Woods learned that in September 2002 Carmin went to a New Age "energy medicine" conference in Wichita convened by orthopedic surgeon Mary Lynch. Dr. Lynch had stopped practicing traditional medicine and now engaged in "consegrity," a practice that originated in Wichita. Dr. Lynch had coined the term "consegrity" from "consilience" and "tensegrity." Consegrity seemed to be a belief in "remote energy healing" that can take place after sessions with a trained practitioner.

At this New Age conference, held in Wichita in 2002, Carmin Ross met Larry Lima. They began an affair. This led to Murray and Ross's divorce and a surprising custody battle. Until the divorce, Carmin had told family and friends that she was essentially raising their daughter on her own because Tom did not want to have anything to do with raising the child he'd never wanted. Joslyn Dugas told the author that Tom virtually had an allergy to his daughter. After the divorce, Tom wanted every right and visitation to which he was legally entitled. Control freak Tom Murray exercised what remaining control he had.

In the CBS *48 Hours* episode on this case, titled "A Mind for Murder," correspondent Richard Schlesinger asked Carmin's parents, "How does a peace-loving mediator-type person react to a nasty custody battle?" Danny Ross answered, "She [Carmin] described it to us that her Mama Bear claws are gonna have to come out."

True-crime author Diane Fanning, citing social science and criminology research, wrote in her 2006 book, *Gone Forever*, about a husband who murdered his wife when he learned she was planning to leave him, "The fact is that the most dangerous time for any woman is that transition period from when she decides to leave, through the months of separation. That is when many women are battered. That is when many women die." Doug Woods thought Murray had controlled Carmin since she was his student and that her murder occurred because over the past few years he had been losing control over her. With, he believed, her impending move to California with their daughter, he was finally losing his last little bit of control over her. Woods wanted Tom Murray to gradually talk himself into a confession.

In July 1981 in Riley County, Kansas, just outside of the city of Manhattan, a seventy-four-year-old woman was attacked by a man while she was sleeping in her bed. The attacker covered her face with the bedcovers, hit her on the head, and raped her. When he left, she called the police. They took her to the hospital, and vaginal semen samples were taken and preserved pursuant to the rape kit procedures of the day. Semen samples from the bed at the crime scene were also preserved.

Shortly after the rape occurred, a twenty-two-year-old soldier stationed at nearby Fort Riley, Eddie James Lowery, was involved in a traffic accident very near the victim's home. Suspected of the rape, he was taken to the Riley County police department, put in an interview room, and questioned all day. He was not provided food. He asked for a lawyer but was told he did not need one. During his interview he was provided all the details of the crime. The session in the police interview room was not audio-recorded or video-recorded.

The police said he confessed.

Lowery said he did not. Legally, he recanted, saying

he was coerced and deceived into making statements while he was injured from the car accident (his clothes were torn and he was bleeding) and impaired from going without sleep or food. But the case went to trial and the judge admitted the "confession."

At the time, before DNA testing was invented, all that the prosecution could show was that the rapist and Lowery were both blood type O. About forty percent of the population in the USA has blood type O. The prosecution argued that Lowery's blood was consistent with the rapist's blood. Lowery's first trial ended with a deadlocked jury.

In Lowery's second trial, in January 1982, with the same evidence and the same arguments, he was convicted of aggravated burglary, aggravated battery, and rape. He was sentenced to eleven years in prison and served his term in Lansing State Prison in Kansas.

After he was released from prison, Lowery was required to register as a sex offender. Each year he was required by law to re-register as a sex offender. In 2002, twenty years after he was convicted, Lowery hired attorney Barry Clark. Lowery said he was innocent of the rape and that if the biological samples had been preserved, DNA testing, a much more accurate method of identification, would prove it.

Fortunately the court had ordered the samples preserved. Portions of the samples were sent to a California laboratory for initial testing. They exonerated Lowery as the rapist. Then the laboratory in the Kansas Bureau of Investigation retested the samples. They agreed. The DNA in the semen collected from the bed and from the victim's vagina did not match Lowery's DNA. Lowery could not have been the rapist. The DNA excluded him.

In April 2003, a judge in Riley County District Court vacated the judgment and conviction of Eddie

James Lowery. He was no longer a convict. He was no longer a sex offender.

Unlike Lowery, Murray would repeatedly be offered food, drink, bathroom breaks, an attorney, and the opportunity to leave. Murray was asked to make a voluntary statement, but he was not coerced into a confession. He was not told details of the crime.

Police all over Kansas had learned from the Lowery case. They would not make the same mistake again.

11

On Friday, November 14, the Lawrence news media learned that something had happened at the Sears kit home at 1860 East 1150 Road. When they arrived they saw that more than ten police cars, a command center bus, and police tape surrounded the house. The identity of the victim was being withheld, but a death had occurred that the police classified as a homicide.

A reporter located the previous tenant, Cynthia Breitenbach. Breitenbach said that a woman from Manhattan had moved into the house. She thought she had one or two children. She had met the woman briefly when she moved in in August but did not recall her name.

John and Irma Jeane Crown, two of Carmin's nearest neighbors, were interviewed by deputies and later by reporters, but said they had noticed nothing unusual. They didn't even know that a woman lived in the house. John Crown did say that there had been an increase in traffic along East 1150 Road, also known as Douglas County Road 7, because nearby Douglas County Road 1029 had been closed for repairs.

Neighbor Charles Taylor, who lived south of the house, told a reporter that after the police arrived he witnessed a green Saturn SUV being towed away. He had seen the woman who lived in that house driving that vehicle.

Passerby Alan "Red" Arboyle told authorities that between 7:30 A.M. and 8:30 A.M. on Thursday morning, November 13, he had seen a woman sweeping the front porch of that house. An examiner of shoe impressions later told a jury that the shoe impressions on that porch were consistent with the Earth Shoes worn by Carmin Ross.

On Friday evening Angela Hayes called Joslyn to tell her Carmin had been murdered. They were both grief-stricken and in disbelief. Carmin was so lively, how could she be dead?

Joslyn would later tell the author that of all the reasons she had imagined that could have caused Carmin to miss her appointment, the possibility of Carmin's being murdered had never entered her mind.

Tom Murray was not told how his wife died, and he had not asked, but before he left the Riley County police station, the people of Lawrence knew that Carmin had been murdered. The lead sentence Saturday morning in the *Lawrence Journal World* newspaper article about Carmin's death read, "A woman found murdered Friday in her rural Douglas County home has been identified by the Douglas County Sheriff's Office."

The Lawrence paper reported that Carmin Ross, of 1860 East 1150 Road, had been murdered, but the authorities had released no information about how she had been murdered.

A gun?

A knife?

Strangled?

Suffocated?

Beaten?
No information was given.

Tom Murray left the police department, went home,
and made a long-distance telephone call to his friend
Dr. Gay Lynn Crossley-Brubaker. Gay Lynn had
taught in the English department with Murray at K-
State, but was now teaching at Marian College in Indianapolis. Murray was planning to visit her over the
Thanksgiving break. Murray told her Carmin was
dead, he had met with the police all night, and they
were treating Carmin's death as a crime of passion.

Doug Woods was exhausted. Arriving home in Lawrence from Manhattan after the long interview with
Murray, he wanted only to fall into bed and sleep.
    The previous afternoon Woods had had a pounding
headache. Then he was ordered to report to the
crime scene. He headed the investigation. He partici-
pated in the phone calls with Angela Hayes and the
others. He had the ninety-minute journey to Manhattan, then the confrontation with Tom Murray when
he thought he was going to have to tackle Murray
and rescue the child. Then he had the all-night interrogation and the frustration of not obtaining a confession. He was exhausted. However, Sheriff Trapp
had told him to get two hours' sleep and then go
back to Manhattan.
    Doug Woods had grown up with a father who was
a homicide investigator. In his family such a schedule
was the rule, not the exception. He was used to his
father calling and saying, without elaboration or clari-
fication, that he would not be home. His father might
not be home for days, though they might see him on
the television news or see his photo in the newspaper
at a crime scene. They knew he was gone because he
was doing important work.

Doug's family knew from news reports that Douglas County was conducting its first murder investigation since April 2001, when the body of thirty-eight-year-old Dale Alan Miller of Topeka had been found buried in a field west of Lawrence. They surmised that Doug was working the murder case.

The sheriff had ordered him to get two hours' sleep and then return to Manhattan to continue the investigation. Therefore, Doug was determined that he was going to sleep for two hours, then go back to work.

And that was what happened. He returned to being wholly mentally absorbed in the chase.

Doug went back to Manhattan, to Tom Murray's house, where he met with the Riley County crime scene investigators. They had found a luminol reaction on the garage floor on the driver's side next to where Murray parked his maroon Saturn sedan. The reaction indicated to them that Murray had dropped blood when he exited the car. Other things could cause the luminol reaction, however, even horseradish, but the test was relatively inexpensive and was used as a first step to tell investigators where the promising areas were to search for DNA evidence.

This was good news.

The investigators photographed everything. One never knew what might later be important evidence in a homicide trial, if it ever came to that.

One of the things photographed was the fuel gauge on Murray's Saturn.

Doug spoke with Robert and Angela Hayes. They said that while caring for Helen in Murray's home they had smelled a strong odor from the fireplace. They thought it was the smell of bleach and something that had burned. Doug checked the fireplace but couldn't smell what the Hayeses had said they smelled.

The crime scene investigators also checked the fireplace but did not find anything unexpected.

Nine days after Carmin's murder, Tom Murray had his wood-burning fireplace destroyed and replaced with a gas fireplace. The stone from the original fireplace was sent to the landfill. Contaminated, it was now worthless as evidence.

Helen would later say she and Daddy had played a "burning game" in the wood-burning fireplace.

At 3:00 P.M. Saturday afternoon, Sheriff Rick Trapp held a news conference. He disclosed that Carmin Ross, a forty-year-old attorney and single mother, was found killed at 1860 East 1150 Road, near Lakeview Lake. The sheriff's department went in response to a call from her fiancé in California after he had been unable to reach her.

"We found what we believe is a crime of violence," said Sheriff Trapp.

The news media reported that Sheriff Trapp still disclosed no details about how the woman was killed.

In their Sunday morning editions, the *Lawrence Journal World*, the *Manhattan Mercury*, and the *Topeka Capital Journal* each printed substantial reports.

The *Manhattan Mercury* reported that former Manhattan city prosecutor Carmin Ross, who had also served as K-State's director of employee relations, had been found murdered in her rural Lawrence home. Her ex-husband was K-State English professor Thomas Murray.

The *Topeka Capital Journal* reported that Carmin Ross was not practicing law but had been working as a self-employed mediator. She had earned degrees in English and law at Ohio State University. The police had made no arrests but were following leads, including leads outside of Douglas County.

The *Lawrence Journal World* described the crime scene as "gruesome." Sheriff Trapp was quoted as saying that the crime scene investigation work done by Douglas and Shawnee County coroner Dr. Erik Mitchell, and the Lawrence Police Department's CSI unit was thorough and painstaking. They had been there since Friday afternoon and probably would not leave before Monday.

A reporter reached Char Shropshire, who had worked with Carmin in the employee relations office. She said she was too upset to talk.

Another reporter called Thomas Murray's home. He wrote that a man answered but had no comment.

On Monday, Douglas County officers stopped cars traveling in front of Carmin's house and asked the drivers if they remembered anything about the previous Thursday morning. A roadblock was set up at the intersection south of Carmin's home, and traffic passing on the Trucker's Turnpike was stopped, as well as the heavy volume of traffic that traveled north on 1850 Road past Carmin's home.

Cadets slogged through the creeks south and north of Carmin's home and to Lakeview Lake, probing and looking for the murder weapon, clothing, anything that might be relevant to the case.

Sheriff Rick Trapp said that area residents should not be alarmed but should be cautious. Trapp said, "Until we learn more, maintain the usual safety precautions: Keep your doors locked and keep your lights on."

Additionally, the sheriff department spokesperson, Lieutenant Kathy Tate, asked the public to report anything that might help solve the crime. Tate said, "Maybe people don't think that their information is particularly pertinent, but we would prefer that they contact us and let us make that decision." The local news media published and broadcast the appeal.

12

Interview Room #2

"She was a peace lover," Murray said of Carmin. "And me too. I mean, we would protest the violence in the Middle East and all that stuff together even after she was living apart and we were separated.

"I forgot what I was saying. Why was I telling you that?"

"The mediation," Woods reminded him.

"Yes. So I think that she believes that I lied when I took Helen to this eye doctor appointment when Carmin was not in town. Then I told Carmin about it afterwards, sort of nonchalantly. 'Well, the appointment went well. We don't have to go back for six months.' She got a little huffy.

"She said, 'You went to the eye doctor without me.'

"And I said, 'Yes. I told you I was.'

"And she said, 'I told you I did not want you to.'

"So it was sort of that kind of thing. So there were some kind of cross, angry, slightly angry, words at the mediation. I mean, you could ask Nancy Hughes. She could probably characterize it better, more objectively. It was nothing.

"So, I'm not good at directions. Getting from one

place to another. But I had directions. I had done it a couple of times already, getting from Fraser back to Carmin's house. And I confirmed with Nancy how to do it and with Carmin. And I said, 'I'm not going to follow you. I am going to do this on my own.' So, I made it back to her house. I didn't take any wrong turns. I made it back.

"And we went in the house and I wrestled with Helen a little bit. I think Helen took me up to her playroom. No, I think it was the other time I was there. I think I wrestled with Helen a little bit on the, on the, um, is there kind of, um, Indian-looking—I forget what you call them. What do you call them? Pellum? It's an expensive carpet we had. But, anyway, it doesn't matter.

"Yes, we have this carpet on the floor and Helen and I were wrestling on it. Then about probably five o'clock, or a little after five o'clock, maybe a little later, I said, 'You know it's going to take us a while to get back to Manhattan, Sweetie.' To Helen. It takes me a little longer than most people because I have a thing about staying, I don't ever drive over sixty or sixty-five miles per hour, so it takes me a little longer to get places. I didn't want to get home so late that we wouldn't have time to eat before we got to bed. (9:01:30, for only the third time, Murray looks at Woods. Then he again looks away. Murray's body is facing east.) So we got home and it was later than I thought. It was almost seven."

Woods asked, "So what time did you leave Carmin's?"

"I think it was about five o'clock."

"In the evening?"

"I think so. That was Tuesday. And then Helen and I stopped at—Helen calls it her favorite Chinese restaurant in town—to eat, and then we went home."

"You stopped in Manhattan to eat?"

"Yeah."

"What time did you stop and eat?" Woods asked.

"I don't know," Murray answered. "It might have been like a quarter to seven or seven. It was late and Carmin had just told me that she thought Helen needed more than ten or ten and a half hours of sleep a night.

"She said, 'Shoot for something a little closer to eleven and a half or twelve.'

"And I said, 'Okay.'

"So, I'm looking at my watch knowing that Helen and I have to get up kind of early the next morning. That was Wednesday."

(November 12, 2003, the day before Carmin's murder.)

"Why was that?" Woods asked.

"Because I have to take her to her child care person, the preschool person. I usually get her there about a quarter till nine, and then I have to go and if I don't do that then I don't get a parking space and I park off campus on the green zone."

"So what time did you think you got home after eating?"

"Tuesday night?"

"Yes, sir."

"Well, it was, I don't know exactly. It was later than I wanted. (9:03 P.M. At this moment Murray turns completely south, eyes open, and looks at the blank wall. He again has his back to Detective Woods.) I think it was going on eight o'clock because Helen wanted to walk in the dark. It's a kind of game we play, and do other things, but I said, 'We have to brush our teeth and get ready for bed.' We did that. I think we were asleep by eight fifteen or eight twenty Tuesday night."

"Did you hear from Carmin again on Tuesday night?" Woods asked.

"Not Tuesday night. But she called again Wednesday night. Helen and I were sitting on the couch and Helen was not feeling well. She was all congested when the phone rang. I said I was tired too. I said, 'I'm not going to get that, Sweetie, do you want to run and get it?' But no. And then we could hear from the answering machine that it was Carmin's voice. Helen said, 'Pause the movie.' We were watching some movie. She went and got it [the phone] in the bedroom and I got it in the kitchen and I could hear that she and Carmin were talking, so I turned off the machine. That was Wednesday night."

"What time was that call?"

"Oh, we tend to call between, it might be anywhere between six thirty and eight o'clock. Carmin was probably calling earlier rather than later, thinking that I was going to try to get Helen to bed."

"Do you always call?" Woods asked.

"Every day," Murray answered.

"It's an everyday thing?" Woods asked.

"Yes. But this time it was going to be different because I heard—and I was surprised about this—I heard when Carmin was helping to get Helen in my car, she said, 'Now you want me to call you every other night?' And Helen said, 'Yes.' So I thought, 'Oh. That's a change.' So I figured it was going to be if she called, we saw her Tuesday, so she would call Wednesday night and Friday night and then we were going to do the switch again in Topeka on Sunday. So she called Wednesday night. And then, yes, Wednesday night. And then Thursday was when I got the e-mail from her. Wait a minute. When did I talk to her on the phone? Because she said, 'Did you get my e-mail?'"

(The prosecutor would later claim that Murray slipped up here, in his statement at 9:05:20 P.M., Friday, November 14, 2003. The prosecutor would claim that Carmin asked Tom that question not over the phone but just before he murdered her.)

"And I had gotten it, but I hadn't responded to it. It was about having Helen a little bit early to Topeka on Sunday. But anyway, then I checked my e-mail on—"

Woods asked, "So which came first, the phone call or the e-mail?"

Murray said, "Let me think about it. I got the e-mail at work Wednesday afternoon. I'm sure about that. But I didn't answer it. Then we got the call Wednesday night."

Woods asked, "What was the gist of your e-mail?"

"It was saying what I said. It's all small talk. But I need Helen back by noon on Sunday because she's going to a birthday party. And I would like to have the crate that was on the front porch, which we had talked about. And that box of Christmas decorations, that's mine. I want that. And there was something else. Oh, do you think you could bring the car topper with you when you come on Sunday? But I didn't have time Wednesday. I gave midterms in two of my three classes on Wednesday and I didn't have time to enter student stuff. And I didn't have time to answer it. So Thursday I got my midterms graded. And then played with Helen all afternoon. Then when Helen went to bed that night, and I think she was asleep, I think I looked at the clock and it was like eight-oh-seven or something like that—pretty early for us."

"You said Helen was in bed a little bit after eight?" Woods asked.

"She was asleep because I always lay down with her until she goes to sleep. I cuddle with her, then I sneak out after she dozes off. I'm pretty sure I glanced at the clock. I remember seeing eight-oh-seven. The first thing I did was go up to the office and because I thought, well, I want to answer that e-mail and see if

I got any other e-mails today. So I did that. I answered that e-mail that I just described to you. But there was another e-mail from Carmin Thursday night. If I remember right, if I remember right, when I hit the reply thing, and, you know how it says 'on such-and-such a day at such-and-such a time you said this,' and I think that she wrote the message—it was either—I know there was a two in it. It was either twelve or two, and she had written the message that afternoon. I got it that night and I answered it."

"So you are saying that she wrote the message at two o'clock on Thursday afternoon?" Woods asked. (He's nailing down Murray's claim of the time. Later analysis of Carmin's computer would show that her last e-mail was sent to her sister Heather at 9:09 P.M. Wednesday, November 12.)

Murray answered, "Well, I couldn't swear to that. But I remember there being a two in it. It was either twelve or two. I thought it was two, but it might have been twelve-oh-two or two-oh-two."

"Okay," Woods said. "In the afternoon, though?"

"I think so," Murray answered. "But that was Thursday. Then, today, I did not get an e-mail from Carmin. I was not expecting anything. I mean, because when I sent her my e-mail, the e-mail I responded to, the one I described to you. Otherwise, the last thing I said was, 'See you Sunday.' So I wasn't expecting to talk to her again. But then I got this other e-mail from her. It was a one-line or a two-line thing. The one that she wrote early that afternoon. She said, 'Can you please remind me what Johanna and Kenny named their baby?' So I answered it with one or two lines Thursday night. And then we were expecting a call tonight. And, in fact, we were just getting ready to go to bed when you guys came. I thought it was kind of funny that Carmin hadn't called, although sometimes she loses track of time. She was never very good about—she didn't like clocks. She didn't like time. And I figured, well, she'll probably call later or leave a message like she often does. Helen would hear it in the morning. So on the one hand I was thinking it was a little strange that she hadn't called. But on the other hand it—sort of fit into a pattern. I didn't think much about it. And that brings us up to now."

13

Murray said that he did not talk with Carmin on Wednesday night, November 12. He said that his last conversation with her was at her house on Tuesday, November 11, at 5 P.M., after their mediation meeting.

But a check of the e-mails sent by Carmin and received by Murray, and a review of phone records for Wednesday showed that Carmin had sent Murray two e-mails. She had provided a list of Helen's things that she wanted Tom to bring when they exchanged custody.

On the police tape at 9:05:20 P.M., Tom said that in his last conversation with Carmin, she had asked, "Did you get my e-mail?"

The only time that Carmin would have asked that question would have been either on Wednesday, when Murray said that they had not spoken, or on Thursday morning before she was murdered.

In her opening statement, prosecutor Angela Wilson told the jury, "His own words will help to show you that he is the one responsible." In her closing statement, she emphasized to the jury what she called Murray's slipup. The way the prosecution interpreted the evidence, they had Murray on tape saying that he had at least a brief conversation with Carmin on Thursday morning, just before he murdered her.

14

Interview Room #2

Detective Doug Woods asked, "Earlier, you said something about a phone call. Did you get a phone call or was it an e-mail? Did you get a phone call from her Thursday night, or were you just referring to the Wednesday night phone call?"

"No. I didn't get a phone call from her Thursday. I don't think—I'm sure I didn't. In fact, I didn't talk to her on the phone Wednesday. It was just Helen who answered it."

"This Larry guy. They are married now? Are they both living in Lawrence?" Woods asked.

Murray answered, "No. As far as I know he is in San Diego now. This is the other interesting thing that Carmin said at this mediation we had Tuesday. I forgot that she said, 'I wanted to tell you that Larry is moving to Lawrence.'

"I said, 'Oh.' Thinking, 'Hey, this is great! Maybe they're not going to move to San Diego after all.' But I said, 'Is this temporary or permanent?'

"She said, 'Well, for now, it's just temporary, but he is going to move here,' and that's all I can—that's all she said about that.

"I think, as we speak, he is probably in San Diego.

I think Carmin described it, I mean, I don't know much about it, but it was outside of town. It's sort of in the greater San Diego area. Kind of a rural place. Helen told me that across the street they have horses and somebody has chickens. So I'm picturing kind of a farm rural existence. But then I saw a picture of Carmin and Helen in a swimming pool. But I think that might have been Larry's brother. I don't know.

"I have asked a lot of questions," Murray continued. "And Carmin, one of the things she's done over the last thirteen or fourteen months is draw very definite boundaries. She sort of alienated people. She's sort of estranged herself from her family in the context of this New Age business. It was kind of bizarre. I mean, her mom and dad were using words like they thought she was possessed or had been brainwashed, you know. Her dad thought she was psychotic, he told me in June, because of the things she had been doing and done were so far out of character.

"I just talked to a person that Carmin used to work with, named Shar, who called me the other night. And she said, 'Tom, I got your new number. Is Carmin there?' And I said, 'Oh, you haven't heard the story?' And I told her the whole thing sort of the way I told it to you. Her first response was 'Is Carmin on drugs?' I said, 'Well, I can't imagine that, but I don't know. The old Carmin would not have even thought about it. But the new Carmin was so far away from the Carmin that I knew that I don't really know.'

"But anyway, that brings us to this," Murray concluded.

Detective Woods asked, "Tuesday night, you would have gotten home around eightish, you think?"

"Tuesday night," Murray answered. "That's the night we went to the Chinese restaurant? I think we got home around eight."

"And then you had to get up early the next morning. Who watches Helen?" Woods asked.

"Not real early," Murray answered. "I mean, I get up about six and Helen gets up around seven."

"Who watches Helen during the day?"

"I take her, well, the woman who came to be with Helen while I'm with you, Angela. Her little girl is Helen's best friend."

"What is Angela's last name?"

"Hayes. And they have hired a college student named Lacey who has been with both of them, both of the girls, now, for a couple of years. They both love her [Lacey]. I dropped her off at Lacey's on Wednesday morning."

"Wednesday morning?" Woods asked, to confirm.

"Yes."

"Where does Lacey live?"

"I mean, I didn't drop her off at Lacey's. Lacey goes to the Hayes house. Because I'm in class it's not convenient for me to go back and get her. One of them, Rob or Angela, brings Helen back to our house. Then I have another student who has a key and she is there by twelve noon."

"You said, 'Rob and Angela bring Helen to your house'?" Woods asked.

"Rob or Angela bring her on the way to taking Mikala to kindergarten. They drop Helen off at our house and Peiwen is there waiting for her. She stays with her until I get home from work Monday, Wednesday, Friday evenings."

"You said, 'Monday, Wednesday, and Friday'?"

"Yes. I have a Monday-Wednesday-Friday schedule this semester, on classes."

"So, then Tuesday and Thursday mornings, are you open?"

"Yes. Tuesday and Thursday mornings are my time. It's really the only time I have when I'm not with

Helen. My time to get my research and, this week, it was all the midterms I had to grade."

"Okay. So then, Tuesday and Thursday, Helen was with Rob and Angela."

"Yes. She goes with Lacey over to the Hayes house. She goes there Monday through Friday."

"What about Tuesday and Thursday afternoon?"

"Then she is with me. That is our special time together. We might go out and about to town or just stay around the house and play or whatever. But we're always together the rest of the afternoon, the rest of the day."

"So, do you have her a week at a time, normally?" Woods asked.

"We've been going on an every-other-week basis.

"I don't know if this matters. That is something else that Carmin and I talked about at the mediation. My impression was that this every-other-week thing was working out pretty well. But Carmin wanted to adjust it a little bit. She's got Helen going to a preschool in Lawrence. I don't know the name of it. Stephanie is one of the women who runs it. But one of the things we are trying to work on with Helen is, she is just very, very shy. And Carmin said she is making such great strides with Stephanie at the preschool. That is Monday, Wednesday, Friday in Lawrence. She would like her to be there every Monday, Wednesday, Friday. So she suggested for the next semester that I pick Helen up, say, Friday at the end of preschool and have her back Monday before preschool starts so that Helen could go to preschool every Monday, Wednesday, Friday morning. I think we were going to talk about that this next Tuesday. That is when our next mediation is scheduled."

"Do you and Helen do anything Wednesday evening?" Woods asked.

"Wednesday evening I got her in bed pretty early after the phone call from Carmin. We brushed teeth and I think she was asleep, uh, actually. The other thing we are trying to work on is that she starts putting herself to sleep. I think I might have left the room a little bit before she was asleep. I might have walked out about eight on Wednesday. Usually by eight I'm comatose. So I sat down and I watched *West Wing*," Murray said.

"Thursday," Woods asked, "daytime, what time did you drop Helen off?"

"That's a good question. Because I don't have to get to class my eye is never on the clock. It's always, like, well, let's keep moving. We don't stop to play games, but we don't have to rush. I would have to ask Lacey for sure. I wasn't really watching."

"What time do you have class on Wednesday morning?" Woods asked.

"Monday, Wednesday, Friday I teach nine thirty, eleven thirty, and one thirty."

"So Wednesday morning you would have dropped Helen off at what time?"

"It was about a quarter till nine. Then I hightailed it to my parking place. Wednesday I had a meeting, a promotion meeting, a reappointment meeting, that lasted till about four thirty," Murray said.

"You had a meeting when?" Woods asked.

"Wednesday afternoon." Murray answered.

"It was what kind of meeting?" Woods asked.

"We were meeting to discuss the reappointment of one person and a promotion of another person to full professor. It's called a reappointment and promotion meeting.

"I got home at ten after five o'clock because I remember writing down that I was going to pay Peiwen $31. I give her $6 per hour. She was there from twelve to five ten, so it came to $31. Then Helen and I played a little while and then we had dinner."

"Did you stay in or eat out?"

"We don't go out much. We stayed in. We had already ate our special treat out this week, so we stayed in and ate. She was in bed—well, she got the call from Carmin, it must have been between six thirty and seven—and we finished watching the movie we were watching, and I had her in bed by eight. I watched television for a while, then I'm always in bed by ten."

"Thursday morning—what did you do Thursday morning?" Woods asked.

"Thursday morning we got up like always. We played a little on the way getting ready. I think you know I wasn't hurried or anything. I think I had her to Lacey by, it would have been probably a quarter to nine and nine because my intention was, I had brought, I had two classes' worth of midterms that I had to get graded.

"I always get the test back the very next day after people take them. I never miss doing that. So I knew I had to get them graded the next morning. My intention was, I was going to the campus office and grade them there because, I don't know why, but I got to my usual parking spot and, you know, it was all filled up. I thought, 'I really don't want to sit in this office anyway,' so I drove home and probably got home by, I don't know, I wasn't looking at the clock, around nine fifteen or twenty. No, it would have been nine thirty, because I dropped her off about nine. Then I proceeded to grade—actually, I got them all done, all the midterms, handed them back today. Then Helen got there about ten after twelve. Normally she eats before she comes, but—"

Woods interrupted. "So you think she got home about ten after twelve on Thursday?"

Murray answered, "It was about that. We ate lunch together, which was unusual. Normally she eats with Lacey. But when Angela dropped her off she said, 'She hasn't eaten lunch.' She said, 'She wants to eat lunch with Daddy.' "

(Woods believed that at the time Murray was addressing, he had just returned home and finished cleaning up after murdering Carmin.)

"So we had our lunch together there at the house," Murray said, "and then we played the rest of the day until dinnertime, and ate, and it was nothing spectacular. It was just a regular day."

15

Interview Room #2

After describing the day Carmin was murdered as "It was nothing spectacular. It was just a regular day," Murray continued, "We didn't go out or anything. I asked her [Helen] if she wanted to [go out], but she said, 'No, I just want to stay home with you.' And I said, 'Okay.' We played that evening. I think again I had her in bed eight or eight fifteen. That's the time I'm shooting for, and that was Thursday. Then today, again, I had her over to Lacey about a quarter till [eight forty-five]. Actually, I got there a few minutes early. And I walked in and I saw these projects that Mikala and Lacey, Mikala and Helen, had been working on. Then I went to campus. Today I got home about five ten or five twenty, because I remember I was going to pay Peiwen about $32 for today. So I gave her the check. We ate dinner tonight and had our evening."

"Thursday night, what time did you go to bed?" Woods asked.

"Regular. I'm always in bed at ten."

"Sit tight here for just a minute. I need to make a quick phone call. I'll be right back. Do you need anything? Bathroom? Water? Pop?"

Murray answered, "No." Woods left the room and Murray was left alone, but was still being recorded.

In the interview room by himself at 9:26 P.M., Tom Murray starts talking aloud. He puts his left hand on his stomach. His right hand remains hidden under his leg.

"Oh, God. Oh, God. I could be sick."

Murray is quiet for a time, then twists, folds, straightens, and intertwines his arms, palms briefly up and out, moving in ways that are difficult to describe, finally settling in a posture something like an ancient multi-armed Hindu statue.

"Helen. Oh, God.

"Helen's not going to have a mommy.

"Helen's not going to have a mommy.

"Oh, God. I could get so sick.

"Helen.

"Helen.

"How am I going to tell you, you don't have a mommy?

"Oh, my God.

"How am I going to tell Helen?

"Mommy died.

"Mommy went to heaven.

Murray took a drink of water.

"Oh, that's not smart.

"Helen.

"Danny and Judi are going to be devastated.

"Oh, my stomach.

"I'm going to be sick.

"This has got to be a dream.

"Wake up."

At 9:32:29 P.M., when he concluded his soliloquy, Murray looked directly into the camera, as if to be sure that it had recorded his performance. Detective Schlerf would testify, "On the wall to his right is where the microphone is mounted on the wall, and I took significance to this because during the times that we were not in the room he was talking to himself, and it appeared that he had taken notice of the camera and the microphone, and that the narration was more for our value than anything else."

While Murray was alone in the room the Douglas County detectives and two Riley County detectives, Brad Schlerf and the coincidentally named Doug Wood, met and continued to monitor Murray. Schlerf pointed out Murray's shifting body posture, gestures, and infrequent eye contact. They brainstormed about how to proceed. Woods decided he would begin asking some leading questions, taking Murray back to Tuesday, then bringing him to Thursday, when he would ask whether Murray drove to Lawrence on Thursday morning.

Because of Schlerf's experience it was decided that he would return to the room instead of Armbrister. Schlerf would be able to directly see Murray's body language. This took about twenty minutes.

Woods returned to the interview room with Schlerf. Schlerf sat in a chair to Murray's right while Woods sat at the other end of the table. In his pretrial notes Schlerf wrote, "I took the seat across from Murray to observe his physical responses to Detective Woods's questions." Schlerf thought that to this point Murray's behavior was "out of character" for what was typical for innocent men involved in a death investigation. Schlerf testified that "he was being very talkative. Generally when we speak with someone after a death notification, they're not very talkative other than trying to inquire what happened. He was giving a great deal of detail. The norm would be some sense of confusion, of trying to understand everything that's being presented to him. In this case he was doing all the talking and with a great deal of detail at that."

*   *   *

"How are you doing, Tom?" Woods asked. It is 9:44 P.M.

"I think I'm going to be sick," Murray answered.

Woods said, "This is one of the other detectives from Riley County," referring to Detective Schlerf. Schlerf took his seat and did not speak.

"What are you thinking right now, Tom?" Woods asked.

"How to go home and figure out how to tell my daughter she doesn't have a mommy."

Detective Woods said, "I need to ask you some more questions, okay? You came down here on your own free will. You drove down and have been very cooperative. I appreciate all of your cooperativeness and forthrightness. I need to ask you some more pointed questions. But before I do that, I need to read you your rights. You're not under arrest, okay? You understand that, okay? Is that okay with you?"

"Yes," Tom Murray answered. He did not ask for an attorney. He did not say he wanted to leave. He did not ask for a member of the clergy or a counselor.

"What I'm going to do is, I'm going to read these rights to you. I understand that you are a very well-educated man. I know you know language very well. But I still have to do this. What I'm going to do is, I'm going to read these aloud to you. And these spaces [indicates spaces on a document he is showing Murray], if you understand what I read to you, will you please initial those if you understand, okay?"

Murray nods his head, indicating yes, but he also answers verbally. "Okay. Do I have to wait till you read them all?"

Murray is eager to get on with it. This is a bother.

"First of all, the place is the Riley County PD interview room. The date is eleven, fourteen, two thousand

three, and the time is nine forty-five. Okay, Tom?"
Woods asked.

"Yes," Murray answered.

"Before I ask you any more questions, you must
understand your rights. Number one, you have the
right to remain silent. Do you understand that?"
Woods asked.

"Yes," Murray answered.

"Okay. Anything you say can be used against you
in court. You have the right to talk to a lawyer for
advice before we ask you any questions, and have your
lawyer with you during questioning. If you cannot afford a lawyer and want one before we ask you any
questions, one will be appointed. If you decide to answer any questions now without a lawyer present, you
still have the right to stop answering anytime until you
talk to a lawyer. Do you understand your rights?"
Woods concluded.

"Yes," Tom Murray answered.

"Would you please write the 'Yes' in there [indicat-
ing the document] if you understand your rights?"
Woods asked. After Murray did so, Woods asked,
"Are you willing to waive your rights and speak with
us? Talk to us?"

Murray answered, "Yes."

Woods said, "And if you agree to all that, will you
please sign that and date that, please? The date is
eleven fourteen." After Murray did so, Woods said,
"Now, I sign this as your witness that you did this
freely and voluntarily and I didn't threaten you in any
way or anything like that, did I?"

"No," Tom Murray said.

"Did I promise you anything?" Woods asked.
Doug Woods is now sitting closer to Murray. He has
moved his chair to the east side of the desk. Murray's
posture is opening somewhat. Murray's left elbow is

on the desk. His right hand remains hidden between his legs.

"No," Tom Murray answered.

"Have I been mean to you in any way?" Woods asked.

"Uh-uh," Murray answered.

"Okay. How would you say you have been treated while you have been here, or at your house?" Woods asked.

"Professionally. Very well," Murray answered.

"The time is now nine forty-eight [9:48 P.M., Friday, November 14, 2003], Tom. Let's just, you know, kind of start back over here. We have to start back over. The part I want to start back over is yesterday morning. Actually, let's go back to Tuesday. One of the first questions we use is: Do you have any questions for me?" Woods said.

"No. I don't really understand what we're doing," Murray said. "But I mean, first off, when you came to the door I was assuming that Carmin had a traffic accident. (Murray looks down at the floor, avoiding all eye contact.) But now, I'm assuming this wasn't a traffic accident. Something else happened. I'm kind of curious to know what happened. But you'll probably tell me when you tell me, I guess. That's one of my only questions." Murray then turns away and waves with his left hand.

Woods is irked that Tom Murray does not come straight out and ask how his ex-wife died. Woods has been maintaining a calm, polite, deferential demeanor. But now he becomes a bit aggressive and says, "I come to your house to tell you that your ex-wife has died. You seem to be visibly upset about that news I gave you. I understand the concern for your daughter and so on. You drive down here on your own free will. You agreed to come down here and talk to me. You have yet to ask what happened to your ex-wife."

"I've been thinking about this the whole time," Murray said, "but I just assumed it was a traffic accident until we are getting into all of the questionings and the details. But you'll tell me that when you are ready, I guess." Now Murray's feet begin tapping. He has not been tapping his feet before. He also now begins turning his head to face Doug or Brad when he talks.

Murray's posture is slouched forward, as it has been during much of the interview. Schlerf noted that Murray was tapping his feet "nervously" (Schlerf wrote in his notes) and was sheltering his right hand in his lap. A review of the tape showed that to this point Murray had concealed his right hand the entire time of the interview to this point. His right hand was either under his left leg (he was sitting on it) or it was covered with his left hand or it was between his legs.

16

Tom Murray's doctorate was in English and he taught in English departments. Most university English departments are in the school of liberal arts or humanities, and most Americans think of college English courses as teaching correct English composition. Dr. Thomas Murray had taught English composition, but his scholarly work was in English linguistics. Linguistics is the scientific study of language, is more of a social science than a liberal art, and is often taught in psychology or general social science departments.

Murray had to go to great lengths to justify his linguistics research methods. He wrote, and edited with Carmin, two books on legal and ethical issues in surreptitious (secret) recording. He spied on people to listen to their language.

This verbal voyeurism may have given Murray a thrill. Thomas Murray was a window-peeper of argot, a snoop of lexicon. He was a spy of language, but the key point was that he was a spy, a deceiver, who was not present for the purpose that others were present for. He always had a plausible, socially acceptable basis for his behavior.

It wasn't just Murray's methods that struck some people as perverse, but the topics as well. He researched the once taboo subculture of those engaging in the sexual practice of dominant-submissive control and pain known as sadomasochism. His research was published in his best-known book, *The Language of Sadomasochism*. Sadomasochism is a sexual practice, called perversion by many, that is, sometimes criminal.

The American Library Association periodical *CHOICE* wrote a review of Murray's book on sadomasochism. Quoted on Amazon.com, the review does not say the book is of use to teaching or writing or scientifically studying English, but it does say that it is of benefit to those studying abnormal psychology. Thomas Murray's academic research topics and methods were sometimes odd, as was he.

Linguistics, which became accepted as an academic discipline in America only after World War II, is the scientific study of language. Linguists use statistical tools to analyze language, just as crime scene investigators use statistical tools to analyze fingerprints and DNA.

In 1968 the field of forensic linguistics was initiated in the United Kingdom. Linguistics professor Jan Svartvik studied the 1950 criminal "confession" of Timothy John Evans. In 1950 Evans had been executed in England for the murder of his baby. He was later exonerated and reburied in hallowed ground. The murder for which Evans had been executed was attributed to the serial killer John Reginald Christie. This story is told in the 1965 book and 1970 motion picture *10 Rillington Place*. The Evans case was one of the reasons that Britain abolished the death penalty in 1965. It was proved that an innocent man had been convicted, sentenced to death, and executed. By statistical and logical analysis, in 1968 Professor Svartvik concluded that the person who made the rest of the statement did not make the part of Evans's statement that was the confession, which was purported to be a

verbatim transcription of what Evans said while in police custody. In other words, although Evans made
most of the statement, the "confession" portion was
fraudulent.

Linguistics professor Malcolm Coulthard similarly
analyzed the statement of Derek Bentley, executed in
England in 1953. He concluded that Bentley's purport-
edly verbatim statement was edited by the police such
that its semantic meaning was so transformed as to be
unreliable. In 1998, primarily due to Professor Coulthard's work, a court posthumously overturned Bentley's conviction.

In 2000, Vassar College English professor Donald W.
Foster published his book *Author Unknown*, in which
he shared stories of how he determines "literary fingerprints." Among other things, Foster's analyses of
their writings correctly identified Joe Klein as the pre-
viously anonymous author of the best-selling political
novel *Primary Colors* and Harvard graduate Dr. Ted
Kaczynski as the author of the Unabomber's Manifesto.

In the United States, there are two standards for
admission into court of statistical-based evidence such
as linguistics, fingerprints, and DNA. The *Frye* standard was first used in 1923, and the *Daubert* standard
was first used in 1993. In *Frye*, the standard is the
acceptance of the practice as being scientific by a con-
sensus of scientists in the relevant field. If the majority
of scientists in a given field accept a practice as adher-
ing to the scientific method, then the courts will accept
it. In the *Daubert* standard, the judge has to know
enough science to determine whether the practice is
based on the scientific method. Kansas federal courts
apply the *Daubert* standard; Kansas state courts,
where Murray's case was tried, still use the older
Frye standard.

In 1962 historian Dr. Thomas Kuhn's book *The*

Structure of Scientific Revolutions was published. Kuhn quoted Nobel Prize–winning physicist Max Planck. Near the end of his life, Planck explained in detail how it was only after a long and hard fight that the scientific community accepted quantum mechanics: "A new scientific truth does not triumph by convincing its opponents and making them see the light, but rather because its opponents eventually die and a new generation grows up that is familiar with it."

Planck and Kuhn argued that *scientific* reality is accepted by scientists primarily through social means, not through logical proof independent of the society in which the logic and proof are used. The "in-group," the clique, of the specific relevant body—physicists, medical doctors, psychologists, linguists, biologists, etc.—has to accept it before the community at large will accept it. That is also what happened in medicine, with the slow acceptance of the germ theory findings of Drs. Holmes and Semmelweis. Medical doctors rejected the germ theory for more than a decade until it was accepted by a majority of scientists.

In criminal court, the scientific evidence against Carmin Ross's killer would be accepted or rejected according to the *Frye* standard, the view held by Planck and Kuhn. The Kansas Supreme Court adopted the *Frye* test in 1947. *Frye* requires that before expert scientific opinion may be received into evidence, the basis of the opinion must be shown to be generally accepted as reliable within the expert's particular scientific field. In other words, the court must be convinced that a majority of scientists working in that particular field accept the principle and practice at issue before the court should accept it into evidence. The court wrote, "If a new scientific technique's validity has not been generally accepted or is only regarded as an experimental technique, then expert testimony based upon the technique should not be admitted."

The Kansas Supreme Court has since explained: "*Frye* was deliberately intended to interpose a substantial obstacle to the unrestrained admission of evidence based upon new scientific principles. . . . Several reasons founded in logic and common sense support a posture of judicial caution in this area. Lay jurors tend to give considerable weight to 'scientific' evidence when presented by 'experts' with impressive credentials. We have acknowledged the existence of a '. . . misleading aura of certainty which often envelopes a new scientific process, obscuring its currently experimental nature.' "

This "social acceptance" requirement is echoed in psychological studies of scientists, though they are generally reluctant to permit research into their own processes. Cognitive psychologist Dr. David Faust wrote in his book *The Limits of Scientific Reasoning* that scientists are reluctant to have the tools of scientific research applied to themselves. But, Faust wrote, when such studies are done, it is found that scientists are prone to make all the silly mistakes and colossal errors in reasoning that they ridicule in nonscientists.

17

Professor Don Hedrick, the Kansas State University English department Shakespeare scholar, agreed that Shakespeare's *The Winter's Tale* is an apt analog to Tom Murray's situation. In Shakespeare's play, a man believes his wife is having an affair. He becomes furious and tries to have her killed.

In an e-mail to the author, Professor Hedrick wrote, "As it happens, I did a production of the play at our Manhattan Arts Center, our community theater, in August of the year that Tom was under suspicion [2004], and thus just before his eventual arrest. While I maintained skepticism about whether Tom was guilty, I realized that it was possible, and the possibility that a generally mild-mannered person could snap and become extremely jealous was often, in class teaching as well, in my thoughts as I taught the play and directed it. (I was, of course, also thinking about Tom when I taught *Othello*, and very delicately and tentatively noted in class that surprising events like this did happen, as we know from life.) My thoughts about Tom did, in fact, influence my directing of my colleague Michael Donnelly, who played the jealous husband, Leontes. I remember directing him at one point not to think so much about the 'motivation' of his character but instead to show a sudden, irrational,

explosion of emotion on stage. He tried this out, bolt-
ing from his sitting position entirely unexpectedly, and
it was truly frightening to everyone who saw it. Michael made the stage business a permanent part of our
run, and our local arts reviewer for the *Mercury* even
commented that this was the first time he'd seen the
role acted so believably, even having seen it played
once by Joseph Fiennes in London. So, your hunch
about that play, if it was a hunch, turns out to be
rather on target."

Interview Room #2

"Let's go back to Tuesday, then, to your mediation
meeting. How upset were you when you found out
that Larry was going to move in with her?" Woods
asked.

"No," Murray said. "I wasn't upset. I thought it was
a good sign that he was coming to Lawrence. I thought
it was a sign that—I mean, Lawrence is more counter-
cultural and sorta funky than Manhattan. Carmin, I
think, liked that.

"I was thinking they could buy some land and build
there, or whatever they were going to do there, and
it's sure better than being a couple thousand miles
away. So I was heartened by it."

Woods confronted his suspect. "That is not exactly
the same story that the detectives who are currently
talking to Nancy are telling us."

Murray said, "I was not upset. I'm not sure what
Nancy's saying, but—"

Woods interrupted. "Nancy said that you were visibly kind of upset that this guy was moving to Lawrence to be with your ex-wife."

"No," Murray asserted. "What upset me was that
when I said, 'Is it temporary or is it permanent?' and

she said 'Temporary.' That upset me because I'm thinking, 'Great, we're going to have to go through a custody court thing again.' But when I heard he was coming to town, I thought that was—I was heartened by that."

Woods changed topics. The interview subject is upset but may be on the way to confessing, so for the moment Woods decided to redirect the subject's attention with a simple question. "When is Helen's birthday?"

"December nineteenth," Murray answered.

"Okay," Woods said. That was an easy, nonthreatening question and answer. But Woods was now going to go into dangerous territory.

"I assume Helen was now going to have a birthday party," Woods said.

"Yes," Murray answered.

"And you're not invited to Helen's birthday party, are you?" Woods asked.

"Yes, I was," Murray countered.

"Are you sure about that?" Woods asked.

"Yes, I am sure," Murray insisted.

"Did you tell Nancy something different?" Woods asked.

Murray is knocked off stride. "No," he declared. "Originally, see . . ." He stammered. "Nancy doesn't know the whole story. Originally, the party was to be at my house. Then Carmin decided she wanted to have it at her house. Originally, I was not to be on the guest list. I think that was at a mediation before this one. We might have talked about that. I said, 'Come on. It's going to be really odd for Helen if Daddy's not at the party.' Carmin said, 'Larry is going to be there and I know that you don't have no great love lost.' And I said, 'Well, I have no respect for Larry, for making himself available to a married woman.' But I said, 'I am confident that I can put whatever aside and focus on Helen. Helen is my reason for being, sort of, and I can do whatever I have to to be at that party, and it will be just fine.' And Carmin said, 'I don't want all kinds of negative energy at the party.' And I said, 'Don't worry about it. It will be fine.' So, a day or two later she e-mails me and she said—this is in a long list of things—she said, 'About the party, come.' And she said, 'I'll get back to you with a definite time.' And she said, 'I'm thinking it's going to be late afternoon or early evening.' So, yes, I was invited to the party."

"So she changed her mind, then?" Woods asked.

"Yes," Murray answered.

"Okay," Woods said. "Initially, you were upset. If I were a divorced dad, I would have been upset."

Woods *is* a divorced dad.

"I was more surprised than anything. I mean, you've got to have Dad and Mom both at the party," Murray said.

Woods said, "It makes it a little awkward, now that this new dad figure was going to be in the house, too. I mean, to me, that would bother me."

"No," Murray said. "He's not a, he's made it very clear that he does not want to be a dad figure."

"But he's going to be a man role in her life, right?" Woods said.

"Well, sure," Murray said.

"He's going to have some impact on Helen's life," Woods said.

"Absolutely true," Murray said.

"Positive or negative, it may not be agreed with some of the impacts he has on her life," Woods said.

Murray said, "Frankly, while I have no respect for him, everything that I have heard about him, from both Carmin and from some woman in Wichita at this energy medicine center, and when you read his Web page, he sounds like a nice guy, so—"

Woods interrupted. "How upset were you when you found out your wife was having an affair?"

"I found it out—" Murray began.

Woods interrupted. "Tell me that."

"She had told me that she had met somebody and that she realized that she loved him more than any other person on every level. By which, she meant they kind of have some kind of energetic, you know, connection. I said, 'Did you sleep with this person?' And she said, 'No.' In fact, I don't really know when they consummated the thing. I have no idea. But I know it was an intimate relationship because about two weeks later, this was in October of 2002, mid-October, I remember that because it was the day right before my uncle died. I was walking by where Carmin had her desk in the basement.

"At the time the e-mail program we used was called Juno. We had some power outages at the house. The transformer had blown and whenever that happens, when the e-mail program is on you wind up losing messages and address book entries and all kinds of stuff. So I had said, 'Let's be sure we always exit out of a program when we are done.' Carmin had taken Helen to play at a friend's house in town and I was walking by her desk on the way to something and I saw her e-mail program was running. So I thought she forgot to turn it off again. So I walked over to get out of her program and just glanced at the message on the screen. I saw some words in there that did not seem right. So I read the message and it was clear that it was, how to describe it, sexually suggestive. And I thought it was from this, it was signed, 'Larry.'

"And I thought—well, I was on the floor. I was paralyzed. Could not move. Could not breathe. I was shaking like a leaf. And then I remembered Carmin and I had had a discussion just the previous day. She said that, unintentionally, every time she sent an e-mail, a copy of it was being sent to a file. She had sent a mail file and wanted to disable that, but she didn't know how. So I remembered that. So I got into the 'mail sent' file and I saw this string of messages that she had sent Larry. And, again, I mean, it was, I remember. I am good with language. She said, one of them was that she didn't want to bathe herself because she didn't want to wash the scent of his body off of her. He wrote that he found her hairs all over the bed. And so I'm thinking that she lied to me and that they had consummated this thing. So I went upstairs and I called her and I said, 'You've gotta come home now. Leave Helen there.' So she did.

"And I was on the floor of the entryway. I said, 'Tell me that you're not having an affair with this guy.' And she said no, they were not. I said, 'Carmin, I have seen the e-mail messages.' She said, 'We didn't.' How did she say it—'No intimate body parts touched.' I mean, as I told her later, I was disappointed. I was, I guess there was some anger there. But you say, 'How angry were you?' I don't know if you can quantify it. I mean, I don't think of myself as real, you know, like, throw things around my house when you get angry kind of person. I have never done that."

Woods said, "So this man has his breaking point."

"Well," Murray said.

"Some have a quicker fuse than others," Woods said.

"I suppose that's true. I suppose that's true. I can't remember if I said this earlier or not. I had reached the point where I was okay with the divorce. I mean, I had actually reached the point where I had realized that, as much as Carmin had compromised some things that she believed in, for me, I had done some compromising too. I was not entirely happy with it. I had fallen into this single life again. I was. I can't say that I was happy with it. But I was not unhappy with it. I mean, I was getting used to it again," Murray said.

18

These events occurred early in the first decade of the third millennium, and it was already hard for many people to remember that widespread use of computers in the home, school, and workplace, and use of the Internet, had started only in the final decade of the second millennium. In 1999, the FBI started a pilot project, Regional Computer Forensic Laboratory (RCFL), to address computer crime and evidence, including crimes of violence such as murder. The program grew rapidly, and one of the centers became designated as the Heart of America RCFL (HARCFL), in Kansas City. When Tom Murray's computers were taken, because the Lawrence Police Department was part of the M-Squad, and the LPD was a HARCFL participating agency, Murray's computers were analyzed at HARCFL.

It did not take long before they found that Murray had used the Yahoo search engine to conduct his crime research.

On October 7, because Helen was sick, Carmin missed a child custody mediation appointment. She kept trying to find a sitter until the last minute, so she had not called Tom to advise him of her problem or to reschedule. At that meeting, Murray had planned to give her and the mediator a written document that

he titled "A Modest Proposal." In it he proposed that
Helen live with him because she had already formed
"significant ties to Manhattan." But, other than Murray, Helen's only Manhattan ties were to her babysitter and her preschool. Later in the proposal, Murray
declared that Helen should change schools. The document was entirely self-serving for Murray.

The title Murray selected for the document was om-
inous. "A Modest Proposal" is the title of Jonathan
Swift's 1729 satire proposing that if young children
were a burden to their poverty-stricken parents, they
should be killed and eaten.

Murray was very angry that Carmin missed the appointment. On October 8, beginning at 3:11 P.M., his
computer search inquiries were "How to murder
someone and not get caught," then "Extradition to
United States."

The murder and extradition inquiries would later
raise eyebrows.

But, as of October 8, Carmin had not yet told Murray that she was planning to move to California with
Helen. She missed the October 7 mediation appointment and had not yet told him. There was no reason
for him to think that he was going to have to move
to California if he was to be near Helen.

On Friday, October 17, Murray searched on the Internet for poisons.

On Tuesday, October 21, Murray and Ross met with
mediator Nancy Hughes at their rescheduled gather-
ing. Murray presented his "modest proposal." Carmin
replied with an emphatic "no."

On Wednesday, October 22, for much of the day
Murray made Internet inquiries. Computer detective
Dean Brown testified that on October 22, 2003,
Thomas E. Murray's computer was used to search the
Internet for the following terms:

"murder for hire" at 11:25 A.M.

"how to hire an assassin" at 11:26 A.M.

"how to make a bomb" at 12:54 P.M.

"how to kill someone quickly and quietly" at 1:15 P.M.

"how to kill someone" at 1:20 P.M.

"saxotoxin" at 1:26 P.M.

"where to find saxotoxin" at 1:28 P.M.

"how to get saxotoxin" at 1:28 P.M.

"sarotoxin" at 2:34 P.M.

"the best way to murder someone" at 3:24 P.M.

"how to poison someone" at 3:29 P.M.

He also searched for "how to plant drugs," "high explosive," and "drug overdose."

On November 5, Murray searched "the best way to kill someone."

On Monday, November 10, Carmin and Helen were in Indiana. Murray searched for "eyedrops, murder, CSI." This is the only time that either his home or his work computer indicated that he visited the *CSI* television program Web site. He looked only at a script that described how to murder someone with tetrahydrozoline, which is the active ingredient in Visine, which had been used in a *CSI* episode. Tetrahydrozoline purported to be a perfect poison—odorless, tasteless, and colorless.

In his Internet searches Murray never entered terms such as "how to write a script," "how to obtain a Hollywood agent," or "how to write for *CSI*."

Murray did research on Rohypnol (flunitrazepam), a date rape drug.

In the Tuesday, November 11, mediation session, Murray learned for the first time that Carmin's fiancé would be moving to Lawrence after their wedding on November 27. In a few days, Helen would have a family unit with a stepfather, living not in California but right in the same house. Larry planned to live in Lawrence until the child custody matter was resolved. Carmin expected to obtain primary custody of Helen, and then they would move to California.

Murray was emotionally raging. He was near a full boil. In an e-mail to a friend he wrote, "I can't just sit back and have my daughter taken away from me. I'm increasingly coming to feel like an animal that's been backed into a corner."

On Wednesday, November 12, Murray's only searches were for ways to drive from Manhattan to Carmin's house without a record being made of his passing. Because he believed that cameras would record him using the turnpike or passing near tollbooths, his online map searches showed a route using Kansas Highway 40.

Thursday, November 13, was the only morning Tom Murray was known to be in Manhattan, but did not check his e-mail. Every other Thursday his computer showed activity, except for the morning Carmin was murdered.

There are three distinct links between mediation sessions and Murray's murder-related computer searches. First, a mediation session that Murray attended but Carmin missed on October 7 is followed on October 8 by Murray searching for "how to murder someone and not get caught," then "extradition to United States." Second, Carmin's rejection of Tom's "Modest Proposal" on October 21 is followed on October 22 by Murray entering at least fourteen murder-related inquiries, including "how to murder someone" and "the best way to murder someone." Third, Murray learned that Carmin wanted to take Helen with her to California at the mediation session on November 11, which is followed on November 12 by Murray searching Internet maps for ways to travel from Manhattan to Lawrence without passing turnpike tollbooths, where he believed there were cameras. Mediation, then murder research; mediation, then murder research; mediation, then search for a murder-er's route.

Carmin, in contrast, after each mediation session talked with her family and friends and her attorney. She said that she wanted her and Tom to be friends.

ACT II

Real villains will hide all evil traits,
so they'll appear to be too good to be true.

—James Bonnet, *Stealing Fire from the Gods*

19

Interview Room #2

"Are you seeing anybody now?" Woods asked Murray.

"No," Murray answered.

"Have you dated much since you divorced?" asked Woods.

"Never. I don't have time to. I mean, all my energy is going toward Helen," Murray answered.

"When Helen's not with you, what do you do with your time?" Woods asked.

"Research," Murray answered. "I have an article and a book going. I read a lot. I mean, I don't go out. One of the complaints that Carmin had was that I was never social enough for her. I mean, I'm just not, I'm not a go-out-and-party kind of guy."

"Dinner and conversation—nothing like that is at all interesting to you?" Woods asked.

"No," Murray answered. "In fact, I had a conversation with a colleague today who went through something very much like I went through with Carmin, she went through with her husband. He left her and immediately moved in with somebody else. She said within six months she was starting to get interested in seeing somebody. Just this afternoon I said, 'Well, I can't picture myself ever doing that.' I said, 'I've been there, done that.' Sort of got kicked in the teeth. I don't want to do that again. Plus, I have baggage. I mean, I have a five-year, almost a five-year-old daughter. I'm just not interested in doing that."

Woods asked, "So after your meeting, you go back to Carmin's house. You find your way over there. How long do you think you were there that time?"

Murray answered, "Let me think. We got there, I might have gotten there at four thirty or so. I'm sure I was out of there by . . . if I got home at seven and I left the restaurant it takes me about an hour and forty-five minutes to two hours. I might have been out of there by five o'clock."

"It sounds like to me pretty much that your world totally revolves around your daughter," Woods said.

"I have my daughter and I have my career, my profession," Murray said. "Carmin had suggested when I said, 'Please, don't go to San Diego.' She said, 'You can come with us.' I said, 'But I'm twenty-one years in the profession. I'm rooted here. I'm sort of at the top of the food chain. I can't just go knock on the door of the first school you see and say, 'Here I am. Hire me.' I said, 'I'd be giving up my career, not just my job.' And she said, 'Well, if I don't go to San Diego, I'm going to be giving up essentially the same thing.' I said, 'No. It's not the same thing.' I said, 'You don't have a career right now. You have this dream of being a healer, but you're not.'

"But I don't know if she ever saw that. But, anyway, we weren't, that was one of those things we weren't communicating on, we weren't connecting on," Murray said.

Woods said, "Back to Wednesday night, or actually, Wednesday morning. You got up. You got Helen out of bed."

"Yes. I parked at nine A.M. and I was there until Wednesday. I had a meeting," Murray said.

"An appointment and reappointment meeting," Woods said.

"Yes," Murray said.

"Thursday, you and Helen picked, or Helen's sitter, went to your house around sometime after noon. She was watched by—what's the girl's name again?" Woods asked.

"Lacey," Murray answered.

"Who watches her at your house in the afternoon?" Woods asked.

"On Monday, Wednesday, Fridays?" Murray asked.

"Yes," Woods said.

"Peiwen," Murray replied.

"She would have been there Wednesday afternoon?"

"Peiwen Wang," Murray said.

"She was there Wednesday afternoon?" Woods asked.

"She was there Wednesday afternoon," Murray said.

"You guys made dinner and played and stuff, right?" Woods asked.

"Yes. She loves to pretend," Murray said.

"What time do you think you dropped her off Thursday morning?" Woods asked.

"I don't know. I wasn't on the clock. But it's my habit to be there between eight thirty and eight forty-five, when I have to go to class. So I'm guessing it was around eight forty-five. But it might have been as late as nine. But that would be kind of pushing it, I think," Murray said.

"When you come to Lawrence, like, say, Tuesday, what is the route that you drive?" Woods asked.

"I get on 70 [U.S. Interstate Highway 70] and I go

to the very first exit to Lawrence, the one that says 'Lecompton Highway 10,' and I get off there. You go through a tollbooth and you turn left. Go as far as you can, turn right, and go a couple of miles and you turn left on Carmin's road," Murray said.

"Okay, that was the route you would have driven Tuesday night?" Woods asked.

"That's coming home," Murray answered.

"So when you pulled out of her driveway you turned right?" Woods asked.

"No. No, you pull out of her driveway and you go left," Murray said.

"Okay," Woods said.

"You back up to the main road and you turn right. You then get on the highway," Murray said.

"Out of her driveway, you would have turned left?" Woods asked.

"Left. You go as far as you can and you turn right. Then I don't think you turn again. I think you see a sign for 70. Then you turn left and there's the tollbooth. I think that's right. I have only done it two or three, three or four times. But I think that's right," Murray said.

"Since you guys divorced, she moved here when?" Woods asked.

"To Lawrence?"

"Yes."

"About August first," Murray said.

"You said you've driven to Lawrence how many times?" Woods asked.

Murray said, "I have driven to Lawrence several times with the mediations, but I've driven from my house to her house—"

Woods interrupted. "So anytime you come to Lawrence, do you always use I-70 and the turnpike?"

"No. If I go to Fraser I get off at, I think it's the second exit at 69," Murray answered.

"But you use I-70 the entire time," Woods said.

"Yes," Murray said.

"You told me earlier that you had been to four or five mediations. Is that correct?" Woods asked.

"I don't know exactly. It might be four," Murray said.

"What do you do at Fraser Hall [in Lawrence]?" Woods asked.

"That's where Nancy meets us. That's the psych, I think the psych clinic is there," Murray said. Murray's body is wildly torqued; his legs are turned so that his knees are facing south, his right hand is hidden between his legs, but his torso and face are facing northeast, toward Doug. It is 10:07 P.M.

"How many times have you driven straight to Carmin's house?" Woods asked.

"Let me think a minute. Normally, we meet in Topeka in the parking lot of Sam's Club to switch Helen, trade Helen. I know one week when Helen was sick and she could not come to my house I went to Lawrence once or twice to visit and help take care of her. I was there, you said, 'How many times have I driven from my house to her house'?" Murray said.

Woods said, "Yes, to Carmin's house."

"It might just be once," Murray answered. "It might just be once or twice. I think the other times I've been there I came from Fraser Hall."

"Okay, but driving directly from your house, you're telling me that was one or two times, okay? Always taking I-70?" Woods said.

"Always taking I-70. Yes," Murray said.

At 10:08 P.M. Woods asked the question he'd been leading up to: "Thursday morning, did you drive to Lawrence?"

Murray sighed, lowered his head, breaking eye contact, slumped in a posture of defeat, and answered emphatically, "No!" Then he resumed eye contact with Doug Woods. Brad Schlerf said that this was kinesic reaction that told us we were on to something.

"I told you, after I dropped Helen off I drove to my building. I decided not to work there. So then I drove home and I graded my midterms Thursday morning," Murray said.

"So you didn't come to Lawrence at all on Thursday?" Woods asked.

"No. I wasn't in Lawrence on Thursday," Murray answered.

"What about Wednesday evening?" Woods asked.

"No. No, I couldn't be there Wednesday evening. I was with Helen," Murray said.

"Okay. So, Thursday morning, you had some free time and you were going to grade your midterms and so on?" Woods asked.

Murray was facing Woods, looking at him eye to eye, but then he closed his eyes. "I had from the time that I dropped Helen off until the time that I got her back again, yes, about three hours, give or take," he said. His answer was given with his eyes closed. A linguist would take the text of Murray's words and conclude that he had just said that in those three hours he had graded midterms. However, in the interpretation of his body language, under these circumstances, because he closed his eyes when he said it, he had just told a lie.

"Is there anybody that can vouch for you Thursday evening?" Woods asked.

"Let's see. I was sitting in my kitchen the whole time. I don't think the phone rang. The guy who lives across the street. He's retired military. Tim. I don't know whether his garage door was up when I pulled in, but if he, probably would be the only one, I guess," Murray said.

"So he wouldn't know if you were home all morning Thursday morning?" Woods asked.

"Well, he wouldn't know if I was home all morning, but he would know when I pulled, he would have seen me, probably, pull back in," Murray said.

"What time do you think you would have gotten back to your house after you dropped Helen off?" Woods asked.

"I wasn't on the clock, but I'm going to guess between nine and nine thirty, something like that. Nine. Nine fifteen. Because I had a good about two and a half or so hours' worth of grading to do. I got it all done and I gave those back today. I have another batch that I have to get back on Monday," Murray said.

Woods and Schlerf wanted to discuss Murray's answers. They exited the interview room. It was 10:10 P.M. When alone, Murray immediately looked at Woods's handwritten notes, which, he, eager to talk with Schlerf, had inadvertently left on the table. Via the monitor in room 236 Brad saw Murray and exclaimed, "Hey, he's looking at your notes." Woods immediately returned and grabbed his notes. Murray had read the notes for about one minute.

Murray then assumed the posture of Rodin's famous bronze and marble statue *The Thinker*, a posture with chin on hand in sober contemplation. Murray looked directly into the camera.

20

Three weeks after Carmin's murder, Detective Doug Woods traveled to the campus of Ohio State University in Columbus to learn more about Carmin Ross and Tom Murray and interview people who knew them.

Tom's dad died when Tom was nine. Apparently his mother had difficulty coping with life's details, and Tom quickly became the de facto head of the household. After age nine, he did not have a normal childhood because he was attending to bill paying and other activities normally performed by adults. One person thought that in his childhood Tom distorted his needs for the needs of his surviving parent. This left him with emotional needs that Carmin fulfilled.

Woods learned that when Carmin Ross and Tom Murray met in 1984 Murray was a twenty-six-year-old Ph.D. who was teaching English and Carmin was his twenty-year-old student. Carmin was working toward a bachelor's degree in English.

The faculty and former students whom Woods interviewed said Murray was unpopular. They acknowledged that he was distinguished, intelligent, and capable, and in the classroom he was a superior teacher, but his natural personality was controlling, cold, aloof, and imperious.

In contrast, Carmin was so smiling and friendly that wherever she was, she soon became the most popular girl. The lithe five-foot-six, one-hundred-pound Carmin was beauty-pageant lovely. When she entered a room all eyes turned toward her. With her bubbly personality, she was always the life of the party.

Perhaps to compensate for his own unpopularity by having a popular girlfriend, perhaps to prove his superiority, Murray seduced his student. This violated university rules. Instructors are in a position of dominance over students and have the power to determine the success or failure of students' careers. Because of this unequal master-servant status, sexual relationships between faculty and students are forbidden in universities everywhere, including at Ohio State University. Murray ignored this rule. Carmin was starry-eyed over the attention that this tall, handsome, well-off, and brilliant man showered on her. She succumbed to his advances.

At first, Carmin's parents and three sisters were wary of the relationship. When they met Murray, however, he was at his most charming. Because Murray wanted to marry Carmin and "have a bunch of children," her parents and siblings came to approve of him. When Carmin turned twenty-one, she and Tom married in Columbus, Ohio. Carmin earned her English degree and then graduated from law school.

Against Carmin's wishes, the Murrays then moved to Manhattan, Kansas. Tom quickly became a full professor at Kansas State University. Carmin worked as a Manhattan city criminal prosecutor, though she had never wanted to live there.

Carmin wanted to become pregnant and start a family. Tom refused. Contrary to his earlier indications, he said he never wanted children. This constant conflict in their lives was their private civil war and ultimately determined their fate.

*   *   *

When Detective Woods returned to Kansas, he found that Murray's students said he was grading their midterm exams as they were handed in. Some were handed back during class. Woods concluded that Murray had lied about grading papers that Thursday morning.

In addition, Woods found that some students at Kansas State University, in contrast to those he interviewed at Ohio State University, loved Professor Thomas Murray.

But certainly not all students at Kansas State University admired Murray. Murray had been student Paul Fecteau's assigned advisor. Fecteau wanted to make English a career, and he did. He became a popular English teacher at Washburn University of Topeka, Kansas. He's been published and produced and has written a novel, a nonfiction book, and a screenplay. In the summer of 2006 Fecteau told the author he went to Murray for advising only once. In their single private meeting Murray, objectively, was unfailingly professional in the text of what he said. Superficially, he was well mannered. But he seemed unctuous and smarmy and insincere, except when he showed his true cold, impersonal, and discouraging side. Murray said that creative writing as a career was so difficult that he could not advise Paul to pursue it, which Fecteau took as an insult. Thereafter, Paul sought counsel only from other English professors. He'd heard the same thing from other students—don't go to Murray for counsel.

On investigation, it seemed that Murray was able to charm some students because Carmin had tried to coach him to become less cold and aloof and more likable. This is supported in part by Murray's dedication to Carmin in his 1995 linguistics textbook, *The Structure of English*. It read: "C D R-M" (Carmin D.

Ross-Murray] has taught me nothing about linguistics, but a lot about living."

Woods learned that Murray was what is commonly called a "control freak." Not only was he smug in his intellectual superiority, but he showed it in control of his classroom and in his personal life. As an example, Carmin's family said that on the Friday after Thanksgiving when the women would go shopping while the men watched football, Tom Murray would go shopping with the women. They believed this was because Tom wanted to keep an eye on Carmin. He tried to control her life.

21

On Wednesday, June 30, 1993, nineteen-year-old Pittsburg State University student Stephanie Schmidt was raped and murdered by a man she worked with at Hamilton's, a Pittsburg, Kansas, restaurant. (Pittsburg is just east of Parsons, Kansas.) Donald Ray Gideon was on probation, supposedly on a supervised release pursuant to rules of the Kansas Department of Corrections, and worked at the restaurant as a dishwasher. He was also Stephanie's neighbor, so they saw each other often and knew one another. Gideon had served ten years in prison after being convicted of a brutal rape of a young woman who was attending college. Neither Stephanie nor the restaurant manager knew why Gideon had been in prison. Gideon had lied and said that in case his parole officer contacted him, he was on parole after serving time for a bar fight.

For nearly a month, Stephanie was missing. For a month, radio, television, print media, and flyers asked the public to be on the lookout for Stephanie Schmidt, who turned twenty on July 4, 1993. She was described. Her last known whereabouts was her birthday party at Bootleggers Bar and Grill in nearby Frontenac, Kansas. She celebrated with her college friends, then planned to go to her parents' home in the Kansas City area to celebrate her birthday with her family. No one knew what had happened to her after she left the tavern. Everyone hoped Stephanie was still alive.

Shortly after Stephanie went missing, one of her friends, a young woman who was also attending Pittsburg State University, went to see Professor Julie Allison in the psychology department. Dr. Allison was personable and accomplished, admired by many of the young women on campus, and they felt comfortable coming to her. The young woman told Dr. Allison a surprising story: Stephanie had come to her, told her she was dead, had been murdered, but that everything would be all right. Dr. Allison told the author that she and the student discussed the matter thoroughly. They discussed all the various possibilities, including the likelihood that her experience was a dream or other psychological artifact, but the student calmly, confidently, and firmly said that her experience was different, but was just as real as what she was experiencing now. Stephanie was dead. Stephanie had communicated with her.

This episode led Dr. Allison to become a researcher in the field of after-death communication, a legitimate area of research for psychology. There is no claim of supernatural activity by social scientists. They collect, correlate, and present data on people who report being visited by loved ones who are missing or are known to be dead. With her student Kelli Gariglietti, Dr. Allison wrote a seminal paper: K. P. Gariglietti and J. A. Allison (1997), "Lay-persons' perceptions of after death communication," *Journal of Personal and Interpersonal Loss* 2:71–82.

On Friday, July 2, the police started looking for Stephanie. On Sunday, July 4, the news media asked the public for information. On Tuesday, July 6, Don Gideon did not show up to see his probation officer. The police started looking for him and told people that Gideon had been convicted not of a bar fight but of brutally raping a twenty-year-old college student in Parsons, Kansas.

On Friday, July 16, 1993, *America's Most Wanted* broadcast a segment about the missing Stephanie Schmidt and Don Gideon. The next day Gideon called the police and turned himself in. He was in Volusia County, Florida, but had already tried to escape into Canada from Washington. Canada had refused Gideon entry because of his felony conviction. He had traveled from the center of the country to California, up the coast to Canada, and then all the way back across the country to Florida. Gideon didn't tell the authorities where to find Stephanie's body until July 27. She was buried on August 2.

For his crimes, Gideon was sentenced to ninety-nine years' imprisonment.

The horrifying events had a life-changing impact on Stephanie's family and friends. Her family started the Speak Out for Stephanie (SOS) Foundation, which increased public awareness of the legal issues related to Stephanie's murder and was instrumental in legislative changes including but not limited to public access to the names and whereabouts of registered sex offenders and a law authorizing civil confinement of sexual predators.

Another young woman, another of Dr. Allison's students, was deeply affected in 1993 by Stephanie Schmidt's murder. Twenty-year-old Angela Wilson worked with Stephanie on the student newspaper, the *Collegio*. The experience inspired her to go to law school and become a prosecutor. In 2005, in her first murder case, still haunted by the ghost of Stephanie Schmidt's murder, she would prosecute Tom Murray.

22

At 10:08 P.M. during the November 14, 2003, video-recorded interview, Murray told the police that the previous day, November 13, he was in his home all morning grading papers. It took him at least three hours to finish. He had taken Helen to the babysitter's that morning so that he would be undisturbed at home while he graded papers. Today, on the fourteenth, when he dropped Helen off at the babysitter's, he told the babysitter his brain was still "mush" from grading the papers.

Both of the women at the day care, Angela Hayes and Lacey Bonine, said you could set your watch by Tom Murray's schedule. He always arrived with Helen at 8:45 A.M. Both women said that November 13, 2003, was different. When Angela came downstairs at 8:20 A.M., Helen was already there with Lacey and Murray had departed. Angela thought her clock must be wrong. But Lacey Bonine said Murray had dropped Helen off early, about 8:15 A.M. About four hours later, at 12:25 P.M., Angela took Helen to Tom Murray's home. Like all day-care providers, she kept careful records of when children arrived and departed.

But on Friday, November 14, according to the women, Murray was back to his normal schedule. He arrived with Helen at 8:45 A.M. that morning.

When each of Murray's students was interviewed, it was confirmed that Murray had been grading papers as they were turned in. He returned many students' papers on Wednesday, November 12. He had no papers to grade on Thursday morning, November 13. He had lied to the police.

In addition, the students in Murray's Friday morning, November 14, linguistics class, said that morning he explained that the previous day his daughter, Helen, had injured him while they were playing octopus. He showed the class his injured finger on his right hand. The students did not remember Murray ever sharing personal information like that before.

Babysitter Lacey Bonine said that Thursday was the anomaly, because on Friday he dropped Helen off at the normal time, 8:45 A.M. Murray also told her that his brain was mush from all the grading he had done the previous day.

When Lacey was shown the clothing the police had tested, the clothing that Tom Murray said he had worn that day, she said those were not the same clothes. She remembered Murray wearing brand-new shoes of a different color. The shoes were of a different type and were so new that they had no creases. The shoes the police were showing her now were old shoes. The coat was of similar color but a different length. She swore that those were not the same clothes.

Just before Carmin's murder, Tom Murray had his hair cut very short, a buzz cut, almost bald. No one had a recent photo to show this, but everyone agreed about it. In the preliminary hearing, Gay Lynn Crossley-Brubaker testified that when she saw him at Carmin's memorial service, she was shocked at how short his hair was.

23

Interview Room #2

Detectives Woods and Schlerf returned at 10:26 P.M.

Woods said, "Are you doing all right? Do you need to go to the bathroom or anything?"

"I'm sleep deprived. I haven't slept more than three hours," Murray answered.

"Why is that?" Schlerf asked.

"Helen stopped at the Chinese restaurant Tuesday night and she ingested a little cheese. She has a thing with dairy and refined sugar. It causes congestion. She refuses to blow her nose, so when she gets horizontal with snot in her nose, instead of breathing silently, she snores. Her bed is right next to mine in the bedroom and very often she crawls up into bed with me to cuddle next to me. With her loud breathing I haven't slept more than two or three hours each of the last three nights. Plus, I'm guessing that it's going to be way past one o'clock before I go to bed tonight," Murray said.

"How is your health?" Schlerf asked.

"My health?" Murray responded.

"Are you in good shape?" Schlerf asked.

"Physically, you mean?" Murray asked.

"Uh-huh," Schlerf responded.

"Yes. I think I'm in excellent shape," Murray answered.

"When was the last time you went to the doctor?" Schlerf asked.

Murray looks at Schlerf when he answers. Murray is now turning to look at the detectives when he speaks.

"It's been a few years. I think I had, what do you call it, colonoscopy. I think I had one of those two or three years ago. But I'm in excellent—I mean, I work out six days a week. I think I'm in excellent shape," Murray said.

"Where do you work out?" Schlerf asked.

"In my basement. I have stuff down there."

"Do you have any kind of injuries? Swollen muscle? Things like that, that you get from working out?" Schlerf asked.

"I've had a problem with my left shoulder for years. Right now, it's not bothering me," Murray said.

"Have you recently had any kind of injuries? You know, sprained wrist? Stubbed toe? Anything like that?" Schlerf asked.

"You mean down to the most minor thing?" Murray said.

"I mean something that would physically—you would have to work around it, you know," Schlerf said.

"I don't think so. Work around? I don't think so. Like favor one leg or the other?" Murray asked.

"Yes. Pulled muscle. You had to limp a little," Schlerf said.

"I've had a pain behind my right knee for years, too, but that's not acted up. I think the answer's no," Murray said.

"Okay. Do you have any cuts, scrapes?" Schlerf asked.

"Yes. Take a look at this," Murray said, showing his right hand.

"What is it?"

"Yesterday—what is today?" Murray asked.

"It's Friday." Woods answered.

"Yesterday, I was playing octopus with Helen. Octopus is where I come at her and tickle her and stuff. I was laying on the carpet in the living room on my back with my arms stretched out. This part of my finger was down on the carpet and when she picked up her leg, her heel, she went 'boom' on my right, here on my finger. Did that ever hurt. You can't say anything because she's so sensitive that if she knows she hurt you. Look at it, I mean, you can tell it's swollen a little bit," Murray said.

Murray shows the officers his hands and wrists. Schlerf and Woods both stand and walk over to look at the marks Murray is showing them. This is about the only time all three men are clearly visible in the recording.

"Bruise there," Murray said, indicating his wrist. "But it doesn't really hurt. It hurt at the time."

"It's not so bad," Schlerf said.

"No. And I've got some little things, you know, cleaning out the gutters. I've been sticking my hand down the downspouts and screws catch me here and there," Murray said.

"So you've got some scrapes on your arms," Woods said.

"No. Not on my arms. But my hands are dinged up," Murray said.

"Nothing recently, within the last week or two?" Schlerf asked.

"Yes. I was up on the gutters, I think last Friday. So that's a week. Just yesterday afternoon after lunch, Helen was, when Helen wanted to come home with me, I had bought a fresh pineapple. I was cutting it apart and sliced into my hand there, and she said—she hates the sight of blood—and she said, 'Oh, Daddy, is

it bleeding?' and I said, 'Yeah. But just a little one,' "
Murray said. Again, both detectives are standing and
looking at Murray's injuries.

"Hold your hand up for me like that," Woods instructed. He wanted to see the cut on Murray's right
pinky finger.

"Calluses," Murray said. "I tried to cut off. This is
when I when I was on the ladder. I caught hold of
the gutter because the ladder started to slip."

"Pull your shirt up for me," Woods instructed.
Looking at Murray's arms, Woods asked, "What's on
your arm there? What are the bruises on your wrist
from?"

"This? I guess that's from playing with Helen, too.
That's the only time I get stuff like that," Murray said.

"And your other wrist?" Schlerf asked.

"No," Murray said, indicating no bruise.

"Are you right- or left-handed?" Woods asked.

"Right," Murray answered.

"Can you hold that arm up for me?" Schlerf asked.
"It's kind of hard to see from the side."

"Oh!" Murray said. "I've got something there,
too."

"You said you're right-handed. Right?" Schlerf
asked.

"I'm right-handed, although ever since I've been a
teenager I try to do everyday things both ways. I
mean, I try to shave left-handed and brush my teeth
left-handed," Murray said.

At 10:32 P.M., Detective Schlerf said, "When you
talk, you talk left-handed. You're constantly gesturing
with your left hand. I don't know if you've ever noticed you do that."

"No, I didn't notice that," Murray said.

"You just did it again," Woods said, laughing.

"I may do that in class, too, in fact. In fact, I guess

I do, because I have chalk in my right hand so my left hand is free," Murray said.

"Just so I can check, you have a couple of little injuries here to your hands. Do you have anything on your chest or your back?" Schlerf asked.

"No. You can take a look if you want to," Murray said.

"Do you mind if we take a look?" Schlerf asked. He's referring to lifting Murray's shirt.

"You can just lift it up if you want," Murray said, referring to his shirt. "If you want moles, I've got them." Murray is wearing blue sweatpants that have a bright yellow waistband and white pocket interiors.

"Let me see. Why don't you go ahead and take it off so I can see your shoulders. It would make it a lot easier," Woods said.

When Murray lifts up and removes his pink wolf pack sweatshirt, his skin is seen to be almost shockingly marked with moles. His torso and arms are muscular and trim. His waist is flat. He appears to keep in very good physical condition.

"Turn around."

Murray does.

"Okay. You can put it right back on," Woods said.

"Helen elbowed me in the head last night with her fist or elbow or something a couple of times," Murray said. "I get that every night when she's in bed with me. That's nothing."

At 10:34 P.M. Schlerf decides to affirm that Murray is oriented to the situation and says, "Do you understand what our job is? Our job is basically to try and find the truth of everything that happens and to understand what happened. When we can understand why it happened, and, us being here today is nothing more than that. Just trying to understand the things that happened in Carmin's life over these last weeks or two or whatever. So you know part of why you are here. You have been in her home, correct?"

"Yes. A few times," Murray answers.

"You have stayed pretty much confined to the living room, you know. When somebody comes in my home and they're a guest, I pretty much sit in the living room while we chat," Schlerf says.

"I've been all through the house. I've been up to Helen's play area on the third floor. I was in Helen's bedroom. I don't think I was ever in Carmin's bedroom. I just stuck my head in. I think I've been in every bathroom. In fact, as recently as Tuesday I was in the bathroom downstairs. I went to the bathroom there," Murray said.

"You were in her bathroom on Tuesday?" Woods asked.

"Tuesday, I was in her bathroom," Murray said.

"What one would that have been?" Schlerf asked.

"There's one right as you go in the front door. There's a bathroom there," Murray said.

"And that would have been the one you used on Tuesday?" Woods asked.

"Yes. Because on Tuesday I did not leave the living room," Murray said.

"She's a fairly neat person," Woods said.

"She gets that from me," Murray asserted.

24

Detectives Brad Schlerf of Riley County and Doug
Woods of Douglas County had each traveled interesting career paths that prepared them for this type of
homicide investigation.

While Woods was a Lawrence native, Schlerf was
born in New Jersey, grew up in Florida, and arrived
in Manhattan when he was assigned to Fort Riley
while he was in the U. S. Army. In Florida, Schlerf's
parents volunteered for their local fire department
and ambulance service. At age fourteen, Brad
Schlerf also became a volunteer firefighter. He also
became SCUBA-certified, and he loved swimming in
the ocean.

After high school graduation, Schlerf joined the
army. Scoring near the top of the ASVAB (Armed
Forces Vocational Aptitude Battery) tests, he was told
he could pick a job. He became an aircraft mechanic,
did his job well, and was soon assigned to VIP flights.
He then became an aircraft inspector. In January 1991
he was sent overseas as part of Operation Desert
Storm.

When he returned to the USA he left the military
and took a well-paying job as an inspector for Lockheed.

But he had a desire to become a police officer. He told the author he could not explain that desire other than to say he had been inclined toward public service since he served as a volunteer firefighter at age fourteen. No one in his family had been a police officer. When he left his good-paying job at Lockheed to become a police patrolman, he took a two-thirds cut in pay. In September 1991 he decided to live in the Manhattan, Kansas, area because he had liked it when he was assigned to Fort Riley. He thought this was a good place to live. He had success in the police department, and in 2001 he was promoted to become a Riley County detective.

When he became involved in the Murray case, Schlerf had broad investigative experience as a detective and was busy working on his own homicide investigation, the Opal Trumpp case. Murder cases were not quite as rare in Riley County as in Douglas County, but they were not frequent. Four years earlier Opal Trumpp had been shot to death in her basement. The only suspect was her husband, who found her body, but they had not developed him other than as a suspect. The case had grown cold.

Less than a month ago a woman had told Riley County police that her husband had murdered Opal Trumpp. She said that he was in a drunken rage and threatened to murder her. To prove to her that he could do it, he claimed that he had committed murder before and told her how he murdered Opal Trumpp. The woman provided information about Opal Trumpp that the police had never released, including that she was wearing pajamas under her sweatpants and that she was wearing a sweatshirt with a Christmas tree design. Trumpp was an officer of the Leonardville Bank, and the woman said her husband planned to force her to go to the bank and open it for him. When she refused he shot her, first in the chest and then in the head. Schlerf was investigating the Trumpp homicide when he was sidetracked by becoming the resource and liaison officer on the investigation of Carmin Ross's murder.

25

Detectives deduced that while Carmin was unconscious her murderer walked into the kitchen, selected a Wolfgang Puck boning knife, and then returned. That knife was missing from Carmin's set. It was the only thing missing from the house and it was never found. It was perfectly consistent with Carmin's stab wounds, which were carefully measured at the autopsy.

Because Carmin was facedown, the killer tried stabbing her in the back but struck bone several times in her spinal vertebrae and scapula. The blood smear mark on the carpet showed that the killer then dragged Carmin away from the front door, knelt over her, rolled her on her back, pulled her up by her sweater to raise her shoulders to expose her neck, then stabbed her thirteen times in her larynx. The blows came from the killer's right hand. Carmin was alive until after the stabbing. The coroner reported that she inhaled blood into her lungs from her neck wounds. Then she died.

The Wolfgang Puck boning knife's blade stuck out beyond its handle. If this knife was held in a down grip, where the pinky finger was nearest the blade, and then struck point first into a hard object, such as bone, the blade's sharp extension would cut the pinky finger.

Thomas Murray had cuts on his right-hand pinky finger consistent with the cuts that would be expected from that scenario.

For about the first two hours and thirty minutes of his video-recorded interview Murray concealed his right hand. When Detective Woods saw his cuts, Murray explained that he had cut his finger coring a pineapple. He dryly said, as if bored, that the pineapple core might still be in the trash can.

At trial, the prosecution pointed out that Thomas Murray was right-handed. Had he cut a finger while coring a pineapple, as he said, he should have cut his left hand, because one does not hold a knife in a down grip to core a pineapple.

On Saturday, November 15, 2003, when Doug Woods opened the lid of Murray's trash can and looked inside, he and the other officers exchanged looks of disbelief. This trash can was immaculate. It had been scrubbed spotless. Woods told the author, "This was the cleanest trash can in the world."

There was only one object in the trash can. Right in the center, as if placed there with great care, was the core of a pineapple.

26

Perhaps the greatest crime novel in world literature is Fyodor Dostoyevsky's *Crime and Punishment*. In that masterpiece a brilliant young student, Raskolnikov, is exposed to the following idea, and he accepts it:

> "Let me ask you a serious question. On the one hand you have a stupid, silly, utterly unimportant vicious woman, no good to anybody, who doesn't know herself why she goes on living. . . . On the other hand you have new, young forces [young people, students] running to waste for want of backing, and there are thousands of them . . . promising . . . who might be saved . . . from ruin and corruption . . . with her money! Kill her, take her money, on condition that you dedicate yourself with its help to the service of humanity and the common good: don't you think that thousands of good deeds will wipe out one little, insignificant transgression? For one life taken, thousands saved from corruption and decay! Why, it's simple arithmetic! What is the life of that spiteful woman weighed against the common good? No

more than the life of a louse or a cockroach. . . .
She doesn't deserve to live."
—Fyodor Dostoyevsky, *Crime and Punishment*,
  1866

In July 1984 Thomas E. Murray delivered a paper,
"On Solving the Dilemma of the Hawthorne Effect,"
at the Fifth International Conference on Methods in
Dialectology, held at the University of Victoria, British
Columbia. Murray recommended that for linguistic
research, people should be recorded secretly, so that
they were unaware that they were being recorded. In
subsequent discussion of Murray's recommendation,
other linguists wondered whether the authorities
would arrest the researchers the same as they arrest
those who otherwise illegally invade people's privacy.
Could what Murray recommended be a crime? If not
a crime, could it expose the researcher and his or her
institution to civil liability? And even if it was legal
under the criminal and civil laws, was it responsible
of social scientists to conduct this research? Was it
ethical?
   Murray defended his conclusion that linguists
should secretly record people's conversations in his
book, cowritten with Carmin Ross and published in
issue 76 of the American Dialect Society, *Legal and
Ethical Issues in Surreptitious Recording* (1991). After
Carmin reviewed the criminal and civil legal issues,
Tom addressed the ethical issues. On page 48 he
wrote:

   The philosophy of ethics takes as its central
   tenet that issues of right and wrong can be decided in one of only two ways: either one must
   rely on some established and agreed-upon collection of moral rules, or one must be guided by
   the good and bad consequences of one's actions.

Murray then addressed a series of hypothetical moral dilemmas, including the *circumstances* when the "horrible death of a human being" would be morally wrong and would *not* be morally wrong.

This is an astonishing paper, read in light of later events.

After discussion, Murray concluded that moral rules must be "abandoned" in favor of arriving at "best consequences."

Murray's conclusion spawned tremendous discussion around the world in the community of professional linguists, so much that five years later he wrote a second book, issue 79 of the American Dialect Society, *Under Cover of Law: More on the Legality of Surreptitious Recording* (1996). He further addressed legal and ethical concerns and reinforced his conclusion that linguists had the scientific duty and ethical right to secretly record people's conversations because the ethical thing to do was whatever achieved the best result for the best people.

Tom Murray believed that surreptitious recording was justifiable. He was the moral arbiter, like Raskolnikov. If there was a woman who was so inconvenient that the world—his world—would be a better place if she was no longer alive, he would find her elimination to be morally justifiable.

27

During Murray's prosecution, on Thursday, February 24, 2005, his neighbor Kathy Love testified to a conversation she had with Murray several weeks before Carmin's murder.

Prosecutor: "What did he [Tom Murray] tell you about his marriage?"

Love: "Just that they weren't married any more and that his wife was planning on taking Helen. His wife had a boyfriend in California, and they were planning on moving to California with the daughter."

Prosecutor: "Did he tell you how he felt about that?"

Love: "Sad. He wasn't happy about it."

Prosecutor: "Did you, at this point, when you came over to the house on this day, did you know they had divorced?"

Love: "I don't really talk with the neighbors, so, I knew something was going on. They always left every summer, and so, they were home that summer. He was home that summer. I saw him. And then I saw Tom and his daughter at the swimming pool, just the two of them, and Carmin wasn't there. So, I kinda had a feeling something was going on, but I didn't have all the details."

Prosecutor: "Was there a point when you went to get your daughter?"

Love: "Yeah. She was upstairs, so then I went upstairs. I played a little bit with the toys and then helped them pick up and then went on home."

Prosecutor: "Prior to going upstairs, what were you and the defendant discussing as you were heading up to get Christy?"

Love: "We were talking about, with my sister dying, that had been a hard time. And then he said it had been a hard year for him with the divorce. And then he said, 'I hate to say this, but it would be better if she weren't alive.' "

Prosecutor: "Do you know who he was referring to when he made that statement?"

The witness nods her head affirmatively and says, "Carmin."

Prosecutor: "And where were you when he made the statement?"

Love: "In the front entryway at the bottom of the steps."

Prosecutor: "At this point, was this when you were heading up to get Christy?"

Love: "Right."

Prosecutor: "Did you say anything in response to the comment 'It would be better if she wasn't alive'?"

Love: "Not that I can remember. Nothing significant."

Prosecutor: "When you came downstairs with Christy, was there any further conversation with the defendant?"

Love: "No. The girls were there so we just went ahead and left."

Prosecutor: "When did you learn about Carmin Ross's death?"

Love: "When the detective came to the house on Saturday."

Prosecutor: "You say Saturday?"

Love: "Right."

Prosecutor: "That would be November 15th, 2003?"

Love: "Yes."

Prosecutor: "What was their purpose for being at your house?"

Love: "If we knew any information."

Prosecutor: "At that time did you tell them about the remark that the defendant had made that 'it would be easier if she wasn't alive'?"

Love: "No, I didn't."

Prosecutor: "Did you remember it at that time?"

Love: "Yes, I did."

Prosecutor: "Can you tell the jury why you did not share it with the officers on November 15th?"

Love: "The reason I didn't share it at that time was because he lived just behind us. I thought if he was capable of doing that type of thing, then I didn't want him to be angry at our family. For the safety of us in our family, but then, I thought if he didn't do it I don't want to say anything that would ruin his reputation either. So, I was hesitant about saying anything."

28

Interview Room #2

"Okay. Is there a reason why we're going to find your fingerprints anywhere besides the living room? If, Tuesday, you were pretty much staying in the living room, or in your daughter's room, or in the bathroom?" Detective Schlerf asked.

"I might have been in the kitchen," Murray said.

"No. Since Tuesday. I mean, was there something?" Schlerf said.

Murray leans back in the chair, which is a new posture. He crosses his legs for the first time. His right hand goes under his right leg. His left hand goes to his face. "Let me think. Let me think. I was in the bathroom on Tuesday. Did Carmin ask me to, because I had brought. I can't remember. What the name of the company was. Maybe Spiegel. I had given her a catalog that had come to me because we were interested in getting Helen a Christmas present like a little car of some kind or a little motorcycle. Carmin had said, 'Be on the lookout for it.' So I had brought this to her. I think I followed her into the kitchen. I did follow her into the kitchen. Why did I do that? Maybe she had her catalog out there. But I walked through the dining room past where she had her work area and the table and chairs. I walked into the kitchen. Wrestled with Helen. Went into the bathroom. But I was all on that first level. I know I did not go up the steps," Murray said.

"What size shoes do you wear?" Schlerf asked.

"It depends," Murray answered.

"What are those right there?" Schlerf asked.

"Twelve or thirteen. Probably, I think, twelve," Murray said.

"How many pairs of tennis shoes do you own?" Schlerf asked.

"This is it," Murray answered.

"What other kinds of shoes do you have?" Schlerf asked.

"I have a pair of—they used to call them desert boots—and I have a pair of dressier shoes. And then just house slippers. Oh, I have a pair of black, sort of like penny loafers, except I think they have sort of like little tassels on them," Murray said.

Schlerf asked, "New Balance tennis shoes, and sort of like army-type desert boots?"

"No, they're . . ." Murray said.

"Hiking boots?" Schlerf asked.

"No. They used to call them desert boots. They're about probably fifteen years old," Murray said.

"Describe them for me, then," Schlerf said.

"They're made out of a light tan leather. They come up to about here [indicating on his leg]. I could show them to you in my closet. They are not messy on the bottom like this. I think they are just smooth," Murray said.

"A moccasin?" Schlerf asked.

"It's not a moccasin," Murray answered. "You can wear them out. They are hard-soled."

"Let me see the bottom of your shoes," Woods instructed. Murray lifted one of his shoes. Woods looked, then said, "How about the other?" Murray lifted that shoe, then Woods said, "Okay."

"You were saying, black loafers, house shoes," Schlerf said.

"I know I didn't wear these on Tuesday, if that's what you're going for," Murray said.

"Okay. What did you wear on Tuesday?" Woods asked.

"Tuesday, I had my dress shoes on because I had a pair of slacks and a sweater on. I didn't wear my tennis shoes with that. I don't know the brand," Murray said.

"A couple of things that we need to do so that we can identify what fingerprints and items of clothing and things, fiber kind of things that are maybe at her house that belong to you, okay?" Schlerf said. "What we would like to do is, I have a facility downstairs where we can do your fingerprints. If you agree to doing that, so that we can compare it and eliminate your fingerprints. Also, if we would be welcome to go back to your home, okay, and look around. And you've got some shoes there and clothing items we might look at. Your car. Sometimes carpet fibers from your car, you know, can get stuck within the crevices of your shoes and things like that. If you don't have any problem with that, we would like to be able to look in your car and look at your home."

"Are you going to do that tonight?" Murray asked.

"The child, I believe, is asleep. We had her [Angela Hayes] call here just a little while ago," Schlerf said. "We will try and figure out how we can do that as discreetly as we can to not disturb her sleep. Is there any reason why your fingerprints would be in the house [Carmin's house]?"

"Oh, heavens, yes," Murray answered. At this time, 10:40 P.M., Murray turns toward the person he was speaking to. He continues to do this frequently throughout the rest of the interview, but not always. "They are going to be everywhere. All of the furniture, I helped move it. I don't know anything about the nature of fingerprints. I don't know how long they last. But, when, for example, Helen was sick about three weeks ago, one of the things I did that day, because Helen was located on the couch, she went between the couch and the bathroom because she had the runs. Because of the size of my feet and my knees it was uncomfortable for us to be there. So Carmin said, 'Let's move this table out away from the couch.' So we did that. But then, when I left, and I must have been there probably two or three hours, we moved it back again. Like I said, I helped her move and a lot of stuff in that house came from the cabin."

Schlerf makes a note that Murray is providing excessive detail.

"When you say 'table,' which table are you talking about?" Woods asked.

"She had a kilim rug, she had this blue couch adjacent to the fireplace, and then there's kind of this rustic-looking—I have one just like it at my house—a rustic-looking sort of a coffee table in front of it. She had, I don't know, a candle or something on it. That's the one that we moved," Murray said.

"So you moved it by yourself?" Woods asked.

"No. No. She and I, we did it together. I think either one of us could have done it, but since we were both there we just, we did it together," Murray said.

"So you picked up an end to move it to wherever she was moving it to?" Schlerf asked.

"We only moved out from the couch, you know, like eighteen inches or so. Just so we could give us all room to get in and out because that's where Helen was the whole time," Murray said.

29

*We find in the rules laid down by the greatest
English judges, who have been the brightest of
mankind, that we are to look upon it as more
beneficial that many guilty persons should escape
unpunished than one innocent person should suf-
fer. The reason is because it is of more importance
to the community that innocence should be protected than it is that guilt should be punished. . . .
When innocence itself is brought to the bar and
condemned, the subject will exclaim, "It is imma-
terial to me whether I behave well or ill, for virtue
itself is no security." And if such a sentiment as
this should take place in the mind of the subject
there would be an end to all security whatsoever.*
—John Adams, 1770, Closing argument in defense of
British soldiers accused in the Boston Massacre.
(Criminal defense attorney John Adams later became president of the United States.)

Judge Robert Fairchild of Lawrence, Kansas, was
haunted by a ghost. It was the same ghost that
haunted the English judges, Constitutional framers,
and John Adams. In criminal trials, it is more important to protect the innocent than to convict the guilty,
because when society recognizes that its government

is so untrustworthy, so unreliable, that the innocent are convicted along with the guilty, then revolutions occur. That was a key reason for the American Revolution. The American Declaration of Independence declared that England's King George was ruling the American colonies with absolute tyranny, depriving us of the benefits of trial by jury, obstructing the administration of justice, making judges dependent on his will alone, making law arbitrary, and protecting his agents by mock trial. When government does not provide justice, then the people revolt.

In America in recent years an astonishing number of people who had been found guilty beyond a reasonable doubt and condemned to years in prison, life in prison, or execution, had later been fully exonerated due to DNA advances or by other means. This happened so often that on Saturday, January 11, 2003, Illinois governor George Ryan commuted the sentences of all 156 people on his state's death row to life in prison, saying, "Our capital system is haunted by the demon of error: error in determining guilt and error in determining who among the guilty deserves to die. . . . Today I am commuting the sentences of all death row inmates."

Every judge thinks that a wrongful criminal conviction, a fundamental miscarriage of justice, could happen elsewhere, but "not in my court." But could it? All the judges that it had happened to had thought it could not happen to them.

Robert Fairchild was as well prepared to become a judge as anyone. He learned economics as an undergraduate at Texas Tech, then earned a law degree from the University of Kansas. He practiced law while serving a term in the U.S. Air Force Reserves, taught part-time at the law school, and in 1996 was appointed to the bench.

In 2003 Judge Fairchild went to Memphis, Tennessee, to attend a one-week program for judges at the Institute for Faculty Excellence in Judicial Education. There, he began more deeply researching and developing his PowerPoint presentation that he titled "Not in My Court." He eventually presented it to all 156 district court judges in Kansas and 75 judges in Nebraska. Its purpose is to help judges avoid wrongful convictions.

Judge Fairchild found that most of the time when an accused person is wrongly convicted, it happens because of eyewitness error, prosecution misconduct such as suppression of exonerating evidence, use of false testimony, improper closing argument, or police misconduct such as coerced confessions. Judge Fairchild can provide nearly endless examples of wrongful convictions, as well as recommendations as to what should be done to prevent their repetition.

Robert Fairchild would be the judge in Tom Murray's trial. This judge was dedicated to seeing that accused people receive fair trials. It's possible that for his type of circumstantial-evidence case, Tom Murray could not have had a better judge in all the United States.

30

Interview Room #2

Murray said, "I can deduce that Carmin did not die in a car accident or of natural causes. And [pause] you either think I had something to do with her dying or you're trying to eliminate me from—I don't know if I'm a suspect or what the case is. I'd have to say that I'd be a logical suspect, though, if I were doing this. I know that you're just doing your job. I would do it the same way because I am the new ex-husband and we do have this, I don't know whether it's contentious, but we had this disagreement about where Helen is going to live next year."

Woods leaned over to Murray and said, "I can understand why that'd piss you off. I mean, I'm a divorced person, too. And I have a child. And situations like that will come up where she's had to have a job in another state." Woods is trying to show Murray their commonalities and display empathy.

"As I told Helen," Murray said.

"You know, well, you obviously seem like you're a really good father. You care about Helen very much," Woods said.

"I told Carmin on the phone, you know, if we didn't have Helen, I would be fine with not seeing or hearing from Carmin again. She interpreted that to mean that I actively didn't want to, but I wasn't being mean-spirited, just in a spirit of let's get on with our lives. I think I might have said something like, 'Isn't it too bad that we have a child together because we're going to be in one another's lives forever, you know, until I die, since I'm older and I'm a male," Murray said.

"You can look at it this way: most kids nowadays grow up in a divorced home," Wood said.

"That doesn't make me feel better," Murray said.

"That doesn't make me feel better, either, but it's the way things happen," Woods said.

"My kid is not most kids. She's my kid," Murray said.

Woods crossed his legs. "I agree with you, but you also have to understand that that's just the way things go. Dealing with the fact that she wanted to take off and go to San Diego. I can imagine how irritated it would make a person," Woods said.

"Well, I think there was a chance that she was going to stay. Frankly, Nancy was doing her best. I mean, she brought it up at almost every mediation, the possibility of a Lawrence—well, the proposal I had on the table was to have Helen based in Manhattan and to have Carmin come and go. She could come up the beginning of the month, stay half the month, and then go back to wherever she lived. I was going to pick up the lion's share of the expenses to take care of her home and stuff. She would only have to do that during the school year, you know, because during the summer

Carmin Ross and her
daughter one month
before Carmin's murder
Courtesy of Joslyn Dugas

Photo of isolated farmhouse where murder occurred
Courtesy of Robert Beattie

Tom Murray first told police he was here, home, grading papers when Carmin was murdered. *Courtesy of Robert Beattie*

Murray later told police he decided to drive to tiny Paxico, Kansas, shown here, to look at antique pillowcases.
Courtesy of Robert Beattie

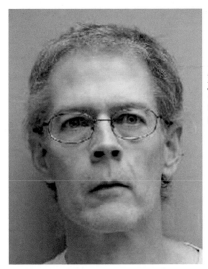

Mug shot of Professor
Tom Murray, PhD
*Courtesy of KS Dept.
Corrections*

Riley County Interview Room #2
Courtesy of Brad Schlerf

Riley County
detective Brad Schlerf
Courtesy of Brad Schlerf

Kansas State University and a Riley County police car
Courtesy of Robert Beattie

Carmin and Tom discussed their marriage on long walks here on the Konza prairie. *Courtesy of Robert Beattie*

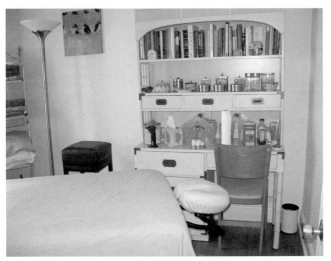

Carmin's missed appointment for acupuncture was the first indication something was wrong. *Courtesy of Robert Beattie*

District Attorney Charles Branson ordered the prosecution to proceed. *Courtesy of Charles Branson*

Murray's trial took place in the Douglas County Judicial Center.
Courtesy of Robert Beattie

Judge Robert Fairchild presided over the sensational trial.
Courtesy of Robert Fairchild

After Angela Wilson's dramatic arguments, the Kansas Supreme Court affirmed Murray's first-degree murder conviction.
Courtesy of Robert Beattie

Prosecutor Angela Wilson
Courtesy of Angela Wilson

Angela Wilson wearing the bracelet she wore during Murray's trial;
it had victim Carmin Ross's photo as a heart-shaped charm.
Courtesy of Robert Beattie

and Christmas and stuff, she could take Helen wherever she wanted to for her time," Murray said.

"Answer me a couple of questions," Woods said.

"Yes," Murray said.

"You've obviously surmised why we're talking," Woods said.

"Well, it doesn't take a rocket scientist," Murray said.

"Right. So tell me why something like that would have happened," Woods said.

"Something like what?" Murray asked.

"Something bad happening to Carmin, and you being responsible for it," Woods said. He is trying to get Murray to begin confessing.

"Well, like I said, because I am the new ex-husband, and—" Murray said.

Woods interrupted Murray. "No. Tell me why I shouldn't look at you."

"No. I said if I were you, I'd be looking at me. I think you should," Murray said.

At the preliminary hearing Schlerf would testify that this is an atypical response. Murray did not take offense, whereas typically in cases when an innocent man is accused of murder he becomes very defensive.

"So tell me what a great guy you are, then. And tell me why I shouldn't be pointing a finger at you a little bit right now," Woods said.

Murray answered, "You've got to know me. I'm sort of the original Boy Scout. I mean, I've always been the serious one in the quiver."

As if to emphasize that he was a straight arrow, at this point his body language completely changes. From being slumped over, he leans back in his chair and sits up straight. His tone of voice changes. Detective Schlerf described him as becoming more analytical.

"One of the points I made at the mediation before

this last one," Murray continued, "was, Carmin likes to make her own rules when she plays a game. In fact, we used to have a joke; we called it 'Carmin's Rule.' It was on the order of Murphy's Law. Carmin's Rule says that if the usual rules in any game don't produce the intended outcome, or necessary outcome, Carmin will do whatever she wants to get the necessary outcome. Well, I'm not like that. I always play by the rules.

"Why shouldn't you look at me? Well, because I'm about as mild-mannered as they come. Although, I mean, you said 'every person has their breaking point.' And I guess I might argue with that. I don't know— different people deal with anger and stress in different ways, you know," Murray said.

"Oh, I agree with you," Woods said.

"I process things verbally. I say things out loud and, you know, it diffuses the nature of the situation for me. Or, I talk to friends. I mean, I have a friend in Indianapolis I talk to regularly. We're going to go there for Thanksgiving, Helen and I. And she's been very—every couple of weeks, we'll call and maybe talk, thirty, forty, an hour," Murray said.

"This is a female friend?" Woods asked.

"Yes. She [Gay Lynn Crossley-Brubaker] used to be in our department here. Then things were not going to go well for her in her review, so she took a job at some Catholic school in Indianapolis [Marian College]," Murray said.

"Okay," said Woods.

Murray is still concealing his right hand, gesturing with his left. It is 10:48 P.M. Murray said, "She took pity on Helen and me for Thanksgiving. She said, 'Why don't you come to Indianapolis?' And I said, 'You know, if you guys are open to it—I know Helen was just there'—Helen and Carmin were there to help her dad celebrate his sixtieth birthday a week or two ago—I said, 'I have Wednesday open.' I'm going to arrive on Tuesday and leave on Saturday. Thursday and Friday are spoken for, but Wednesday is open. I could drive up, borrow Gay Lynn's car, and drive up and we could see, because Carmin's, two of her sisters live right there, right next to Mom and Dad, and then the other one would probably be coming down from Michigan. And she just wrote back today and said, 'Well, we would love to see you, you know, you're our son, but we're going to be in Kentucky at Dan's mom's house.' So, why shouldn't you look at me? I don't know, because I'm a wonderful person. I don't know, my students would be better to. . . . And, in fact, while you were gone, you know, I had asked if I had anybody who could vouch for my presence at the home."

While Murray was talking, Brad Schlerf reentered the interview room with a digital camera. It is 10:50 P.M.

"Thursday morning?" Woods asked.

"The answer's 'yes,' " Murray said. "I have about thirty-five people who can do it. But, it's kind of indirect, but it might be the best I can do. I gave exams on Wednesday at eleven thirty and at one thirty. I had the meeting at three thirty. Went home and had dinner. Played with Helen. As I think I said, I'm comatose by eight. I watched *West Wing*. [The "Separation of Powers" episode in which the climactic drama was a "showdown."] Didn't do grading that night. Graded them the next morning. Played with Helen. One class has eighteen or nineteen and the other class has fourteen. It takes five to ten minutes to do the test. I mean, you could do the math and see how long that takes. I did that Thursday morning. Oh! And the other thing is, well, I can't say I've never lied. Carmin and

I used to joke and argue about that, but I'm an honest person. I'll tell you straight out what I think about something, whatever the case is."

"But then, too, look at it from my point of view," Woods said.

"You have to be suspicious," Murray said. "I understand you're just doing your job. I understand that."

"Nobody has mistreated you or anything," Woods said.

"No. I realize it's nothing personal," Murray said.

Brad Schlerf said, "What I'm going to do, I want to take a couple of photographs of you, okay? And you do have some cuts and things here on your fingers. So I want to take a look at them real quick, okay? Go ahead and pull your sleeves, both of them, up to your elbow."

Murray did, and photos were taken.

"Put them together, so I can get them in the same frame," Schlerf said.

Murray did, and photos were taken.

Murray said, "Actually, I think this is the one with the pineapple."

Seeing bruises on Murray's wrist, Schlerf said, "Turn this one like a knife edge, turn it the other way so your thumb's down." He deliberately said "knife" to see if Murray would react.

When Murray turned his wrist he said, "That hurts."

Schlerf asked, "Why does that hurt?"

"Because I'm going past the point of resistance. I don't know where I ever got these," Murray said, referring to the bruises on his wrists. "Where they came from? I guess playing with Helen."

After some more photos and discussion about fingerprints, Murray is left in the room alone. He speaks aloud about his injuries. Brad Schlerf told the author that he was sure that Murray was narrating for the camera. "Let's see. I think this one I did with a knife. And this one, I just don't know how I got those. I'm guessing." At 10:56 P.M. Murray bangs his wrists on his legs, near his knees, as if he is holding a child and bouncing a child. "I bet that's it." Three minutes later he does it again.

When Woods returned, Murray said, "I'm still wondering about these." He points to the bruises on wrist. "The only thing I can really think of, and this is going to seem kind of lame, but I know yesterday I was playing with Helen like this." Murray acts as if he is bouncing a child on his knees while holding the child with two hands. His wrists bang on his knees. "Among other things. And she had me do it for a long time. Maybe that bruised it. But the odd thing is, there is no pain here." (Indicates the bruise on his wrist.) "So, it's not, I can't even figure out why it's discolored. I mean, normally, a bruise would be—"

Woods interrupted Murray. He'd heard enough of Murray's explanation. He wanted to talk with him about consent to search his car.

31

Alas, my love, you do me wrong,
To cast me off discourteously.
For I have loved you well and long,
Delighting in your company.
           —*Greensleeves*, old English folk song

Carmin's father, Danny Ross, had been an executive in a large corporation but now operated his own consulting business. He and his wife, Judi, were devastated by the news of Carmin's death, as were Carmin's three sisters, Heather, April, and Samantha. After being informed on Friday evening they all arranged to come to Kansas immediately. They went to Tom Murray's home to comfort Helen and Tom.

At Tom's home on Saturday morning, Danny Ross went to take Helen's car seat out of the Saturn. They were going to take Helen with them on a drive. Doug Woods interrupted him.

"Don't touch that car," Woods ordered.

Both Doug Woods and Danny Ross were sleep-deprived and stressed. They glared at each other.

"I'm getting my granddaughter's car seat," Ross said.

"You can't touch anything in that car," Woods replied.

"You're saying that my granddaughter has to drive around without being in a car seat?" Ross asked.

"I'm saying that you cannot touch anything in that car. Sir, I want your granddaughter to be safe, but we are investigating your daughter's murder and we have not released that car and you can't touch it," Woods said. Woods was sympathetic to Ross's situation, but he could not let him take Helen's car seat out of the car until the CSI team was finished, and they were not finished.

Danny Ross stomped off. He was heartbroken and furious about everything. This was just one more thing. He said he'd probably get a traffic ticket now for driving Helen without a car seat. They'd have to buy another car seat, then the police would release the car and they'd have two. This was all a waste because Tom was not involved in Carmin's murder. Keeping his car in custody was silly.

The Ross family decided to arrange two memorial services. Carmin had lived in Manhattan, Kansas, most of her adult life. After graduating from Ohio State University she and Tom had moved here in 1988. She and Tom had divorced in June, and Carmin moved to Lawrence in August, less than four months ago. Carmin had lived in Manhattan for fifteen years, and most of her friends were here. They would have a memorial service in Manhattan at the church Carmin attended, then a funeral back home in Indiana.

Just as Carmin embraced alternative healing practices by her devotion to consegrity and acupuncture, and just as she embraced alternative dispute resolution by moving from the adversarial system of law to the problem-solving method of mediation, Carmin embraced a nontraditional church. She attended and volunteered at Manhattan's First Congregational United

Church of Christ. The church's pastor is openly gay. The church's Web site's biography of the Reverend R. Kent Cormack says that his spouse is William T. Pugh, who also serves as church organist. A graduate of Yale Divinity School, Reverend Cormack presided at Carmin's memorial service. About two hundred people attended.

At the Wednesday, November 26, memorial, Reverend Cormack spoke of Carmin and what she did in the community and what she did in the church. The Noah's Ark scene in the mural in the church's nursery was painted by Carmin, he pointed out. Carmin loved volunteering in the nursery. Cormack and the other mourners returned frequently to the theme of love.

Angela Hayes said, "Better than anyone I've ever met, Carmin knew how to love."

Patricia Howell, who had worked with Carmin, said that Carmin became a mediator because she thought there were better ways for people to solve their problems than through the legal system. "She described herself as a 'recovering attorney,'" Howell said.

Carmin's youngest sister, April, told a story of how she had once seen a spider and wanted it killed, but Carmin picked it up and took it outside to remove April's distress, saying that the spider wasn't hurting anybody. Carmin never wanted to kill anything. She was gentle and kind.

Carmin had actively opposed the American invasion of Iraq. One of the photos at the memorial showed Carmin and Helen at an antiwar demonstration holding a sign that read, ANOTHER MOTHER FOR PEACE.

Carmin's family declined to speak with the news media after the service, but three years later in a telephone conversation Carmin's father told the author that Carmin was the nicest person he had ever known. He acknowledged that as her father he was biased, but he couldn't think of anyone he had ever met who was nicer than Carmin.

Two Douglas County detectives attended Carmin's memorial service. They did not go to Indiana to attend the funeral, but Indiana police covertly recorded the service from the outside, to see everyone who attended.

Later, when Carmin's father, Danny Ross, and Doug Woods were bantering in a jovial mood, Woods asked how much Ross's Hummer cost. A Hummer is an expensive vehicle. Ross reacted strongly. "How do you know that I drive a Hummer?" Woods explained that the Indiana police had recorded the funeral and the Douglas County detectives had watched the video. They identified everyone who attended. They continued to look for suspects other than Tom Murray.

Meanwhile, back in Douglas County, the sheriff's department took a team of cadets and for five miles in all directions from Carmin's home fished around under each bridge, in each ditch, and in each creek. They were looking for the murder weapon, clothing, anything that might give a clue or point the investigation in a new direction. Despite diligent effort, they found nothing.

Joslyn Dugas attended Carmin's memorial.

Joslyn did not set out to become a practitioner of Chinese medicine. She earned a B.A. in philosophy and attended graduate school at the University of Southern California Film School. She started learning about Asian medicine while living in Southern California. She appreciated its harmony and complexity and started a new career as a licensed acupuncturist. Angela Hayes, Carmin Ross-Murray, and Tom Murray came to her for her ministrations and advice. Joslyn's intake protocol with new clients included learning their background information as well as their descriptions of their present emotional and physical complaints. This is how she came to know Tom and Carmin.

In a session with Tom after the divorce, Tom admitted to Joslyn that he punished Carmin for what he saw as her betrayal by becoming pregnant.

Tom admitted that he *punished* Carmin because she became pregnant. One of the ways he punished her was by withholding sex.

Tom and Joslyn each had a session in July 2003, after the divorce. Carmin's energies were focused on healing. In contrast, when Joslyn told Tom that she thought it was time for him to begin a new chapter in his life by making new friends and dating, he replied, "I can't do that. Carmin ruined my life."

Tom's energies were not focused on healing after their rift. They were devoted to his battle with Carmin.

Joslyn was bereft at the news of Carmin's death. Initially, she knew only that Carmin was found dead at her home.

By the time of Carmin's memorial, Joslyn felt a suspicion that Tom was Carmin's murderer. She felt ashamed and isolated in her belief. When she went to shake hands with him, she felt totally creeped out. When Tom said that he would contact her soon to make an appointment for a session to help him cope with the stress, she felt frightened. Joslyn concluded that Tom had killed Carmin.

Outside the service, Joslyn compared notes with another grief-stricken friend and learned for the first time that she was not alone. Not only was Tom a suspect, but he was being investigated by the police.

*   *   *

That week, Joslyn was not the only woman from out of town who thought Tom might have killed Carmin.

Carmin was murdered Thursday morning, November 13, 2003. That evening, English professor Gay Lynn Crossley-Brubaker, a former college classmate of Murray's now teaching at Marian College in Indianapolis, Indiana, called Tom. Tom was going to visit Gay Lynn over the Thanksgiving break. She later swore that Tom was "unusually upbeat" that evening.

On Saturday, November 15, 2003, after Tom returned home from his overnight dialogue in Riley County Police Interview Room #2, he called Gay Lynn. He told her Carmin was dead, he had cuts on his hands as if "holding a knife by the blade," and the police were treating him as a suspect.

And, Gay Lynn would swear, Tom repeatedly said, "All I see is the blood, all the blood."

At that time, no one had told Tom Murray how Carmin had died, nor had the news media learned or reported how Carmin had been murdered.

At trial, the prosecutor and Gay Lynn Crossley-Brubaker had this exchange:

Prosecutor: "Did it ever cross your mind that he [Murray] was involved in the homicide?"

Gay Lynn: "Yes."

Prosecutor: "And when was that?"

Gay Lynn: "On the fifteenth."

Prosecutor: "Did you do anything as a result of your thoughts?"

Gay Lynn: "Yes."

Prosecutor: "What did you do?"

Gay Lynn: "I went to the viewing to talk, to try to find out more information."

Prosecutor: "And at the end of the viewing, [Saturday] the twenty-second, did you do something?"

Gay Lynn: "Yes."

Prosecutor: "What did you do?"

Gay Lynn: "I contacted the sheriff's department."

Prosecutor: "Here?"

Gay Lynn: "At Douglas County, yes."

Gay Lynn came forward, just as Sheriff Trapp had asked the previous weekend, and told what she knew.

Besides the catastrophe of Carmin's murder, after the memorial and the funeral the Ross family had one enduring moment of unease, a nagging disquiet that would not leave, because of a single incident. They had all been together, sitting in the living room with their memories of Carmin. Some were still tearful. During a silent moment when no one was speaking, Tom, who had been lost in his own reverie, had suddenly raised his arms, palms up, and exclaimed, "How could this have happened to *me*!?"

No one responded directly to the question he had burst out with, but everyone noted that he had not exclaimed, "How could this have happened to Carmin?" His focus was on what had happened to him.

32

One of the ways that American novelists typically let readers know that a particular character is poor and/or uneducated is to have the character use pronunciations such as gonna *for* going.
—Thomas E. Murray, Ph.D., *The Structure of English*,
1995

Note: The spelling in the following Doug Woods quotes is taken from the court reporter's transcript. This accurately reflects the audio of Woods's pronunciation.

Interview Room #2

Woods showed Murray a paper, which was a consent form. "What this is, this is a Riley County form. I'm gonna have to read through it with you because I don't use this form normally, okay?"

"Okay," Murray said.

"This is probably the same thing we use in Lawrence. This is giving us consent to look in your car, okay? So they're going to have somebody come over and look in your car who is a specialist in processing crime scenes and so on. Let me read this to you."

"Okay," Murray said.

"It says, 'I, Thomas Murray, have been informed by Detective Doug Woods, made proper identification as a law enforcement officer with the Douglas County Sheriff's Office, and under the Constitution and laws of the United States and the State of Kansas, my property is free from search and seizure by anyone in absence of the lawfully procured search warrant, do freely and voluntarily give consent to the above officers to have conducted a complete search of the property and premises located at your car,' which is what year?" Woods said.

"Two thousand three," Murray said.

"A two thousand three Saturn," Woods said. "Okay?" Woods continued reading the paper. " 'May be searched by any member of the above stated law enforcement agency during the night or day of November fourteen, two thousand three, without the issuance of a search warrant directing such search. Further, I do freely and voluntarily consent and agree that any property under my control located on or in the above described premises at the time of said search may be removed by the officer authorized to make said search if said property shall be essential in the proof of commission of any crime in violation of the laws of the United States or the State of Kansas or any ordinances of any city therein whether said crime shall be committed by myself or another person. Further, I do agree and understand that any property taken by reason of this authorization can and will be used against me in a court of law. Written permission to search without a search warrant is given by me to the above officer voluntarily without any threats or promises of any kind at eleven-oh-one P.M. on the fourteenth day of November two thousand three.' So you understand all that."

"Sure," Murray said.

"So, basically you don't have to let us get into your

vehicle. You have constitutional rights not to let us in there without a search warrant," Woods said.

For the first time, Murray crosses his legs. He also stops sheltering his right hand. It is 11:00 P.M.

"But if I said, 'No, you can't do that,' you could still get a search warrant. So, you know, no big deal," Murray said.

"Okay, you fully agree to that and nobody has threatened you, promised you anything, nobody pulled a gun out and put it to your head and said, 'You've gotta let us search your car,' right?" Woods said.

"Right," Murray said.

"Okay. If you agree to that, if you will sign that for me," Woods said. He waits for Murray to sign the form.

But Murray does not immediately sign the form. He said, "You kind of have this look on your face like, 'If this were me,' you wouldn't be signing this."

"If it were me," Woods said, "I would sign it." He hands Murray a pen. Murray doesn't take it. Woods leaves it on the desk.

Murray pauses. At 11:30 P.M. he picks up the pen, signs the form, and then says, "Yeah. I don't know what I've got to lose here. I can tell you exactly what they'll find in the car," Murray said.

"What are they gonna find?" Woods asked.

"I have a small box of emergency stuff in the trunk. Some of Helen's toys. A purse and box of Kleenexes in the backseat. Some change. A pair of sunglasses in the front. You'll see Carmin's fingerprints in the car because she drove it once. Are they going to do the— I watch *CSI* once in a while—are they going to do the *CSI* thing where they spray some chemical and look for blood? There's possibly blood in there, probably," Murray said.

"Are they going to find blood in the car?" Woods asked.

"You'll find it. This thing keeps opening up. I did that, I think I did this trying to cut the callus off. It keeps opening up. So you'll find my blood. But the day that I was there at Carmin's house, I said that Helen was sick two or three weeks ago, at one point Carmin said, 'Will you go get, will you go to, there's a Walgreens, and get some Pedialyte to replenish'— because Helen had the runs—'to replenish the fluids?' I said, 'I'll wind up in Iowa or Illinois. You've got to go get it.' So she drove my car because I had pulled in right behind her truck. We didn't want to mix, you know, move all around. So she took my car and went and got the Pedialyte. But when she got back, her nose was bleeding on both sides. She said, 'I didn't know where you kept the Kleenex. I reached around the back. I looked for them in the front. And I didn't see it. I reached around the back and finally found it.' And you'll find them right behind the front seat on the driver's side. But these were, she described them as gushers. And both sides would bleed at once. She and Helen both have this. So I'm imagining that you know when I went out; there was some blood on where she had grabbed the steering wheel. And there was some blood on, I don't know, but she cleaned it up for me. She used some of this, you know, the spray stuff that you put on fruits and vegetables before you eat them. The citrus spray. She used that or vinegar or something and wiped it with a wet rag. I mean, but there may be. If the stuff on *CSI* is true, and the stuff can show up years later, you know, you'll find that some," Murray said.

"So we'll find her blood in the car?" Woods asked.

"Yep," Murray answered. "You'll find a little bit on the steering wheel, and there's probably some on the gearshift. And the way you say it, it doesn't sound good, but it's from a bloody nose. That is all."

"Okay," Woods said. He is focused on whether or

not Murray is going to sign the consent forms. "The second one here is basically identical wording, but it is to search your residence, okay? Would you agree to that?"

"Absolutely," Murray said.

"You know you have the right to refuse to let us in there, and so on," Woods said.

"Now, you know, again, I don't know whether the stuff you see on TV is true. But you guys going to go in and toss everything and it's going to take me a week to put it back together?" Murray asked.

"No. We don't do that. That's TV," Woods and Schlerf said simultaneously.

"Okay. Can you give me an idea of what you do do?" Murray asked.

Schlerf said, "We're going to systematically go through room by room and look through the items like I was describing for you, okay? That we can eliminate these fibers, hairs, you know, things that may come from you that we're going to find there, or things that come from there that we may find at your place."

"Do you want a sample of my hair?" Murray asked.

"We may," Woods answered. "But, you know, we'll cross these bridges as we come to them."

"Okay," Murray said.

"So, you're giving pre-consent, allowing us to search the residence?" Woods asked.

"Right," Murray answered.

Woods indicated the form. "Same thing again, if you would just sign here."

"Are you going to do this tonight?" Murray asked.

"I don't know yet," Woods said.

"I'm already about half asleep. Here. It doesn't matter," Murray said. He signs the forms.

"Are you doing all right?" Woods asked. "Do you want anything to eat or drink?"

"No. Actually, I'd rather be asleep," Murray said.

"Do you want something to drink or something?

Do you need to go to the bathroom or anything?" Woods asked.

"No one thing," Murray answered. "I assume this included the garage, too. I mean, you probably know this. You're professionals. But the garage does have one of these pull-down ladder things that goes up to a kind of an attic storage area that I finished off in the spring. Don't forget to pull it down and look up there as you go. Up behind you there's a light switch on the wall that will light the place up for you."

"I will make that phone call and let them know that," Schlerf said. "The next thing we will be doing is going downstairs to get your fingerprints."

"May I ask you a question?" Murray said. "How long does blood stay on something, because you'll find Carmin's blood in my house, too."

"It depends upon what it's on," Woods answered.

"Okay," Murray said.

Woods leaves the interview room. Murray is alone. He speaks to himself, "Oh, Helen. I just want to go home and take care of my baby girl."

33

*The sociologist cannot give us this kind of knowl-
edge. That is the novelist's task.*
—Leon Surmelian, Kansas State University graduate,
 Techniques of Fiction Writing, 1968

"A million deaths are statistics; the death of one man
is a tragedy." So goes an old aphorism. English professor Surmelian was saying that the writer's task is to
touch people's hearts, and to do that one should tell
a story about one of those deaths. A tragic tale, well
told, will move people to action more than any statement by social scientists about people in statistical
aggregate.

This story is true, is nonfiction, is verity—
Paul Hess was a successful Kansas businessman and
lawyer. In the early 1970s Hess was elected to the
Kansas House of Representatives and then to the
Kansas State Senate. In the early 1980s he was elected
chairman of the Kansas State Senate Ways and Means
Committee. That meant he was one of the most powerful politicians in Kansas. He had a successful marriage, three sons, and was, as much as anyone, the
state's golden boy. He was so successful that many

considered it inevitable that Paul Hess would become governor of the State of Kansas.

Given its population and situation, for the past eighty years Kansas has had a disproportionate number of politicians achieve national prominence. Kansas senator Charles Curtis was elected as President Hoover's vice president in 1928. Kansas governor Alf Landon was the republican candidate for president in 1936. Eisenhower, from nearby Abilene, Kansas, was elected president in 1952 and 1956. Kansas senator Bob Dole was the Republican candidate for vice president in 1976 and a Republican candidate for president in 1996. In January 2008 Kansas governor Kathleen Sebelius was selected to provide the Democratic Party's response to President George W. Bush's State of the Union address.

In the early 1980s, some politically savvy people thought Paul Hess might become governor and one day become a candidate for president.

Yet, the reader has probably never heard of Paul Hess. Why not?

Because Paul Hess had marital discord, and he thought his wife was going to obtain custody of their three boys. So, Paul Hess, chairman of the Senate Ways and Means Committee, the man who some thought was inevitably going to become governor, and maybe president, took his three boys and tried to flee to a country that did not extradite to the United States. Things went badly for him after that. Not only did he lose his political career, but he was disbarred and imprisoned.

The behavior of one of the most accomplished men in Kansas became shocking when he thought he might lose custody of his children.

Men will do that. Intelligence, education, and accomplishment do not inoculate them against foolish or criminal behavior.

*   *   *

On October 8, 2003, Murray's second Internet search was "Extradition to the United States." Was he going to write about a villain who wanted to avoid extradition to the U.S. after committing a murder?

Whether he was writing fiction or nonfiction, the answer is "yes."

Murray watched the fictional television program *CSI* and said he was writing a script for it or a similar program. He searched for and found a *CSI* episode that used a poison that is one of the ingredients in the eye product Visine. Because that had already been used, he could not sell a script where it was used again, so he would have had to search for other poisons.

And he did.

That's consistent with writing a fictional *CSI* episode.

But then he looked for date-rape drugs and how to plant drugs. That might not be consistent, but maybe he was looking for a B story.

But plot-driven shows like *CSI* don't usually have a B story.

Maybe he was considering writing a screenplay. Movies frequently do have a B story.

Murray claimed he was writing fiction.

The prosecution would claim he was writing nonfiction.

*   *   *

Does the reader want reality? No. Not really. Reality is confusing, reality is boring. It lacks emphasis. The reader has reality up the gazatch! No, reality is not what the reader wants. What the reader wants is extract *of reality.*

—Jon Franklin, *Writing for Story*, 1986

Jury trials consist of two adversaries giving their view of the evidence, making arguments to the jury advocating interpretation of the law and evidence in favor of their side. The opponents are biased and are not trying to be fair. The judge's role is to see that the trial between these two adversaries complies with the rules of law—administrative, statutory, and as interpreted by higher courts. The trial will be "fair" insofar as those rules are fair. No version of the truth, in court or in nonfiction, is complete, or completely fair, but as Justice Oliver Wendell Holmes Jr. wrote, "High-mindedness is not impossible." Judges render judgments and jurors render "verdicts," from the French word derived from the Latin *veri* (truth) and *dictum* (speak). The verdict speaks the truth.

But speakers may tell lies with their words. Do their bodies reveal the truth regardless of their words?

In 1952 anthropologist Ray Birdwhistell, Ph.D., published a book based on years of research in communications. He called the book *Kinesics*, explaining that the title described a new field of academic study that he had developed out of his study of linguistics. He observed both speaker and listener and noted that it was not only the text of their words that communicated meaning but also their postures, gestures, and all the aspects of what we colloquially call body language. Birdwhistell concluded that linguistics accounted for only about thirty percent of communication when two people were physically face-to-face talking with each other.

Birdwhistell spawned a rich field of academic research. Other researchers studied every aspect of human body language that they could. For example, Dr. Edward H. Hess found that when healthy heterosexual men see a picture of a nude woman they find attractive, the pupils of their eyes become twice as large. The size of one's pupil is not under voluntary control. This is an example of a finding in kinesics, a nonverbal response that communicates meaning to any trained observer. The response is not as certain as a reflex, but after large samples are studied, statistical norms can be codified to say that as a rule of thumb, most of the time, people from this culture in this circumstance will have this body language response.

Beginning in the 1960s not only academics but business and government organizations interested in the bottom line started teaching their people how to read body language. Business and government negotiators wanted every advantage that they could get, and they believed that reading the body language of others would help them. Then the term entered popular culture. Julius Fast's 1970 *Body Language* became a runaway best seller. Since that time books and seminars teaching how to read and interpret body language have flourished.

For hundreds, if not thousands, of years actors have studied communicating with body movements on the stage and in pantomime. In the silent-film era of the first decades of the twentieth century actors performed with exaggerated body language. The people who watched silent films were called spectators. When the talkie era arrived, there was a deliberate publicity push by the film industry to call the spectators "audiences," to emphasize the new audio component to movies.

Detective Brad Schlerf learned how to read body language or kinesics as part of his certification in computerized voice stress analysis. This was also part of his training in interviewing suspects. Law enforcement officers across the country are actively learning kinesics as one of a host of procedures and technologies that fall under the umbrella of "truth verification" techniques. Schlerf testified at the preliminary hearing that he used his knowledge of kinesics in the interview of Tom Murray.

34

Interview Room #2

"Are these your car keys, here?" Woods asked.

"Yes," Murray answered.

"We're gonna have them move your car around. You're parked in front and we're gonna have them move your car. We've got a garage right here, so we're indoors. It's getting kinda chilly outside. You can walk with us down there," Woods said.

Murray's car is moved. Murray is fingerprinted. Then Woods and Murray return to the same interview room. Schlerf does not return to the room.

"Is this where I started?" Murray asked.

"Yes. Same room. Even your water is still sitting here. Do you need anything other than the water?" Woods asked.

"No," Murray said. Then he added, "Yes, to go be with my daughter." Murray takes a drink of water. He makes a distasteful face and says, "That's awful."

"What's awful?" Woods asked.

"The chlorine in the water," Murray said. He's a cultured man accustomed to drinking filtered water, not the tap water the police provided him. There was a pause, then Murray asked, "What are we doing next?"

Woods handed Murray an open paper packet holding two large long-handled swabs, like giant Q-tips, for a DNA test. "Pull one of those out for swabbing."

"Is this swabbing for DNA?" Murray asked.

Woods nodded. "Swab one of these around inside your mouth for me," he instructed.

"In my cheeks?" Murray asked. It is 11:45 P.M.

"Your cheeks, over your tongue, every place in your mouth, your gums, swab your gums," Woods said. After Murray finished with the first, Woods said, "Pull the other one out, that end goes in first, do the same thing with that one." (This is for test redundancy, if necessary.)

"Do the exact same thing?" Murray asked. Woods nodded. Then Murray again swabbed inside his mouth and placed the swab in the provided holder.

Then Murray said, "Here's another reason why I shouldn't be considered to be a serious, I don't know if 'suspect' is the right word. I'm guessing because you're interested in the scratches I have, and you're looking for obvious marks, that there's been some kind of a struggle. You're interested in my physical condition. You want to know, and you're asking for aches and pains. So you're wanting to know if I've been in a struggle of some kind. [Murray closes his eyes.] I would never, I would never even think of killing somebody. But if I was the kind of person who could do it, morally, I wouldn't do something like I'm picturing you're suggesting."

"What do you think I'm suggesting?" Woods asked.

"Something really physical," Murray answered. "You know I consider myself more of a thinker than a physical person. [Murray's legs are turned away from Woods.] If I were going to do something like that, I would do some kind of poison or something

in the air, you know, airborne, something really slick.
This is kind of 'no-brainer' stuff. The person or people who are going to be caught are going to be
caught through fingerprints and DNA. It's kind of
like anybody with half a brain is not going to get
involved in something like that. That's what I think
about it."

"People do things all the time that they don't think
about. You may be a thinker, but other people react
to certain situations differently than normal. We
talked about how each person has their breaking
point," Woods said.

"Yes. But you are suggesting, you keep focusing
on this Thursday-morning time frame. You asked me
point-blank if I drove to Lawrence. So, what you are
thinking is that I drove to Lawrence, did something,
and then drove back again. Never mind that in my
mind I can't get there and back inside of the time I
have available, but this is not a spur-of-the-moment
thing, I'm thinking. I'm not the expert, but it's not
a spur-of-the-moment, you know, emotional outrage.
Somebody who has to drive eighty-five or ninety
miles, there's some kind of planning involved. If
what I'm picturing is the kind of thing that really
happened, that's not planning, it's more like, I don't
think, it's more of a spur-of-the-moment. But I don't
know. I mean, you've had all the classes and experience, but that's what I'm thinking," Murray said.

After a pause, because Detective Woods did not
verbally respond—deciding when silence is more pro-
ductive than speech is an aspect of good interview
technique—Murray continued to speak. "I was thinking about that. And I'm sure you'll talk to Lacey.
Lacey Bonine is her name. Maybe she can confirm
when I dropped Helen off that morning. But let's say
I got away from there at nine A.M., and I drove to the
university. Oh, let's say I didn't. Let's say I left right

from there and it takes me about ten minutes to get
to the bridge [bridge over the Kansas River, exiting
Manhattan to the southeast to travel to Topeka and
Lawrence], takes me another between ten and fifteen
minutes [driving south on Kansas Highway 177] to get
to [U.S. Interstate] Highway 70. I don't know, from
the bridge it takes me a good seventy minutes to get
to Sam's Club in Topeka, and that's on the west side
of Topeka. Then I would have to go through Topeka.
And then I would have to find my way to Carmin's
house. I don't think I could do it in much less than
almost two hours, an hour and forty-five minutes for
sure. And an hour and forty-five minutes for the return trip. That's two, three and a half hours, assuming
I left around nine A.M. Angela brought Helen to my
house at ten after twelve, or twelve fifteen at the lat-
est. It's just impossible for me to do that. I can't make
the numbers work out."

"If those are truly the numbers," Woods said. He
was challenging Murray.

"I'm sorry?" Murray said.

"If those are truly the numbers," Woods repeated.

"I don't understand." Murray said.

"If the times you're giving me, certain time periods
right now, but right now there's other officers talking
to people. Maybe your time frames aren't going to
add up," Woods said.

"Maybe not. Maybe not," Murray said. "The time
frame that I gave you for Lacey is just ballpark. I'm
almost always there on Monday, Wednesday, Friday
between eight thirty and eight forty-five. I'm thinking
it might have been as early as eight forty-five. I don't
think it was any earlier than that. But even so, that
would give me, assuming I get back to the house right
before Angela got there, a total of three and one half
hours. I don't think, unless I really pushed it, I mean,
I said before that I don't, it's not that I don't speed,

but Carmin and I used to have this thing. She's got the lead foot. I'm always the one who stays about five miles under the posted limit, with cars always backing up behind me. But that doesn't matter."

Murray continued. "Let's say that I decided on this particular day 'I'm in a hurry. I've got to do this in a hurry.' And I even push it, you know, usually on that stretch when I make the trip from my house to Topeka. Usually, there's anywhere from one to three patrol cars along the way. I can't imagine why I would risk getting stopped for a ticket. And the other thing I thought is, to go from my house to Carmin's house, there's a tollbooth there that is right off the Lecompton Highway 10 exit. There's a thing right above the tollbooth. I don't know what that thing is, but if it records the cars that go by, you could look at that. And you could figure out who was working the tollbooth that day. Of course, I don't know what kind of memory these people have, but you could say, 'Do you recognize that guy?' The thing is, they might recognize me from Tuesday, or get the day wrong. That would screw you good. I'm kind of just getting into this a little bit."

"That's true," Woods observed.

"But from the standpoint of, I'm having fun with it from the *CSI* perspective, you know," Murray said.

"Just don't believe everything you see on TV," Woods said.

"You mean, they don't make those things factually true?" Murray asked.

"No," Woods said.

"Really?" Murray said. "The *CSI* show, I thought it was . . ." Murray's voice trailed off. Then he said, "So, tell me, I may never watch it again."

"I don't want to give away secrets. That's part of my job," Woods said.

"No. I don't want you to give away secrets," Murray said.

Woods interrupted. "There are lots of things on the show that are not realistic. I watched it about twice before I got fed up with it."

35

I find action on a page very boring. If I read about a car chase, it's ho-hum for me. What gets me on the edge of my seat is an interrogation, in which you know the answer is around the corner and it's just two people talking in a room.
—Tess Gerritsen, M.D., best-selling mystery novelist,
  Writer's Digest, February 2008

Writers use basic techniques of narrative drive to grab and keep the audience's attention, such as puzzle, mystery, telegraphing, dangling cause, ironic tension, and dramatic tension.

The most powerful technique is dramatic tension (conflict). This is what most writers strive to present to their audience. The simplest way to ensure conflict (tragic, dramatic, or comedic) is to put two characters who are in opposition in a situation where they must be together, where one or both cannot flee, either because of their external situation (they're prevented from leaving) or because psychologically it is more important in the mind of one or both to be there than to leave. This is called putting the opposing characters in a crucible. Fiction is filled with such stories.

Less often, such a story is found in nonfiction. For example, when one character, a detective, desperately wants a man he believes is a criminal to confess his crime, and when the other character, a suspected murderer, desperately wants to persuade the detective that he is an innocent man.

Either Tom Murray was surprised to find himself in the crucible of Interview Room #2, or he had anticipated this situation, knew what he was going to say when it happened, rehearsed for it, and prepared for its aftermath. Such preparation, to support his story, might include planting a confirmatory item of evidence where he expected the police to search and concocting a story to explain Internet searches on ways to murder as research for a *CSI* script.

36

Interview Room #2

Tom Murray said, "I know there's going to be endless questions and, whatever I tell Helen, she is a very precocious and astute and smart kid. She will take whatever I say and turn it into a fear and this fear will last with her a long, long time. I have to be very careful what I say and I cannot lie to her. I have already promised her a number of times I'm not going to lie to her, ever. But, then I didn't count on something like this. I don't know what I'm going to say. If I do say, 'Mommy went to heaven,' she's going to say, 'Why?' And she'll start to suggest possibilities. 'Did she get sick?' We had a bad car accident last year at this time over Thanksgiving. We were driving to Colorado Springs, going westbound on U.S. 70, and rolled the Jimmy across all four lanes and the center median strip. We started in the right-hand lane of westbound and we wound up on the other side of eastbound. A semi nearly hit us. We came to a stop in an upright position and fortunately we all had our belts on. Helen was strapped in. The first thing I heard after I came to, the first thing I heard out of the back-seat, was, 'What just happened?' But that was an awful wreck and she talked about that for months and still brings it up whenever I have to stop short or maybe get a little too close to a car. She says, 'Are we going to have an accident? Are we going to die? Are we going to be okay?' "

Continuing on the subject of Helen, Woods asked, "What kind of problems does she have with her eyes?"

Murray answered, "When she was about two, her left eye started to trail. It was like one eye was crossed and she started to see two daddies and two of everything. So we took—well, first, I let Carmin do the energy medicine thing. Finally I put my foot down and said, 'This is our daughter. Let's be real and go to a doctor.' And we did. After a long series of therapy games and what not, she wears these glasses now. They do a pretty good job. The muscle has gotten stronger. It does a pretty good job of keeping her eye on center. But when she takes her glasses off to take a bath or something, that one eye still trails just a little bit. They said they can correct it with surgery, but Carmin wouldn't hear of that. I'm thinking that since her vision is not impaired anymore, she doesn't see two of anything, is it worth having an operation, you know, something major like that, just for cosmetic purposes?"

Murray changed the subject briefly, drawing attention to his purple-pink sweatshirt that depicted a wolf pack running in the snow. "Just noticed how I'm dressed. Look at this.

"Can you answer one question for me?" Murray asked Woods. "If not, you'll just say 'no.' But I know I already know the answer to that. I was going to ask if a gun was involved. But if a gun were involved, then it wouldn't have been any kind of physical contact, so a gun was not involved."

Woods was silent. Murray continued, "If I wanted to know the details, and I'm not saying I do, but if I wanted to, would you share any of them?"

"Not at this point," Woods answered.

"Okay," Murray said. "Let me offer one more thing I thought of. I went in to the mediation on Tuesday because Monday Carmin and I had gotten our wires crossed about when we were going to do the switch with Helen. We usually do it on Sunday, but they were just getting back from Indianapolis. I thought we were supposed to meet at Sam's Club on Monday, and Carmin was under the impression that we were going to make the switch after the mediation on Tuesday. So I showed up on Monday at Sam's Club. Nobody there. I go inside, call Carmin, nobody there. So I thought, well, I'm going to drive to her house anyway, so I drove to Lawrence, went by the tollbooth—"

Woods interrupted with a question. "Which date is this?"

Murray answered, "This is Monday after my one thirty class. I left about three. Got to Carmin's about five. Nobody there. There was evidence that they were not yet back from Indianapolis because of the way the lights were on in the house. So I opened the storm door, tried the inside door, it was indeed locked. I left a little pile of mail sitting there. That was the first time I drove to her house without, on the front seat, I had a thing I printed out from MapQuest, how to get from my house to hers. And I did not look at it that day for the first time. So when I got home I crumpled it and threw it in the trash thinking I wouldn't need it again. But I was at her house on Monday, if that means anything. And because we crossed our wires and because I thought the fault was hers more than mine, when I showed up Tuesday I was a little bit ticked off. That was the first thing we talked about in front of Nancy, so I'm sure she'll—"

Woods interrupted. "They're getting ready to start the search on your car, okay? You understand at any time you can stop us from doing that. You don't have to allow us to do that, okay?"

"Well, I would eventually," Murray said. He appeared to mean that he would have to allow them to search his car, but Woods wanted the comment explained.

"What?" Woods asked.

Murray answered, "I don't know how this works, but you can go get a search warrant anytime you want and you know—"

Woods interrupted. "I'm just telling you if at any point you're feeling you want to stop this, you're agitated with me, or you'd like to go home, you know you can stop it."

"Oh, I would love to go home, but I—" Murray said.

"I'm not holding you here against your will," Woods said.

"No," Murray said.

"You're here of your own free will and you're agreeing to stay?" Woods asked.

"You don't have to keep repeating that stuff. You haven't been mean to me and you're not holding me against my will," Murray said.

"I was just letting you know that you can stop it at any time and we'll go get your car back," Woods said.

"Well, let me ask you this. Honestly, what would be my advantage in doing that?" Murray asked.

"I can't advise you on legal," Woods said.

Murray said, "No. I'm not asking for legal advice. I'm saying, number one, if I do that it would definitely throw up a red flag. Number two—"

Woods interrupted. "But you're still within your rights to do that."

Murray continued, "Well, my right is to refuse to

answer any questions, but in my mind that's going to throw up a red flag. Number two, you're going to go to a judge tomorrow and get some kind of warrant and we'll be right back where we were twenty-four to forty-eight hours from now."

"It's up to you," Woods said.

"Plus," Murray said, "I'm thinking I'm going to be cleared by this. I'm going to get to go home with my daughter, so—"

Woods interrupted. "So long as you understand I've got to keep explaining that to you. So if something came up and we went to court and you've got some lawyer now, and that lawyer said, 'You held my client there against his will—' "

Murray interrupted. "I'm not being held against my will."

Woods continued with the remarks of a hypothetical lawyer. "And 'He couldn't stop you guys from searching his car. He was locked in this little interview room and wasn't allowed to leave.' I've let him go the bathroom. I've offered him drinks."

Murray said, "If you're talking legal, it's just you and me. We need a witness here to say, 'Well, yeah, he asked him and the other guy said . . .' "

Woods said, "I can get a witness in here if you want me to."

"Oh, no," Murray said.

"Okay, what I'm going to ask you to do," Woods said, "I'm going to fill this little paper out here for you and we'll go through it and read it again. The Riley County Police Department. Date is now November fifteenth and it is twelve thirty-two A.M."

"Can I interrupt you?" Murray asked. "How long do you think this might go on?"

"The guy looking at the car?" Woods asked. "I don't know. He's more of an expert. He has more expertise in that field. And to do his job thoroughly, you don't rush—"

"I mean," Murray interrupted, "I'm not going to bed and sleep anyway, but Helen is going to wake up at the Hayes house expecting to get in bed with me. She's going to freak out when she can't do that. I was just thinking of her."

"Angela knows how to get ahold of us, so we've talked to her and if there would be a problem with Helen she can call us. But for whatever reason, it's not like, you know, if she would call Helen—" Woods said.

Murray interrupted. "I'm just trying to think of Helen's emotional state. That's all."

Woods decided to proceed with the paperwork. He began reading the paper. "So, I, the undersigned, Thomas Murray—"

Murray interrupted. "E. Murray."

"E. Murray. And how old are you?"

"Forty-seven."

And after again repeating his birth date, address, and phone number, Woods continued reading. "I've been duly warned and advised by Doug Woods, and personally identifying himself as a detective, that—as I read along here with you, will you please initial each one of these rights? What I'm going to ask you to do is write a voluntary statement, but right before you write this statement, you have to understand your rights again."

"Uh-huh," Murray said.

"You have the right to remain silent," Woods said.

"This is about the car search, right?" Murray asked.

"No. No, this is different," Woods said. "This is basically getting into your words, your story of what you just basically told us here on the video in written form. Anything you say can be used against you in court. You have the right to talk to a lawyer for advice before we ask you any questions or have your lawyer with you during questioning. If you cannot afford a lawyer, or want one before you answer any questions, one will be appointed. If you decide to answer questions now without a lawyer present you still have the right to stop answering at any time until you talk to a lawyer. Now, Mr. Murray, do you understand your rights? Just initial that and that one too."

Murray initialed the form where indicated.

"Are you willing to waive your rights and give a statement?" Woods asked.

"Yes," Murray answered.

"Starting there, let's just start with Monday. Give me, in your written form, your day-to-day routine as far as you know," Woods said.

"I'll never get it all on there," Murray said.

"I'll get you some more lined paper," Woods said.

"I really got to write this out longhand?" Murray asked.

"You don't want to do it, you don't have to do it," Woods said.

"No, no, no. I'm not refusing to do it. I'm saying . . ." Murray said.

"Basically, what this is is your story in your handwriting, so when I type up my little report," Woods said.

"So we're starting Monday, though I could go on for pages and pages, depending on how much detail you want," Murray said.

"Do you want to start on Tuesday?" Woods asked.

"No. No. I'll start wherever you want. I'm just not clear on exactly what you want me to do," Murray said.

"Your last contact with Carmin," Woods said.

"Physical contact?" Murray asked.

"Physical, electronic, telephone, that stuff, okay?" Woods said.

"Yes," Murray said.

"Your movements Tuesday, Wednesday, Thursday. Let's do Tuesday, Wednesday, and Thursday, your movements," Woods said.

"Will you be here sort of looking over my shoulder?" Murray asked.

"No. I'm going to leave you alone," Woods said.

"Well, I don't want to do it, then have to do it again," Murray said.

"No, what you write is what you know. Just be as detailed as you can. You're an articulate man. I have no question about what you're going to write being articulate enough. I don't need to know what time you went to the bathroom, if you blew your nose, if you got a glass of water," Woods said.

"Basically, a . . ." Murray said.

"A synopsis of those three or four days," Woods said.

"With ballpark time frames when I interact with Carmin. And I can't type it, I have to handwrite it," Murray said.

"Yes. If you would, please. Just so it's in your writing," Woods said.

"Okay," Murray said.

"I'll get you some more lined paper. At any point, if you want to, as soon as you step out the door, there will be somebody outside the door. Right out here in the hallway. So, if for any reason you need anything while you're writing this. If you decide you want to stop from doing anything. If you're done talking to us. You want to leave. Step outside the door," Woods said. "I gotta keep offering this to you."

"Can I ask you one question?" Murray asked.

"You sure can," Woods answered.

"When I go home, from your experience, am I going to be done, or am I going to have to come back and do some of this again?" Murray asked.

"Hopefully not. But I cannot one hundred percent guarantee you," Woods said.

"I'm not looking for guarantees. I'm just . . ." Murray said.

"Hopefully, yes. If everything pans out, you get to go home and you won't have to be burdened and bothered from these guys from Lawrence again," Woods said.

"Unless something else would come up. Actually, to the extent that I'm helping you solve the case, I'm tickled to death to participate. Answer me one thing. I said that I've noticed that when I go through the tollbooths that they have this thing, is it a camera up there?" Murray asked.

Doug Woods thought it was and nodded his head affirmatively. It later turned out to be not a camera but an electronic monitor for specific commercial trucks.

"It is?" Murray said.

"I believe so," Woods said.

"That's all I need to know," Murray said.

From about 12:40 A.M. to 1:30 A.M., Murray wrote his statement in longhand. This is his written voluntary statement:

On Monday, 10 November, I arose at 5:55 a.m. and was at my customary parking place across from campus by 9:00 a.m. I taught my three classes, then left campus about 2:30 [p.m.] to drive to the Sam's Club parking lot in Topeka by 4:00, where I expected to meet Carmin for the purpose of picking up my daughter, Helen. Carmin did not show up, so I drove on to her house in Lawrence. She was not home, so I left some mail behind the storm door and returned to my home in Manhattan.

[That was page one of three.]

On Tuesday, 11 November, I met Carmin at Fraser Hall on the KU campus at 2:00 p.m. for a mediation appointment with Nancy Hughes. The mediation lasted until a little after 4:20 p.m., after which Carmin and I returned to her house in separate vehicles. I was at the house by 4:30, and played with Helen and talked to Carmin until about 5:00 or shortly thereafter. I left a toy catalog on the kitchen counter, used the bathroom, then left with Helen. I remember that we got back to Manhattan about 7:00, ate at a Chinese restaurant, and finally walked into our house between 7:30 and 7:45. Helen was asleep by about 8:00, and I went to bed about 10:00.

On Wednesday, 12 November, I dropped Helen off at the Hayes residence about 8:45, drove to campus, and had a typical workday. I returned home about 5:10, and learned from my childcare person (Peiwen Wang) that Helen wasn't feeling well. I comforted her and cuddled with her until about 6:45, when Carmin called. When she and Helen finished talking, Helen and I finished the movie we'd been watching, then she went to bed about 8:00. I did my e-mail, in the process, answering a message from Carmin, and went to bed about 10:00.

[That was page two of three.]

On Thursday, 13 November, I dropped Helen off at the Hayes residence around 8:45 or shortly thereafter, drove to campus, then drove home. I proceeded to grade the rest of the midterm exams I had given the proceeding [*sic*] day, drove around a bit to clear my head, then returned home. Angela dropped Helen off about 12:15, and Helen and I played the rest of the day. I cut my hand while carving a whole pineapple, and bruised my right forefinger and (I think) both wrists while playing. Helen went to bed about 8:00, after which I did my e-mail, in the process answering a message from Carmin (I believe she wrote the message either at 12:00 p.m. or 2:00 p.m. that same day). I was in bed by 10:00 p.m.

On Friday, 14 November, I dropped Helen off at the Hayes house at about 8:45, parked across from campus by 9:00, and had a typical workday. I arrived home at 5:10, sent Peiwen home, played with Helen for a while, then fixed dinner. After dinner, we played until about 7:50, at which time we answered the front door and found four police officers. I then called Angela Hayes, who arrived at the house five minutes later; then I accompanied the officers to the police station, where I've been ever since.

[End of page three of three.]

Murray signed each page "Thomas E. Murray." Each page was witnessed and signed by "Doug Woods."

37

A Douglas County sheriff's detective asked the author not to identify him in this book. If news reporters of all sorts, including nonfiction authors, granted all such requests, there would be little accurate nonfiction published. However, in this circumstance, with the detective possibly working undercover in the future, the author decided to grant the request. In this book this officer, and several other officers, in accordance to their wishes, are referred to objectively in context, as they are in the transcript, as "second officer," etc.

Doug had challenged Tom, but they had established a rapport. Doug had appeared to sympathize with Tom's marital and child custody woes. Now, Doug wanted Tom's confession. This dialogue exchange occurred just after Murray asked about the tollbooth cameras and said, "That is all I need to know."

Interview Room #2

"Who says you didn't drive 24 Highway all the way there?" a second officer sneered.

Murray responded, "I have no idea where 24 High-way is."

"That's *the* main highway," the second officer said. "That's one of the main highways that leaves Manhattan. You've lived here for sixteen years. You've gotta know where Highway 24 is."

"I once got lost going to church." Murray said. He reveled in his traveling ignorance.

The second officer laughed.

"You think I'm kidding?" Murray asked.

"I know there are people that have a hard time finding their way around," the officer said.

Woods, handing Murray some paper, said, "There's some more lined paper." He wanted Murray's statement now. "Any reason you want to stop. Need something. If you want to go to the bathroom again. You want something to drink? Coffee?"

"No," Murray said. "I'm here on my own free will. You're not keeping me from the bathroom." Then, indicating the form, he asked, "Do I need to fill anything out at the top?"

"Start writing on this page, then somewhere on here, if you want to make a notation that this is page number one," Woods said.

"And starting with Monday through today?" Murray asked.

"Yeah. All right," Woods said.

Then Murray wrote his statement.

After Murray finished his statement, about one thirty A.M., Woods came back into the interview room and asked, "You all right?"

"Yes," Murray answered.

"You all done writing?" Woods asked.

"I think so," Murray said. "Wait a minute. I just thought of something. What was I going to tell you? It was important." Murray appears to be thinking hard. He becomes frustrated. "Crap! I don't know what it was. It was something about Carmin."

"Are you doing all right?" Woods asked. "You wanna get up and walk around? Go outside and get some fresh air or something?"

"No. I'm going to have to go to the bathroom in a little while. Just give me a minute. I thought about it. I just dozed off when you came in and I forgot. But I remember that I wanted to make another . . ." Murray said, his voice trailing off. "I'm telling you, you're probably tired of hearing me talk about it."

"No. Not at all," Woods said. He wanted Murray to talk.

"Well, I'll tell you—this isn't the thing I was thinking of—but I will tell you one thing about Carmin. She and I used to wrestle in the house all of the time. You know, in fun. If one person did this [indicating Carmin's murder], and if the person who did this, if one person did this, then that person would have had to have been, if some kind of physical contact was involved, the person who did it is real quick, because whenever Carmin and I wrestled, I was always stronger, though, but not a whole lot. She was amazingly strong," Murray said.

Murray continued. "She could move faster than anybody I have ever seen. She would be grabbing me, and poking me in places before I had a chance to really react. We used to kid all the time, if we had a contentious marriage and it ever got serious, I mean, where we were physical with one another, she probably would be able to, well, not beat me up, but she would be able to hold her own."

Murray seems to remember what he wanted to say. "Oh. I know. Yes. On the same lines, when you were looking at my body, I know you're not going to find any bruises, or if you do, they are going to be the size of a foot [indicating a size of a child's foot] that's about this big or a hand that's about that big [a child's hand] and it is going to be from Helen, from rolling around and banging me when we sleep or when we play.

"The statement that I wrote out is substantially the same, although one thing occurred to me, and I know that you're going to look at this with a raised eyebrow, let me find it [looking at his written statement], on Thursday, on the thirteenth of November, I dropped Helen off at the Hayes residence around eight forty-five or shortly thereafter, it might have been as late as nine. Then I drove to campus. Then I drove home. I proceeded to grade the rest of the midterm exams I had given the proceeding [sic] day. Drove around a bit to clear my head. I didn't tell you that before. Then I returned home. Angela dropped Helen off about twelve fifteen. But I did go out and drive around a bit," Murray said.

Murray continued. "But I did not drive to Lawrence. I started to drive to Topeka, but I don't know how far I got. I had the intention of going to Paxico because they have the antique places there."

Paxico is a small town just north of Interstate 70. It can be seen from the highway and is advertised by large billboards visible from the highway. Paxico is about equal distance between Topeka and Manhattan. It survives economically primarily by being a town for tourists traveling the interstate to stop and shop. It has many antique stores. The gas station has old-fashioned pumps.

"The last time I was there I left a note with my e-mail address with the person who works there. I haven't heard anything in weeks. I thought, 'Well, I've got like an hour, an hour and a half, I'm going to drive out there.' And I honestly don't know how far I got, but before I got real far, I know I didn't, I couldn't have got to Topeka. Before I got real far I turned around and came back home," Murray said.

"Did you make it past [Interstate] Seventy?" Woods asked.

"Oh, yes. I was on Seventy. I was on Seventy heading toward Paxico toward Topeka," Murray said. "I just don't know how far I got. I went to clear my head after grading all those tests and to think about the new proposed child care plan that Carmin had given me the preceding day. I have a pretty dull and boring life, but I like it that way."

"Are you normally so fidgety?" the second officer asked, playing bad cop.

"No. I'm cleaning my fingernails. It looks like I'm fidgety, but it's because I'm snapping them," Murray said.

The detectives wondered what Murray had under his fingernails that he wanted out from under them. Carmin's blood? Carmin's skin? It had been more than thirty-six hours since the murder. Surely he'd cleaned them, but maybe he was still worried about what might be found. "I know. Since we've started talking you've done that numerous times," Woods said.

"I need to cut them," Murray said. "I am fidgety. This whole thing has me rattled. Not that you're interested, maybe you are, I don't know, but I've thought about it and I think I can account for every one of these scratches on my hand, if you want to know where they came from."

"Good. I have scratches on my hands that I can't account for," Woods said.

"They all happened in the last two or three days. One's a paper cut. One's from cutting the pineapple yesterday where I bled in front of Helen and freaked her out. And this one, two of these are self-inflicted because I, well, I don't have my keys, but on my key ring is a little penknife that my father-in-law gave me. I try to trim the calluses flush with my skin. I usually nick myself," Murray said.

"Do you need to go to the bathroom or anything?" Woods asked.

"No," Murray said.

"Need a drink? Something to eat?" Woods asked.

"No," Murray said.

"Are you sure? They're still working on your car," Woods said.

"Okay," Murray said. They leave the interview room at 1:37 A.M.

Murray and Woods and a second officer reenter the interview room at 1:44 A.M. Murray is in midsentence when the audio returns. He is complaining that Carmin never locked her door. He is relating how Carmin behaved when they met on the Ohio State University campus, when they started dating while she was his student and he was her teacher. He then describes how he envisioned her murder.

". . . unlocked apartment when she was home and I always said, 'What if somebody comes in the house? What are you going to do?' And she would say . . . Because she was an undergraduate she would walk across the Ohio State campus at two o'clock in the morning without anybody around and I would say, 'If somebody comes up to you, what are you going to do?' And she always came back with, 'I can talk myself out of any situation.' And I always said, 'No, you can't. There's always some crazy person out there who is not going to listen to whatever talk you have.' I'm just picturing as much as I can how all of this went down. She tried to talk herself out of this situation," Murray said.

"Okay. That's good to know," Woods said.

"I don't know this, but I'm betting that the front door was unlocked because I told her, 'Look, you can do what you want, but when Helen is there, I want the front door locked. I don't care if you live in the country.' She always said, 'Living in the country is safe. We're not in the city.' So I'm the co-parent here, I insisted that the doors be locked. Now, I don't know if she did it, but, so, for whatever that's worth," Murray said.

38

At 12:38 A.M. on Saturday, November 15, Murray said
that he now remembered that after he finished grading
papers, he then drove to Paxico, Kansas. There was
an antique store there with antique pillowcases. He
wanted to look at them and maybe pick up a few.
Admiring antique pillowcases was a hobby of his.

Murray's claiming to have a hobby of admiring antique pillowcases struck Doug Woods as odder than
Murray's accompanying his wife and sisters to the mall
on all their shopping trips.

But Woods learned, through his investigation, that
though collecting antique pillowcases is a hobby that
some people do have, Murray did not make any pur-
chases of antique pillowcases that morning, nor had
he ever. And the people in the antique shop had no
recollection of seeing Murray that morning, or ever.
There were no antique pillowcases in his home, no
books or magazines or hobby periodicals about antique pillowcases, and no one who knew him had ever
before heard that Murray had this interest. Murray
said he now remembered that he had taken Helen to
the babysitter at the normal time, graded papers, then
driven toward Paxico. He changed his mind about
going into the antique shop and returned to Manhattan. He had driven just to "clear his head."

*   *   *

After Murray finished making his shifting explanations, he was asked to make a written statement of everything he had done and every place he had been from November 11 to November 14. Just before he started writing, Murray asked one question, then made one statement.

At 12:42 A.M. he asked, "Are there cameras at turnpike tollbooths?"

Woods, mistakenly believing at that time that there were, answered, "Yes."

Murray said, "That's all I needed to know." Then he wrote his statement.

When he finished writing, he said that he had not driven to Lawrence and they could check the turnpike cameras to verify that.

When Woods investigated the turnpike he saw a device that looked like a camera. The turnpike authorities explained that this was a special radio monitoring device for specific commercial trucks that traveled through the turnpike. The Kansas turnpike had no cameras.

The Interstate 70 drive south of Manhattan is the Eisenhower Memorial Highway and was the first stretch of U.S. interstate to be built. It was built because General Eisenhower was so impressed with the German Autobahn in World War II. It's eerie, but photos of any random portion of the WWII German Autobahn look like any random portion of a modern U.S. interstate highway.

Traveling west of Manhattan on I-70 one passes Fort Riley, then Abilene, then crosses a bridge over the Solomon River, which in this story causes one to recall the tale of the judgment of Solomon, found in 1 Kings, chapter 3. Two adults who each want sole custody of a child bring it before King Solomon for a decision. The king declares that a sword shall be taken and the living child shall be cut in two, each adult to have half a dead child. One adult cries out and pleads with the king to change his decision and give a living child to the other. The other says that it is fine for the child to be divided and killed.

The king awards the child to the adult who wanted the child to live.

Traveling east of Manhattan on I-70, one sees some magnificent vistas of open range to the horizon. One passes just south of Wamego (seeing the Oz Museum billboard) and Paxico (advertising its antique shops), then arrives in the state capital of Topeka. This is where Carmin and Tom would typically exchange custody of Helen, in Topeka's Super Wal-Mart parking lot, which has easy access off the main four-lane highways that each would drive.

The easiest and swiftest route between Topeka and Lawrence is to take the six-lane Kansas Turnpike, but one may also take Kansas Highway 40, which is a narrow, winding, two-lane road with many sharp turns and often no shoulder, and which most often has slow-moving farm tractors and combines on it. If one chooses that route, one passes sights not seen on the turnpike, such as a "Purebred Nubian Goat" milk farm and a monument, extant but difficult to see, celebrating the pro-slavery movement in the "Bleeding Kansas" era.

On Friday, November 14, 2003, before Thomas Murray drove to the Manhattan police station, officers noted that his vehicle's fuel gauge showed that he had exactly one-quarter of a tank of gasoline. They had a photograph that showed the fuel gauge. Murray had told them that he had filled his tank on November 11, and they later verified this with his credit card receipt for purchase of fuel on that date at a cost of $13.83. Woods knew the location of the gas station and had

Murray's detailed volunteered statement of each and every place he had driven after that.

Douglas County detectives checked with several car dealers until one was found who loaned them a Saturn sedan of the same make, year, and model as Murray's. Two detectives filled the Saturn's tank with gasoline at the same station that Murray had, and from there they drove everywhere Murray said he had driven from November 11 to November 14, 2003. This included the babysitter's, Paxico, Kansas, and a Manhattan Chinese restaurant. The car still had over half a tank of fuel. They called that Trip A.

Then, in what they called Trip B, they again filled the tank at the same station, again went every place Murray said he had driven, but then added a drive from Angela Hayes's home in Manhattan to Carmin's home in Lawrence, and then back to Murray's home, using the Highway 40 route. They photographed the result, which was identical to the photograph of the fuel gauge in the photograph of Murray's Saturn taken on November 14. One-quarter of a tank of fuel remained.

During the police knock-and-talk of Carmin's neighbors after her body was found, neighbor Julie Schwarting said that she saw a maroon Saturn sedan in Carmin's driveway the morning Carmin was killed.

Murray drove a maroon Saturn sedan.

On November 13, 2003, Tom Murray sat on the throne of that Saturn and drove to his fate.

39

Interview Room #2

"Well, that's what Carmin told me," Murray added. "And she also said, 'I don't lie' so . . ."

"We brought a little bit better camera and we need to take some better photos," Woods said.

"What do you want to do?" Murray asked.

"Just take some more photos of your hand," Woods answered.

"Okay," Murray said.

"It would probably be better if you just stood up," Woods said. "Let's start with your right hand flat on the paper first, and spread your fingers apart."

A second officer asked Murray, "Why don't you go ahead and pull your shirt up?"

Woods asked the second officer about the camera. The Riley County camera has auto-focus. It's a good one, though the battery died and needed to be replaced. The officers attended to the camera, then asked Murray to pose and expose his hand and other body parts through a series of positions where they photographed him. After Murray was told that the processing of his car and his house would take all night, he was asked about his bleeding.

"Where are you bleeding from now?" Woods asked.

A second officer said to Murray, "Picking at yourself still."

Murray replied, "These things keep opening up."

"If you quit picking at them they would quit opening up," the second officer said.

Murray began questioning the officers about their jobs and careers. "At some point when this question presents itself and you feel like it, I would be interested to know what do you have to do to be a detective above and beyond just a regular officer? I mean, do you take special courses?' "

Woods answered, "No. They send us to training all the time and you get higher. You can work your way up from a patrolman." On police departments here as elsewhere there was a pyramid of advancement that was similar to military hierarchy or union rank.

"That's what I mean," Murray said. "Do you work your way up?"

"I worked narcotics for two and a half years," Woods said.

Murray asked, "How do they—I don't know what I'm trying to ask—how do they select people they want to be detectives and say, 'You're detective material.' What do they look for?"

"Testing and interview process. How you write. And you have to be observant," Woods answered. He did not mention that a lifetime of being coached to be observant by a detective father helps.

"On reports?" Murray asked, focusing on the writing.

"Yes. And investigative abilities. And there are some guys that don't want to do this," Woods said.

Murray asked, "In detective work, is there anything that's a higher detective?"

"A lieutenant, in our department. It's different in each department," Woods answered.

They took photos until 2:40 A.M.

40

Interview Room #2

"So, you know, we are going to go through that car, and you know we are going to find that blood, so you've gotta come up with an explanation. I asked you point-blank, 'Did you drive to Lawrence on Thursday?' No. You neglected to put in the part that you decided to drive to Paxico, which would have put you on I-70 where you know somebody saw you. And you know we are going to find that out. We may already know that. But I am not telling you everything I know. But you know that you were on I-70 Thursday morning," Woods said.

"Yes," Murray said.

"Then you told me you take I-70 every single time. Then you go to the point of, 'Oh, was there cameras at the turnpike?' Okay. Then we jump over to the fact maybe you drove a different highway. Then we come up with the story 'Oh, I went to Paxico.' Now, why didn't you tell us that in the first place?" Woods asked.

"I didn't say I went to Paxico," Murray said.

"You were headed to Paxico. You got out on I-70. You know somebody saw you out on that highway," Woods said.

"No," Murray said, "I don't."

"You didn't, you neglected to tell us about your trip to Lawrence on Monday when you went up to the house," Woods said.

"I didn't think about it, Doug," Murray said.

"We're talking about Monday through Friday. We want very detailed day-by-day on what your thing was and you leave all this stuff out," Woods said.

"And, as I've explained, over the last three nights," Murray said, "I've slept a total of about four hours."

"And I understand that, but you knew something bad had happened to your wife when I came to your house and told you that your wife had died," Woods said.

"Oh, absolutely I did," Murray said.

"And when you figured out when we got here that she didn't die in a traffic accident . . ." Woods said.

"I knew that when you were at the front door," Murray said.

"And you knew that she didn't die of natural causes," Woods said.

"I knew that at the door," Murray said.

"And we sit here and we talk and you have yet to ask me what happened to your wife," Woods said.

"I have told you specifically I don't want to know," Murray said.

"Stop. I am not done talking to you. I'll let you talk in a minute. I've sat here for eight hours and listened to you talk, okay?" Woods said.

"Okay," Murray said. "I'm sorry."

"We go back to that, you know, you keep leaving little details out of every little part of your story. The blood in the car. Why is her blood in your house?" Woods asked.

"Can I talk?" Murray asked.

"Answer that question for me," Woods said.

"Because as recently as Halloween night she cut a

piece of candy to give to Helen and sliced open her finger," Murray said. "First of all, the truth counts for everything."

"I believe that," Woods said.

"Second of all, you're putting things together in an interesting way to suit your purpose," Murray said. "I understand that is your job. I know it is not personal. Of course, I am nervous sitting here. I was nervous when I saw four police officers come to the front door. And from then till the time we left again one of them was escorting me every place I went, into the kitchen, into the bedroom."

"And I told you we were investigating a death," Woods said. "I don't know you from that wall. Maybe you are this cold-blooded guy."

41

Like Lawrence and Manhattan, Parsons, Kansas, is a small town. It is smaller than Lawrence and Manhattan and it is in southeast Kansas near the borders of Oklahoma and Missouri, not in the northeast part of the state. Parsons was founded in 1870 by the Kansas and Texas Railroad and named after Levi Parsons, the railroad's president. The local shorthand for the railroad became "Katy" for K-T, Kansas-Texas Railroad, and each spring the city still celebrates its Katy Days festival. Important things happen here and some well-known people have come from here. Shaun Hill, 2007 starting pro football quarterback for the San Francisco 49ers, is from Parsons. The most famous person to come from Parsons is the late silent-film actress ZaSu Pitts, who has a star on the Hollywood Walk of Fame and whose image is on a U.S. postage stamp. And, of course, in the 1950s, acclaimed Kansas lawman Jim Woods was raised in Parsons, Kansas.

A big guy, Jim played in the line when he was on the school football team. Jim's dad was a banker, but from his junior year in high school on, Jim wanted to work in law enforcement. He couldn't point to any one thing that inspired him, but he knew he wanted to be a lawman. After graduation Jim worked for a year as a manual laborer for the Katy Railroad to earn money for college. He then went west to Wichita, Kansas, to attend police science courses at what was then Wichita University. He obtained a job in the Sedgwick County jail, took classes, and when he could, he rode along with Wichita police officers, including Walter Norman and Phil Bond. He did well in school, but when in 1963 a job opened on the LaBette County sheriff's department back home in Parsons, he applied and received the appointment as a deputy sheriff.

In those days all of Kansas's sheriffs were elected and state civil service laws, such as there were any, did little to protect civil service jobs. With every change of sheriff there were wholesale changes in staff and deputies. When the LaBette County sheriff was not reelected, the new sheriff did not retain Jim.

Jim applied for a job in the Johnson County (Kansas City) sheriff's office. A new sheriff had been elected there, he had a housecleaning, and he wanted "hard chargers." Jim Woods was a hard charger. He was hired.

Jim married a woman he met in Parsons, a nurse, and moved to Olathe, Kansas, in Johnson County. He had not been there long when a friend, a state trooper, told Jim that the Douglas County sheriff was looking for a deputy of a certain "hard-charging" character and he thought Jim might be the man he was looking for. Jim applied, was hired, and in 1965 the Woods family moved to Lawrence, Kansas.

In 1970 Jim Woods was hired to be an agent of the Kansas Bureau of Investigation (KBI). KBI agents are considered to be among the best investigators that the state of Kansas has, the cream that has risen to the top. Jim had a stellar career as a KBI agent. He was even named a "Kentucky Colonel" by the governor of Kentucky in appreciation of his work in solving a drug case that took him from Kansas to the Bluegrass

State. Woods spent most of his KBI career as a homicide detective. All three of his sons grew up steeped in cop culture and became law enforcement agents. They grew up with a refrigerator in the garage that held not only soda pop but items that Dad would have to temporarily store there (such as body parts or fluids) that they were not to touch. They grew up knowing that Dad might suddenly be gone for long periods of time on an investigation. They knew Dad might call and say he'd be gone and he did not know when he'd be back. He could not talk about what he was doing. He might miss school events, but he would be there if he could. On one occasion he flew in to watch his boys in a game, then flew back out to work on a case. Dad told great stories about his career and hoped his boys might follow him. He schooled his sons in the ways of police work, including the art of obtaining confessions.

All three of his sons became deputy sheriffs. Doug was a Douglas County deputy. Dwayne and Tim became deputies just south of Douglas County in Franklin County. Tim now works in security in Houston, Texas.

For all his success as a law enforcement officer, Jim Woods did not solve his first high-profile murder case. The murder occurred in Lawrence, Kansas, during a turbulent student demonstration, just weeks after Kent State, and it still remains unsolved. That case was famous enough that it's been referenced in at least two published books, Bill Moyers's 1971 best seller *Listening to America: A Traveler Rediscovers His Country* and Rusty Molhollon's 2002 *This is America? The Sixties in Lawrence, Kansas*.

More than three decades later, when Jim's son Detective Doug Woods was assigned a high-profile murder case, it was also in Lawrence, Kansas. Doug would interview the prime murder suspect and would use every technique he had learned from his father and elsewhere to try to obtain a confession.

He could not have anticipated facing an extraordinarily erudite man who was a master of language, a Ph.D., a university professor of English and linguistics, and the author or coauthor of nine books. A man so sure of himself that he declined to hire an attorney. The nearly ten-hour verbal combat between the small-town detective, who had only a high school education but was schooled his entire life by his father to obtain criminal confessions, and the professor of linguistics, schooled in rhetoric and the science of language, may be the greatest recorded linguistic battle between a homicide detective and a homicide suspect in police history.

Forty years after the direction of Jim Woods's career was determined by elections, Doug Woods's case came into question because of elections. In 2004 Kansas sheriffs and six Kansas district attorneys (the six largest counties, as opposed to smaller counties that have appointed county attorneys) were elected to office. Months after Carmin Ross's murder, and months before Tom Murray was arrested for her murder, whether or not Murray would be prosecuted came into question when Sheriff Trapp decided not to run for reelection and District Attorney Christine Kenney had a strong opponent in the 2004 election.

In Kansas, and all across America, in sheriff and district attorney elections two issues predominate: do they prosecute the hard cases and do their prosecutions succeed?

A prominent example of an easy case for the sheriff and district attorney to prosecute was the BTK case in Wichita. Shortly after being arrested, the killer not only confessed but told the authorities where to find the evidence against him in the form of handwritten records, photos, and souvenirs that he had taken from the victims. After that, the legal proceedings were a formality. That's an easy prosecution.

A prominent example of what should have been a successful prosecution was the O. J. Simpson criminal case in California. Simpson, a celebrity in his field, a former pro athlete, was on trial for murdering his ex-wife by putting a knife into her throat. The suspect had a cut on his finger consistent with wielding a knife. He gave the police a long interview without his lawyer present. He was smoothly arrogant. Within minutes of talking with the ex-husband, the police concluded that he had murdered his ex-wife.

But while the Los Angeles police rushed to arrest O. J. Simpson, in contrast the Lawrence law enforcement team took its time building a case against Tom Murray and did not make an arrest for nearly a year. The L.A. judge in the Simpson case permitted the trial to be broadcast live, while the Lawrence judge permitted cameras, but not a live broadcast. The meandering, poorly thought-out L.A. trial lasted nearly a year, while the well-thought-out and tightly planned Lawrence trial lasted less than six weeks. The L.A. prosecutors claimed they had "a mountain of evidence," and they did. They had blood evidence, carpet fibers, and an eyewitness who saw Simpson leaving the crime scene. But through police and prosecution bungling, the evidence was excluded or never introduced and the evidence that was offered gave reason for doubt in the minds of the jurors. In contrast, the Kansas team had only circumstantial evidence, but they would use it wisely, and at trial the jurors had no reason to doubt the suspect's guilt.

But not knowing the future, when the election of the next Douglas County sheriff and district attorney was in doubt, whether Tom Murray would be criminally prosecuted was also in doubt, because the Murray case was a hard case.

On Tuesday, March 11, 2004, Sheriff Trapp, a former FBI agent, announced he would not run for reelection. He was asked by the local news media what this would do to the investigation of the Carmin Ross murder, and he was asked, again, what was the cause of Ross's death. Trapp said he would not release the cause of death because he didn't want to do anything that would jeopardize the investigation. That Ross was beaten and stabbed was still unknown to the public but was known to the killer.

Four days later, on the Ides of March, Undersheriff Ken McGovern announced his candidacy for the sheriff's office.

June passed and no one else filed for the job, so McGovern would become the new sheriff.

The Democrats knew that two-term Republican Christine Kenney was in political trouble because her office had the fifth-worst felony trial conviction record among the six Kansas district attorneys. On Tuesday morning, April 27, 2004, Democrat Charles Branson, a Lawrence attorney and the city prosecutor for nearby Eudora, Kansas, announced that he was entering the race for Douglas County DA. Branson was sharp, personable, and a hard campaigner, but because incumbent Kenney was perceived as vulnerable, he would have primary opposition.

In August, Charles Branson won the Democratic Party primary in the race for the DA position. He thought he won because voters saw his "good ideas. People are ready for a change. I think we can bring some good things to the office, some new things to the office that Douglas County really deserves to have."

The election was hard fought. Branson pointed out that Christine Kenney, during her eight years in office, had personally prosecuted only one jury trial, her budget had increased 46 percent while her case filings had decreased more than 15 percent, and she had avoided filing the hard cases.

To many of the voters, this meant the Murray case. Nearly ten months after Carmin's murder there was no arrest.

For a time during the election cycle, neither Doug Woods nor anyone else knew what would happen to the Murray case.

42

Most stories have a tangible "MacGuffin"—what the focus character and opponent wants to control, possess, or destroy—and the MacGuffin is sometimes in the story's title (*The Maltese Falcon*, for example).

In crime stories the MacGuffin is always the same thing: the evidence that convicts the bad guy. The detective wants it and the criminal wants it concealed.

The cause-effect sequence of story incidents en route to the goal and the MacGuffin require decisions by both the good guy and the bad guy. Some decisions are easy, but some decisions are very hard because the choices are either between the lesser of two evils or between the better of two goods, and it is unclear which is most desirable. Each incident creates hope or fear in the main characters and the audience. There's often a deadline or a finish line that all the characters understand. Once that line is reached, the story is coming to a resolution.

Interview Room #2

In response to being accused of being "cold-blooded," Thomas Murray said, "Well, I know, but hear what I have to say: I was deducing that this is

not—you don't send four police officers to tell somebody his former wife has passed away. You don't have
a police officer go from room to room with this guy
unless you think, well, he might have a concealed
firearm someplace that he is going to pull. Or he might
try to sneak out the back door, or whatever the case
is. So from the get-go I knew (A) something not good
is going on here and (B) I've been implicated in some
way. I don't want to use the word 'suspect' but I suppose, yes, I'm a suspect. I told you earlier, if I were
you, I think I'd be the primary. I would look at me
as the primary suspect. I would have to. And, honest
to God, I am not sitting here trying to anticipate
things."

"Every time I come in here you go, 'Well, there
was one thing I neglected to tell you,'" Woods said.

"Well, I don't know," Murray said.

"'Here's another thing I neglected to tell you,'"
Woods taunted.

"I don't know. Have you been in Carmin's house?"
Murray asked.

"No," the second officer said.

Murray asked the second detective, "Have you been
in Carmin's house?"

"Yes," the officer said.

Murray said, "Okay, when you go in the front door,
you head slightly to the left, there is a bathroom in
there. When I was there on Tuesday, Tuesday after
the mediation, I washed my hands in that sink, dried
them there on the towel. You'll find a drop of my
blood on that towel. Guarantee it. I am not trying to
account for anything. I am just saying I was picking
at this cut when I was in mediation because I was
nervous and there is a drop of my blood on that towel,
I guarantee it."

"You said there is going to be her blood on the
steering wheel on the gearshifter," Woods said.

"I am guessing, Doug, because she is driving. I didn't know. I never saw the blood. She came in and she said, 'I had a nosebleed. Both sides bled.' And she described it as a 'gusher.' But she said, 'I will go out and clean it up.' I never saw it," Murray said.

"Why did she drive your car?" Woods asked. "Why didn't she drive her own?"

"Because my car was parked right behind her car and we didn't both want to go out—"

The second officer interrupted. "She has a big driveway and a yard. It wasn't like it was a two-car, one-car driveway that you couldn't get out. That doesn't make any sense either. I was out at the house."

"I don't have an answer for that. I am not even going to try to make one up," Murray said.

"Okay," Woods said.

"Because you wouldn't even be happy with it, but I am telling you, she took my car. And I understand that you guys are doing your job and I understand that," Murray said. "If I were you, I would probably be saying things the same way. And you have every right to approach this whole thing with great suspicion. But I am doing my levelheaded best to help you and to set that suspicion aside. Of course I am trying to do that. I want to go home and take care of my daughter more than anything right now. That is all. I want to be done with this. Why am I not thinking clearly? Well, besides only having slept a total of about four hours over the last three nights, it's now God knows what time, and I was supposed to be asleep by about ten P.M. The only way I am thinking at is, I think, I am on adrenaline here. I am not asking you to cut me a lot of slack, I am just saying, don't expect—' "

Woods interrupted. "I have been cutting you some slack since we started this."

"I am saying," Murray began, "don't expect me to function now, at this time, the way I would after a

good night's sleep and a clear head. My head is anything but clear. You tell me that my wife, well, you
said, 'Died.' Okay, tell me that my wife died. That's
a huge shock. You take me down here when I say,
'Can we do it in the morning?' 'No, we are going to
do it now.' Well—"

"Now let's stop right there," Woods interrupted.
"That is not what I told you."

"Well," Murray said, "I asked if I could come in
the morning."

Woods said, "I said, 'We need to do it now.' I
wouldn't be at your house if it was something that
could wait. I didn't order you or make you do
anything."

"No," Murray said. "No, I am not saying that you
did."

"Okay," Woods said. "Well, you are wording it like
I made you come down here."

"No," Murray said. "No, I didn't mean that. I did
not mean that. But I asked somebody, 'Can I do it
tomorrow morning?' I think it was the guy with
glasses. I forget his name. He said, 'I think it would
be better if we did it now.' So I said, 'Okay, we will
do it now.' There was no coercion. I am sorry. I don't
know what to do. I am trying to be as helpful as I can
and you don't like the way certain things line up. But
they line up the way they line up. You are talking to
a guy who never so much has been into a fight."

Woods decided that now was the time to try to
prompt Murray to confess.

"I know," Woods said. "But listen, Tom. When
things get emotional, good people sometimes do bad
things. I see it every day."

"Of course," Murray retorted. "I know that."

"A guy that you would say, 'Man, he has never
done anything like that. He would never do anything
like that.' All of a sudden, you are talking to them

because they have done something like that," Woods said. "And it all comes from some kind of emotional trigger, okay?"

"I understand," Murray said.

"You know," Woods said, "you had that with her."

"An emotional trigger?" Murray asked.

"Yeah," Woods said.

"Well, I have had a series of emotional triggers for the last fourteen months," Murray said.

"Exactly," Woods said. "I know you've had a lot of them. You have all kinds of emotional triggers with her. It could cause something like this to happen. And put that on top of all these things that are surrounding you, and this blood everywhere. I mean, I never talked to a guy that had so much blood around him. Everywhere you go there's blood. Somebody is either bleeding from their nose, their hand, or somewhere. Everywhere you're at."

"Well," Murray said, "here's another point."

"Tom," Woods said, "wait a minute."

"All right," Murray said. "I'm sorry."

"That's why we are talking to you like this," Woods said.

"I understand that," Murray said. "I understand that. Here is another point that, if you are me, you might keep in mind, okay? You say, occasionally, emotion gets in the way and causes a trigger and somebody is going to do what they wouldn't ordinarily do."

"It happens all the time," Woods said.

"Well," Murray said, "I have seen enough cop shows and law shows to hear about the temporary insanity or whatever-it's-called defense. But, believe me, I am a rational enough person to think, 'No, let me back up. I am a caring and loving enough person for my daughter to think . . .' Don't shake your head [to Detective Woods]. No. Let me finish. (A) I don't

want her to go through life with one parent because
all the psychological evidence says by the time she hits
adulthood, she won't have any but a very few memories of anything before five years old. That means she
won't remember ever being with Mommy. I would
never deprive her of that. And (B) I have also watched
enough cop shows to know that there is no such thing
as the perfect crime. You are going to get caught. The
bad guy always gets caught. So, if I decide to do a
crime and kill my former wife, I am not depriving
Helen of a life with one parent, I am depriving Helen
of a life with two parents. How in the world would I
do that? She is the most important thing in the world
to me."

Woods said, "You can sit here with that point right
now and think that, but at the time, when those emotional triggers kick in, we don't think rationally. We
don't realize those things are going to happen. We are
not worried about the consequences until afterwards."

"Okay," Murray said. "Well . . ."

"When that emotional trigger happens, anger takes
over and rational thinking moves out the window
ninety-nine percent of the time," Woods said.

"But I told you this before," Murray said. "I don't
know, but I think the kind of trigger you are talking
about is a spontaneous thing that happens, you know,
you are with somebody and 'boom,' you pull out a
gun and you pull the trigger. The scenario that you
are trying to create, or think the evidence leads you
to create, is that I got in my car and drove almost two
hours to Lawrence and did this. And I told you before,
Doug, that that would be a long trigger for me to
sustain."

"With the idea that I am going to drive to Lawrence
and I am going to talk to her, because I don't want
to mess up my parental, how our arrangement is right
now," Woods said.

"I would call her on the phone," Murray said.

"Okay," Woods said. "Talking to people in person is always better, okay? If that was the case, I would be sitting here talking to you on the phone all night long every time I have a question."

"You have a vested interest in seeing my mind," Murray said.

"You have a vested interest in taking care of your daughter," Woods said. "You have a vested interest in being with your daughter a certain amount of time, seeing her grow up, being the daddy that you want to be to her. And that's all about to change for you because we as men, and as horrible as it is in this time and age, we, men, get the shaft in a divorce. You're about to lose that, so maybe we can talk to her rationally and, hey, 'Carmin let's work this out.' Because you were upset initially. You say you weren't upset because Larry is moving to town because, 'Okay, they are not going to take off and go to San Diego. I am still going to be around Helen.' But then she tells you it's a temporary thing."

"That's right," Murray said.

"Right there," Woods said. "It's an emotional trigger. 'Okay, I am going to lose my daughter.' "

"No," Murray said.

"Stop," Woods said. "I am running through this, okay? Why would a reasonable man not think that?"

"Because I am going to win in court, Doug. I've got the case," Murray said.

"You don't know you are going to win in court," Woods said.

"Look at the folder by my telephone," Murray said.

"I'm not going to touch a folder," Woods said. "It all comes down to that one person sitting up there in that booth wearing that robe. And if that person decides the mother is the better parent, you don't get to see your daughter. I am telling you men get the shaft and you know it. You may be 'the World's Best Dad,' but ninety-nine percent of the time the woman always ends up with the child because a child flourishes more with the mother than they do with the father."

"That was true thirty years ago," Murray said.

"It's still true today with the judges," Woods said.

"It's not even true in good old conservative Kansas," Murray said.

"Really?" Woods said.

"That's what my attorney told me," Murray said. "Go ask Sue Jacobson."

"Well," the second officer said, "I can speak to you from about one hundred divorced men."

"Let me ask you this: I am very sorry you are divorced too," Murray said, speaking to the second officer.

"Are the women that you divorced, when you divorced them, were they talking to spirit guides and angels? And were you concerned that they would have . . . You are smiling, but I have this documented," Murray said.

"Oh," the second officer said, "I am sure you do."

"You think I made that up too?" Murray asked.

"No," the second officer said, "I don't think you are making that up. I am just telling you that I know of other situations where a person could be crazier than a shithouse rat and they still ended up with their mother."

"When I was sitting across the desk from Sue Jacobson," Murray said, "telling her all this stuff, she said, 'Look, I don't have a crystal ball in my desk. You never know absolutely sure, but you have a very—' "

The second officer interrupts. "Right. She was developing one hell of an argument for your side. And your wife's lawyer was going to put up one hell of an argument for her side. That is what court is all about. You know that, okay? It all comes down to what that judge thinks where is the best interest for Helen. We don't know. It's all in that judge's head. Your mediator can make a recommendation. You know they get along fine, all those kind of things. But it still comes down to that judge. You're in risk of losing that by one person's thinking."

"There is always a risk, that's right," Murray said.

"And you know as well as I do," Woods said, "just because it's good old conservative Kansas, the men still get it ninety-nine percent of the time. We don't get to see our kids like we should."

"That is not what I was told, Doug," Murray said. "I am sorry."

"Well," Woods said.

"Why do you keep throwing this ninety-nine percent figure when Sue says it is nowhere near that?" Murray asked.

"What Sue is doing," Woods said, "is representing your best interest. She is making you believe that she is going to win your case for you."

"What do you mean?" Murray asked. "That what she is telling me is false?"

"I don't think she is telling you false information," Woods said. "What do you think Carmin's lawyer is telling her? The exact opposite of what your lawyer is telling you."

"She hasn't consulted with an attorney about custody yet," Murray said. "At least, that's what she said."

"Do you know that for a fact?" Woods asked.

"That's what Carmin told me," Murray said. "And she also said, 'I don't lie.' "

"She's not telling you the truth," Woods said. "And [the second officer] may be able to expound on that quite a bit, because she is not telling you the truth."

"As recently as Tuesday, she sat right across the table from me and said, 'I have never told you a lie,' " Murray said.

"Tom," Woods said, "they all say that. You know."

"Well, no, I don't," Murray said. "And I am not willing to generalize like that. I am sorry."

"And when you were going through what you guys [Carmin and Tom] were going through, people will lie, cheat, steal, do whatever they can to win, okay?" Woods said.

"Especially," the second officer added, "when it comes to your child."

"Here's something that will be self-incriminating," Murray said. "Now you can jump all over it, but I had a discussion with another colleague, probably was the beginning of the semester, when I was telling Dave all this stuff that had happened, he and I agreed that every person is capable of doing everything imaginable. I mean, you think everybody is capable, but I think there's a spectrum of possibilities here."

"I think it is kind of like what we talked about," Woods said. "Each person has their breaking point. Yours may be a lot higher than mine. It may be a lot less in the past."

"I am telling you," Murray said, "I have not reached anything that you would call a 'breaking point.' Yet I can appreciate how things look from your point of view. I really can. I think I can. I don't know what I can say. It seems like the more I talk, the more I get myself on your wrong side. Ask the next question, then, if you'd like."

The second officer says, "Okay. Let me ask you a couple things here. And this is, I am just thinking ahead, okay? And you are good at this, so this ought to work out good."

"I am good at thinking ahead," Murray said.

"You are good at figuring these things out, and you are going to see what I am talking about in a minute," the second officer said.

"All right," Murray said.

"And right now," the second officer said, "this is just hypothetical. Let's say, 'What if we interviewed some people that lived around your ex-wife's house who, on Tuesday, saw a stranger in that area, and they described this person in the vehicle and what they described matched you?'"

"I guess it depends on how close the description is," Murray said. "I don't know."

"Let's say 'close,'" the second officer said.

"Well, are you asking me how I would respond?" Murray asked.

"Yeah," the second officer said.

"I guess I would say, well, I am a pretty average-looking kind of guy. You know. I am tall, thin, short brown hair, and that probably describes, I don't know, a significant proportion of the men in Kansas. I don't know. I mean, I am grasping here at straws. I have no idea how many of those men drive a cranberry-colored car. All I can do is tell you where I was, where my car was. I can't account for what anybody else tells you, and I am not trying to except when you say. But, when we have this, of course, it's only natural I am going to come back and say, 'But wait a minute, this happened, and maybe that will explain why you found that, or heard that, or saw that, or whatever the case is,'" Murray said.

The second officer, continuing to play bad cop, said, "So, that would be just another coincidence too. Perhaps there would be somebody that looks just like you and has a car just like you that happened to be there."

"If you're saying somebody saw in the driveway a two thousand three Saturn Ion three that's cranberry colored, and they saw somebody that's six foot two inches, one hundred eighty pounds, this kind of hair, blue eyes, that would be an amazing coincidence. I have no idea what kind of specifics you are talking about," Murray said.

"What about this one? What if we sometime down the road we come and tell you that besides that blood that's in the bathroom, that there was more?" the second officer said.

"Well, there might have been more," Murray said.

"In other places of the house," the second officer said.

"I told Doug earlier," Murray said, "I was picking at this, at these two cuts on my finger, and one on this part of my hand here, all through the mediation, and Nancy probably saw it bleed. I mean, you can ask. I don't know if she did, but I kept, you know, like that, trying to get the blood off. I walked first of all, when I was there Tuesday, I was down on the carpet wrestling with Helen and had my forehead being ground into the carpet. So, here is another amazing coincidence: I was perspiring too. You may find perspiration of mine on the carpet. And you are going to think, 'Oh, my God, now he has a reason for why there is perspiration on the carpet.' Well, I had my coat on, and we were wrestling, and we would wrestle as I come up behind her, and I would lean way over, and my forehead goes down onto the carpet. That's just the way we do it. And I had this, I don't know whether it's Spiegel or some other toy catalog with me that Carmin had asked me to bring, and I was trying to conceal that from Helen, so Carmin's motioning me to follow her into the kitchen. So I follow her into the kitchen and I put the catalog on the counter. I don't know what I touched out there. I don't even remember. I didn't drink anything. She didn't offer me water. So you won't find fingerprints on glasses, but I know I touched things. I just don't know what there might have been blood going from the front door to the kitchen. There might be on where I was wrestling. I don't know, but I know I left a drop on the towel and it was right after I washed my hands so that quick a drop of blood had come out and it got on Carmin's towel and I remarked to her about it."

"So," the second officer said, "it [Murray's DNA] could be on the carpet, too. Is that what you're saying?"

"If I say that, you are going to say, 'Oh, so now you are coming up with an explanation,' " Murray said.

"No," the second officer said, "I am just asking."

"I am saying that I don't know that it's not," Murray said, "but, I don't know that it is."

The second officer asked, "Tom, what if they find it on your dead wife's body?"

"It can't be on her body," Murray said. "Well, I don't think it can. I don't have an explanation. There, you stumped me. I just don't, I mean, if you let me sit and think about it, I might come up with something plausible. But, again, you're sort of baiting a trap and inviting me to walk into it."

"Are they going to find that [DNA on his dead ex-wife's body]?" the second officer asked.

"No," Murray said. "They are not."

"They're not going to find it," the second officer repeated.

"No, they're not," Murray said. "There is no way. I haven't bled on Carmin in the longest time. I mean, I have at some time. Wait a minute."

The second officer asked, "The day, the last day you were there?"

"Tuesday," Murray said.

"Whenever it was," the second officer said.

"No," Murray said, "I did not. Well, okay, I am going to say I did not, but I did have blood dripping off my finger. It wouldn't have gotten on her, though.

It would have gotten on her clothes, I am sure. But that's all I can say. That's the truth. I am being as sincere as I can. I am sorry. You are both acting like you know it's not the answer you want. I don't know. All I can tell you is what is true. I don't know what you want or need to hear."

"The truth," the second officer said.

"Okay. I am a truthful person. I don't make things up. I don't fabricate things," Murray said.

43

Tom Murray guaranteed that his blood would be found in Carmin's bathroom.

Was it?

At trial, on March 3, 2005, the prosecution's DNA expert, Dr. Sudhir Sinha, said, "No."

But then he added that the blood that was found could belong to Murray.

Defense Attorney: "Within a reasonable degree of scientific certainty, you cannot conclude that the sample that was pulled from that baseboard was Tom Murray's blood, can you?"

Dr. Sinha: "No, I'm not saying that. I'm not saying that this blood belongs to him [Murray]. . . . This blood *could* belong to him."

Prosecutor: "Doctor, based on your experience, do you have an opinion with a reasonable degree of scientific certainty [scientific certainty being statistical and problematical] whether Tom Murray's DNA is consistent with the baseboard sample?"

Dr. Sinha: "Well, as far as our standard quality control, we gave the result 'inconsistent, inconclusive.' But as far as my experience looking at it, and looking at the data, and doing several times and always finding the fifteen there, and that it's my scientific opinion that, yes, he is not excluded, and the result looks consistent that out of the mixture he could be one of the persons there present."

According to Dr. Sinha, DNA from three people was in that mixed drop of DNA on the baseboard exactly where Murray said they'd find his DNA. There was Carmin's DNA, DNA that was consistent with Tom Murray's DNA, and a trace amount of DNA from an unidentified person. Doug Woods told the author that trace was consistent with a law enforcement officer who was assigned for a time to be at that baseboard where that trace was found.

Dr. Sinha also testified that Larry Lima was excluded as a source of any of the DNA found in that sample.

To analyze the blood sample, Dr. Sinha examined eleven portions of the Y chromosome, found only in men. He explained that this was like using a magnet to pick up the metal in a haystack.

Of the eleven portions, seven were identical to Tom Murray's. He also testified that because the sample was mixed, and apparently had blood from two different men, he could not make any statistical projection.

Dr. Sinha said that if any one of the eleven portions was different from Tom Murray's, that would have excluded him, but none were different from Tom Murray's, and seven of the eleven were identical.

Murray had anticipated that the police might find traces of Carmin's blood in his car. He explained that on October 5 he was in Lawrence with Carmin when she wanted some Pedialyte for Helen. She asked him to go to the Walgreens drugstore at Sixth Street and Kasold Drive. He said that he did not know where that was and was afraid of becoming lost. So Carmin drove Murray's car to Walgreens while he stayed at her home with Helen. Murray said that while returning from Walgreens Carmin had a massive nosebleed, and that would explain any of Carmin's blood they might find.

Lawrence is a small town about five by six miles in size. At worst, one can be lost for only a few minutes. But Murray should not have gotten lost at all going to Walgreens. It was only three miles from Carmin's on one of Lawrence's main roads, at the busy intersection of Sixth Street and Kasold.

Upon investigation, the detectives found a receipt from that Walgreens for purchase of Pedialyte on October 5, 2003. It was signed by Thomas E. Murray. At trial the defense would eventually stipulate that it was Murray's signature.

Carmin had not driven to Walgreens; he had. Murray concocted a scenario to provide an explanation for why the police might find Carmin's blood in his car and to imply that he did not know the location of Highway 40. When Highway 40 entered Lawrence it became Sixth Street. If he entered Lawrence via Highway 40, to reach Carmin's home he had to drive past the Walgreens that he claimed he could get lost trying to find. To avoid the turnpike cameras that he mistakenly believed were present, Murray would have turned north on Kasold, at the intersection with the Walgreens, and driven the same route that Detective Woods traveled to Carmin's home.

44

Interview Room #2

"Let me ask you this: why, if I were going to hatch a plan to kill my wife," Murray started asking. "Why wouldn't I wait until after the courtroom hearing?"

"Because then," Woods said, "you don't have to go through the courtroom stuff. It's not a crapshoot then."

"But I've already told you, there is no perfect crime. You are going to get caught," Murray said. "The only thing you lose by going to a courtroom is money. What it might cost, ten thousand dollars, I don't know. That's what I've been told, ballpark. I don't mind spending ten thousand dollars for something like that."

"Another problem, if you go there, and you've actually tried to talk to her, okay, we can work something out. You and Larry live in Lawrence. We will remain. Hell, maybe you have even thought about living in Lawrence and commuting back and forth to Manhattan, so that you can be with your child. People do things like that all the time," Woods said.

"Yes," Murray said. "I thought about moving to Lawrence."

"That's a perfectly rational thing to think about.

Convenient, no, but you are going to be there for your child," Woods said.

"Right," Murray said.

"Something happens," Woods said. "She says the wrong thing. And then you get to your boiling point. Your breaking point. Trying to be the thinkable, sensible guy. She says the wrong thing. Says, for lack of a better term, 'Kiss my ass, Tom. I am not doing it. I am taking Helen and we're going to San Diego.' "

"Two things," Murray said calmly. "First of all, she would never talk like that."

"I said, for lack of a better term," Woods said.

"I mean, it's not even close. I mean, she was never, her language was never contentious," Murray said.

"The language has nothing to do with it," Woods said. "I was just using that for an example. She could tell you, 'No, thank you. You were not involved. I'm not going to do that.' "

"The other thing wrong with the scenario is, I am going to drive an hour and forty-five minutes or two hours to get to Lawrence for a one-minute chat before I have to get back in the car and drive," Murray said.

"You've got more than a minute. We've got that figured out. You've got plenty of time. Okay?" Woods said.

"Tell me how much time I have," Murray said.

"A little over four hours," Woods said. "A little over three hours, excuse me. You dropped her off at eight thirty, between eight fifteen and eight thirty."

"Absolutely not," Murray said. "I have never in my life—"

Woods interrupted. "Tom, stop and listen to me."

"Never in my life at eight fifteen," Murray insisted.

"Listen to me," Woods said. "Between eight fifteen and eight thirty is what Angela said. You dropped her off. Angela was home, came down the stairs, and

Helen was already there. We have talked to her. We talked to the babysitter."

"Lacey?" Murray asked.

"She is saying between eight thirty and eight forty. That gives you plenty of time," Woods said.

"Okay," Murray said. "I said eight forty-five."

"You can drive to Lawrence," Woods said.

"Okay, let's start," Murray said.

"Ten o'clock A.M.," Woods said. "You're in Lawrence at ten A.M." [When the murder occurred.]

"I can't drive to Lawrence," Murray said. "I am sorry, okay."

"You can drive to Lawrence," Woods said. "You can be pissed off at the world and drive seventy miles an hour, even though you tell me, 'I only drive sixty miles an hour.' "

"I just don't," Murray said.

"Listen to me, okay," Woods said. "You can make it there in that period. You can make it to Lawrence at ten a.m. You can sit here and tell me, 'I never drive over sixty-five.' You can tell me that all you want. I don't necessarily believe you. Every single time you are on the highway you only drive sixty miles an hour. Fine. You can be in Lawrence at ten."

"Okay," Murray said.

"Your daughter's dropped off [at your home] at twelve thirty," Woods said.

"No," Murray said. "Twelve fifteen."

"I have already talked to Angela," Woods said.

"Twelve-fifteen," Murray said.

"Between twelve fifteen and twelve thirty, she is dropped off. That gives you plenty of time. That's two hours, two and a half hours, and fifteen minutes. You are splitting hairs with fifteen minutes," Woods said.

"Let's go with your scenario," Murray said. "Let's say I get there at ten. Let's say that in my mind I have to be out of there at ten thirty, okay? So I have a thirty-minute window."

Woods said, "I could go over there and talk to her rationally for fifteen or twenty minutes or whatever. If things aren't going well, what is going to prevent you from calling Angela and saying, 'I am in the middle of a conversation with her about Helen. Do you mind keeping her for an extra half hour? Can we arrange something?' You can call Angela or the Oriental girl to come over."

"No," Murray said. "She can't."

"Listen," Woods said, "these things are all options that could come into play."

"But," Murray said, "they're not."

"Yes," Woods said, "they are."

"Peiwen has classes on Tuesday," Murray said. "I couldn't call her."

"You found a babysitter in two minutes at eight thirty tonight to come to your house," Woods said.

"Did you hear what I said on the phone?" Murray asked.

" 'I have an emergency,' " Woods said. "You could have done the same thing on the phone Thursday morning. 'I have an emergency, could you please watch her for another half hour.' That could work."

"I would not ask Angela, describing it as an emergency, I would not ask her to come over," Murray said.

"I think," Woods said, " 'We are discussing my child's well-being' could be considered an emergency. Discussing the point of, 'When am I going to get to see my child? How often?' could be considered an emergency."

"I don't consider that an emergency," Murray said.

"That's fine, Tom," Woods said.

"I am just telling you, Doug," Murray said. "Let me ask you this. What are you going to do if your coroner comes back and says, 'Well, the time of death is eleven a.m.'? Then you are going to say, 'Well, you could speed back to Manhattan between eleven and twelve fifteen.' What is that going to do to your theory?"

"How do you know we haven't already established a time of death?" Woods asked.

"I don't," Murray said.

45

Interview Room #2

At 4:13 A.M., Saturday, November 15, 2003, Professor Thomas E. Murray was left alone in the interview room. He spoke aloud and his comments were recorded—

"I thought for sure I got her there at . . . it was late that day, I thought. Well, I know for damn sure it wasn't eight fifteen. On my best day in the world I cannot get her ready by eight fifteen. . . . He sits there and says, 'if he were to kill his wife,' well, I am sorry, I just have never had that feeling. Why can't you admit to that possibility? . . . I can't believe she was going back to Kelster and preparing for a custody battle and she flat out told me she wasn't. Oh, Carmin. Human beings are such interesting creatures . . ."

At this point Murray stood up and opened the interview room door. He spoke to the officer standing outside the door. Only Murray's side of the conversation is recorded: "Could I have something to write with? A pen? A pencil? Crayon? It doesn't matter. Well, just in the meantime, if I wanted to jot something down that I wanted to remember to tell them. I'd appreciate it. I've got paper. I just need a pen to write with. Thanks. I appreciate it."

After a few minutes Woods returned. "I had one thing I wanted to say to you before you left, but now I have a list of five things. Honest to God. I am not trying to patch holes in the dike. But I think that the things that I have sort of poke holes in your theory. First of all, Doug, I wanted to address the whole Shrek and Baloo coming through the door and doing not-nice things.

"First of all," he continued, "they don't always come through a door. Sometimes they come through the forest. But they are not nice. That's true. But, I think, at least Shrek is in the context of Shrek's being an ogre and not always nice in the movie. But, regardless, the thing I want you to ask Helen, if this reaches a point where you interview her, is ask what Daddy said about hurting Shrek and Baloo.

"And the answer that she'll give, if she remembers, she'll say I refused to play the game because I didn't want to hurt Shrek or Baloo," Murray said. "I told her that I don't think hurting people, hurting bears or ogres, is an option. And we flat-out quit playing the game. And she said, 'Okay, well, don't shoot them, or just shoot them someplace where it will heal.' And I said, 'Sweetie, I am not even going to pretend with guns. We're just not going to do it.' Ask her that."

"The second thing," Murray said, "is, Doug, you deduced early on that I am what you call 'the thinking man.' Okay. You have said I am in this room thinking 'Oh, God! They're going to find blood in the car. Oh, God! They're going to find blood here. And oh, God. I've got to patch this.' And I am coming up with plausible explanations. It seems to me, if I were a thinking man, if I really did this thing, what you're suggesting, and if I did it Thursday morning, in this time frame that you are suggesting, I have had from Thursday morning until whenever you guys got here tonight, or yesterday, a quarter till eight, I have had a day and a half to think the whole thing through. Certainly, it would occur to me that you are either going to find blood. I wouldn't wait until, you know, the twenty-fourth hour to come up with an explanation. I mean, if that were my strategy, I'm just saying, I mean, that's not the way a thinking man works. You've gotta have everything up out in front, I think.

"The third thing is," Murray said, "and I don't mean to be mean-spirited here, I don't mean to impugn the integrity of you guys, or what you are doing, I know you are just doing your job, but it occurs to me that in me, you have not just a likely suspect, but a convenient one: the ex-husband who is threatened with the loss, possible loss, of his child, in your words. Doug, if this scenario falls apart, you're very well back to square one. And, you are right, I have seen enough shows to know that if you don't catch the guy. No, let me back up, to know that the longer the time line goes on after the crime, the lower the percentages of catching the guy who did it. So, we gotta nail them quick. If I put you guys back to square one. It's like, 'No, we've gotta scramble. Who else we going to find? Is it a random thing? Do we have to find someone else who is likely?'

"The fourth thing is," Murray continued, "you told me, Doug, I could walk out of here anytime I want. For heaven's sakes! If I am really trying to hide something, why didn't I get up and walk out and go call the best attorney money can buy and say, 'Oh, my God. You've got to get me out of this.' I am being as willing as I can to sit down and share whatever I can think of with you. I haven't once said, 'I am so uncomfortable I want to leave.' And I told you, I am not going to.

"And the other [fifth] thing is," Murray said, "I asked you about this earlier. I asked you if that thing above the tollbooth is a video camera, and you said, 'Yes.' "

Woods said, "I said it may be, but I don't know for sure."

"Oh, 'may be,' " Murray said. "Well, I am hoping it is. There is absolutely no record of my car going through that tollbooth. And you've said, 'Well, you have lived in Manhattan for fifteen years. You could have gone [Kansas Highway] 24.' "

"You could have taken another car," Woods said.

"Okay," Murray said. "You have to find the car that I could borrow. I don't have a clue. I don't know how to go 24, either."

"You could pop in, just like you said," Woods said. "You could go on the computer, go to MapQuest, and it would tell you exactly how to go."

"But, MapQuest gives you the quickest, most direct way," Murray said.

"You can do it without doing interstates," Woods said.

"Okay," Murray said. "I didn't know that. All right. Well, maybe there's a plausible way. But I am telling you, I don't know how to do that. That would take some, that would take some advance planning. And, before, you said, 'I don't think you planned this out. I think it just happened.' Well, it can't be both ways. I either planned it out, or it just happened."

46

Interview Room #2

"I think it could be both," Woods said.

"But—" Murray protested.

Woods said, "It could be a spur-of-the-moment thing. 'I am mad. I killed my ex-wife.' Then, it's planned out after that. 'I've got to do everything in my power to cover my tracks.'" (The criminal cover-up is planned.)

"But the MapQuest thing would have to be done in advance of that visit," Murray said.

"You could have taken somebody else's car," Woods said. "You could have rented a car. There's a million places you can rent a car."

"Okay," Murray said. "Check every place you can."

"Are you done, Tom?" the second officer asked.

"I am," Murray said.

"Let's see," the second officer said, "there's a couple of other things that I think we had. Do you have a computer at home?"

"I have a laptop at home," Murray said. "And I have a really old, larger-size one. And I have a computer at work."

"Okay," the second officer said. "Internet at home?"

"I can do Internet on the laptop," Murray said.

"And at work, too, probably," the officer said.

"Yes," Murray said. "I usually do it at work because the one at home is really slow. But I have the capabilities to do it, but I rarely do."

"What kinds of things do you look at on the Internet?" Woods asked.

"When at work I go to job listings," Murray said. "I go sometimes to Amazon.com. I go to my e-mail account at work online. I think that is it. If I am researching a class, I was doing part of a class one time on freedom of speech, I once made the mistake of logging on to some porn sites to see what was allowable on the Internet and now I get more spam than you can imagine from things like that. But aside from research or looking at job listings or getting my e-mail, that's about it."

"You ever e-mail Carmin?" the second officer asked.

"Yes," Murray said. "Frequently. I told Doug I e-mailed her as recently as Thursday evening. She wrote to ask me the name of the new baby of friends of ours."

The second officer asked, "Have you ever gotten on the Internet and looked at any Web sites that have to do with crime scenes or polygraphs?"

"Not polygraph," Murray answered. "But I actually got on the *CSI* Web site, if that's what it was. I occasionally have fantasies about trying to make it as a freelance writer. And, especially in the context of perhaps having to relocate and lose my job in academia, I thought, you know, I have friends in the department who wrote a script for *Star Trek* a few years ago. I don't know if it was accepted. But, I thought, well, I could do that. So, I wanted to read and see. So the short answer is, 'yes.' I've done that just once."

"Once," the second officer said. "When did you do that? Recently?"

"Yes," Murray answered. "It was in the last month, I think."

"Would you have any problem with us looking at your Internet history on the computer?" Woods asked.

"You are welcome to all of them," Murray answered. "I give you permission to look at all of them."

"The other thing that came to my mind," Woods said, "was, we talked a little bit about Carmin and the fact that she may have been in the process of visiting with an attorney about this custody issue."

"I find that hard to believe," Murray said. "Because she, as recently as Tuesday, and you can ask Nancy Hughes this, Carmin said, 'I have never lied to you.' Carmin has always been the most straightforward—"

Woods interrupted. "Tom, I understand. 'Ask Nancy Hughes.' I'm telling you, go on and on about what a great person she is, and how she never lies— why did you guys get divorced?"

"Because she told me that 'I was no longer integral to her life path,' " Murray said.

"I thought she had something going on with Larry," Woods said.

"He's the new 'integral person,' " Murray said.

"And you?" Woods asked.

"That's her words," Murray said.

"Well, she can use whatever New Age terms she wants to make it sound good. The bottom line is: she is behind your back with some other man," Woods said.

"That's right," Murray said. "That shocked me."

"You don't know, Tom," Woods said. "You don't know what was getting ready to happen, I guess."

"I know that Helen was number one in her life," Murray said. "She would never put that child in harm's way. If she thought Helen was in harm's way, she would do everything to get her out."

"You thought it was inappropriate that her and Larry were sleeping together in front of Helen," Woods said. "That didn't seem to bother her."

"She told me she was married," Murray said.

"Listen to me," Woods said. "She is not concerned at all about what is going to go on with Helen. She is jumping into bed with a new man in front of Helen. Helen walks in on them and finds them in the new bed together. And who takes her back to her room? Larry does."

"Carmin told me that she and Larry were married," Murray said.

"She's lying to you," Woods said. "Wake up, Tom."

"I took her at her word," Murray said.

"Wake up," Woods said. "My God. You are not an ignorant man."

"Listen," Murray said, "I had no reason not to believe her, Doug. She told me she was married and I believed her. Then her aunt e-mailed me and, in talking about this in e-mail, Betty said, 'Yes, she is married, but it wasn't performed by a minister or justice of the peace because it was too much of this world.' "

"I think you are starting to figure out what was going on," Woods said.

"I had the worst thoughts, too," Murray said. "But I had to believe. In the end, I had to believe that Carmin held Helen in the highest, brightest light. That's always what she was all about. I had no reason to doubt that. I mean, this is her only child, for heaven's sakes. I still don't believe that she would do anything to put Helen in harm's way."

"You wouldn't believe that she had talked to another lawyer about getting full custody?" Woods asked.

"Because she told me that she hadn't. You're right," Murray said.

"She told you she didn't consummate it," Woods said. "She told you she didn't do this. She told you she didn't do that."

"Doug, I still don't have evidence that she did any of this," Murray said.

"Okay," Woods said.

"I am just telling you what I believe. That's all," Murray said.

"I understand that," Woods said.

"If you think I am naive and gullible, maybe I am," Murray said. "We were trying. Carmin and I were doing our best to preserve some semblance—"

"Sounds to me like you were busting your butt doing everything in your power to make this divorce work. But Carmin wasn't doing what you needed her to do. She was doing more of what best suited Carmin and her new man. Her not keeping the happy family unit together as a divorced family," Woods said.

"Then why did she move to Lawrence?" Murray asked.

"To get away from you," Woods said.

"Why didn't she move to San Diego in August?" Murray asked. "She could have gone farther away. I think she wanted to leave Helen in both of our lives on a regular, continuous basis."

"She was fixin' to move to San Diego anyway," Woods said.

"I know," Murray said. "But she delayed it by a year. I think she thought it was that important for me to be in Helen's life."

"What's the possibility of just getting the divorced finalized?" Woods asked. "You haven't even been divorced six months yet."

"Right," Murray said. "I am not sure what you're asking."

"If she put it off for a year, why would she not, instead of when she leaves you, go ahead and move to San Diego? She waits until everything is finalized. Not everything is finalized yet," Woods said.

"Sure it is," Murray said.

"No," Woods said. "Your custody issue isn't finalized yet. You guys were getting ready to go back to court on it."

"For right now, it's final," Murray said. "We have shared custody."

"But you are getting ready to have to go back to court," Woods said.

"The only thing that makes me think she was talking to an attorney about—" Murray was saying when he was interrupted.

Woods said, "I know she was talking to an attorney."

"Let me finish," Murray said. "The only thing that makes me think that now, in the context of what you're saying, is that several times over the last two or three months, she has said, in a sort of a fit of desperation, 'Well, then, let's just go back to court.' And it caught me a little bit off guard. Like, why is she so eager to do that? So, okay, maybe she has been talking to an attorney. She specifically told me, and I think it was in front of Nancy, it was our first or second mediation conference, and Nancy will confirm this, she has been taking notes, Carmin specifically said she had not consulted an attorney on custody issues."

"What she tells you and Nancy has no bearing on real true life," Woods said.

"I am just saying that is what she said, Doug," Murray said.

"Okay," Woods said.

47

In most stories, fiction and nonfiction, the resolution of the story is the ultimate revelation of the characters' true identities. Who is the villain? Who is the hero? Who is the betrayer? In early-twentieth-century America, a common question at many trials was, "Who is the hidden anarchist?" Later, in the 1920s and 1930s, it became "Who hides the fact that he rides with Dillinger or other organized-crime figures?" Then in the 1950s the question became, "Who is the hidden Communist?" For thirty years in Wichita the question was "Who is BTK?" Now, across America the question is "Who is the terrorist?" Later, the precise question will be different, but it will be a question of identity.

In fiction, questions of identity are pervasive. In romances, the question is "Who is the character's true love?" In most murder mysteries, "Who did it?" In comedies, it's often, "When will they realize that the character is not who they think he/she is?" In horror stories, "Who is the vampire?" or "Who is the zombie?" or "Who is the alien?"

In the television program *CSI*, for which Murray claimed to be writing a spec script, the theme song is musical group the Who's 1978 song "Who Are You?" At the beginning of each episode via the song the program tells the viewer what the show is about. It is about discovering identity—the identity of the killer, or victim, or cop, or you. The song screams its question of identity—*Who are you? Who? Who? Who? Who?*

In jury trials, from the public's point of view, the question about the accused is always one of identity. Is he/she the criminal or not?

In the Murray case, a question of identity was whether the district attorney was someone who prosecuted the hard cases.

In this, his first first-degree-murder trial, would Judge Fairchild exorcise the ghost of "Not in My Court"?

Would prosecutor Angela Wilson exorcise the ghost of Stephanie Schmidt?

In his first high-profile homicide case, was Doug Woods going to win a conviction? Was Brad Schlerf's testimony on Murray's body language going to be admitted into evidence before a jury?

And was Tom Murray an innocent aspiring screenwriter or a conniving heartless killer, whom Aristotle would call the worst kind of man, who chose to murder, deliberated on the means to murder, murdered, and then tried to deceive everyone as to his true identity?

48

Interview Room #2

"Well," Murray said, "you are going to love this: there's blood on my mattress pad."

"Probably so," Woods said.

"About four big drops," Murray said.

"Probably so," Woods said.

"Test it," Murray said.

"It will probably come back to your ex-wife," Woods said.

"No," Murray said. "It's Helen's."

"Why would she bleed on your bed?" Woods asked.

"Nosebleed," Murray answered.

"Helen is not the victim of a homicide," Woods said. That was the first time that Murray was told, implicitly, that Carmin was the victim of a homicide.

"All I can do is sit here and tell you the God's honest truth the easiest, best way I know how," Murray said. "If it comes out in spurts rather than in one single long stream, that's the way it comes out. I mean it's only what time now?"

"Five o'clock in the morning," Woods said.

"Yes. And I haven't slept," Murray said.

"Neither have we," Woods said.

"And maybe you're used to it, but I am the guy

who goes to bed every night, in bed, at ten, and hopes to get between seven and eight hours of sleep," Murray said.

The second officer asked, "Why have you not been getting any sleep the last few nights? You said the last two or three nights."

"I explained this to Doug," Murray said. "Helen has a thing with dairy foods and refined sugar. When she eats either, after a certain point they seem to cause all kinds of congestion, snot. When we got back Tuesday night from Carmin's, we went to a Chinese restaurant. Her favorite thing there is crab rangoons. So I let her have a couple. But the center of those things is cream cheese based. I don't know if that's what did it, but when we got home that night, very quickly after that, she started to get all congested. She refuses to blow her nose. And until today, when I got home, today Peiwen said she actually blew her nose. Well, I was so proud of Helen, because she has refused. She just, I don't think she wants to do it and not do it well and have Daddy see her, but she'll go to bed with a full nose. And the breathing is so loud and the snoring that I cannot sleep. You know, it's right in my ear. So, Tuesday, Wednesday, Thursday night, I might have slept each night one to two hours. And, it's just when I reach the point of total exhaustion I fall asleep. Then I will hear this loud ruckus snoring and I will wake up. An hour or two later, then, once my body wakes up. Early in the morning it doesn't go back to sleep again. It's ready for the day. But, that's why it's a longer answer than you wanted, but that's why."

"Well, that's fine," the second officer said. "I mean, it just kind of falls into place with everything else."

"Go look at Helen right now," Murray said. "She's congested right as I speak. You will find in my trash can Kleenexes that have her snot on them. Because what she does in lieu of blowing her nose, is take a

Kleenex and hold it in front of her nose, like this, I mean for a long time, and draw it away occasionally, and get the big long stringy snot. She'll wipe it, then put the Kleenex back. And then complain that she can't eat or drink. And it's, like, 'Sweetie, let's take the Kleenex away.' 'No. Then the snot will get on my face and get on my clothes.' Then we will have to clean it up. You'll find those in the trash can. That will explain or corroborate what I am saying."

"Carmin's family is where, again?" Woods asked.

"Just outside Indianapolis," Murray answered. "Her mom and dad and two of her sisters. And there's another sister up in sort of the western side, about halfway up the western side of Michigan."

"What do you think her mom and dad are going to say?" Woods asked.

"Say to what?" Murray asked. "That their daughter is dead? They are going to be beside themselves. Her father might well have a heart attack. Her own mother, too. I don't know, but that's why I have asked, Doug."

"How would it make you feel if there are other people we have talked to, everyone who we talk to says the first person we need to look at is you?" Woods asked.

"Absolutely not," Murray said. "I just got an e-mail today from Judy—"

"I am telling you that is happening, Tom," Woods said.

"Oh," Murray said, "I was going to say—"

"Now," Woods said, "you are trying to make excuses. I am telling you things that are happening."

"No. No, I am not," Murray said.

"Of course you won't believe anything because you are in this wonderful little fantasy world where no one would think that we would be talking to people, and

Carmin's dead, she was murdered, and 'You better talk to Tom,' " Woods said.

"I told you I am a likely suspect. I told you I would be the first person I looked at. Why wouldn't he say the same thing?" Murray said. "But I will tell you, if you will let me, what her mom wrote in an e-mail today. I said, 'I am going to be in Indianapolis over the week of Thanksgiving. Can we get together? Can we visit you?' And, again, in the e-mail, I said, 'If you think it wouldn't be too awkward, I'll let your judgment, I'll abide by whatever your judgment is.' She wrote back very nicely and said, 'We're not going to be there. We're going to Kentucky to visit Danny's mom. There will be other family members there. But if we were going to be there, of course, we would want to see you. Eighteen years counts for something. You're our son.' I mean, she spoke in loving terms. That's the way they both are."

There was a period of silence. No one said anything.

Murray started saying, "I think you could go find fifty complete strangers who don't know anything about this situation—"

Woods interrupted. "I am not worried about them. I am worried about the people that know you and Carmin. The fifty strangers have nothing to do with this investigation."

"But let me finish," Murray said. "If you were to ask fifty random people, just strangers, here is the situation. We have a recent divorce and child custody up in the air, and you explain the whole thing, and you say, 'Now, the woman is murdered. Who would you look at first?' Well, they are all going to say, 'Well, I would look at the husband first.' This is a no-brainer."

"Maybe your ex-wife is telling them things to make people think we need to talk to you," Woods said.

"Maybe she is, Doug," Murray said. "Maybe she is

the worst person in the world. I don't believe that. If you asked me, I told you, I would look at me."

"I know what you did," Woods said.

"That's why I am still here," Murray said. "I want you to look at me and then at the end say, 'Okay. I guess we are going to have to cut you loose.'"

"You think that that's how it's all gonna work?" Woods said. "That's why we're done here tonight, because this is going to be the end of it? We are going to go home and we are gonna forget about it?"

"I don't know how these things work. But at some point, yes, I am very confident," Murray said. He was almost interrupted, but asked to finish. "Let me finish. I am very confident that you will look at me and say, 'You have answered all our questions and everything adds up. You can go.' And you may call me back in a week or six months or ten years."

"We have told you what we think," the second officer said. "Now tell us what you think. If you didn't do this, Tom, who did?"

"I don't have a clue who did this," Murray answered. "I can look you square in the eye—and I will hold my hand out here so you see it's not shaking—and I'll say, 'I didn't do it.' I did not kill Carmin. If I had it in me to do that, I have not yet reached my breaking-point trigger. It just hasn't happened. Who did it? I don't know. Since we have been estranged, and particularly since she has moved to Lawrence, I don't know the company she keeps. I have no idea. I don't have a clue. I mean, she has a new circle of friends. I told somebody earlier, she has systematically disconnected herself from most of the people she was friendly with here in town. I believe she has replaced them with other friends. But she has always elected not to share that with me. There has always been this wall there. 'Respect my privacy.' Fine. I'll do that. So, I don't know. I don't have a clue. I mean, you haven't told me this, but my mind is continuing to work. I have no idea whether robbery was a motive. I have no idea whether the house was tossed. I have no idea whether there were things missing. I really don't know. I do know she had some things of value. She had an engagement ring worth some money. And some other jewelry. I don't know if that's there or missing. There's a lot I don't know because you haven't told me. I said, 'I don't want to know the details unless you have to tell me,' but I can't answer the question 'Who did it?' I mean, I'll sit here and say this until I am blue in the face. You can choose to believe me or not. All I can do is tell you the truth. And if push comes to shove, if I am actually arrested and charged and tried, I'll look right at the jury and I will tell them the same story. And if I get twelve people like you, well, woe is me. Whatever happens to people who are found guilty of a crime like this, it will happen to me. Sometimes life sucks. I have discovered that over the last fourteen months. And there won't be anything I can do about it."

"What's going to happen to your daughter, then?" Woods asked. "Who is going to raise her, Tom?"

"Hell," Murray said, "I don't know. Either she'll go with, I assume she'll stay in the family. Probably go with Grandma and Grandpa or one of the sisters-in-law."

"Is it gonna be hard on her?" the second officer asked.

"Well, of course it is. I told you, Mommy and Daddy are way up here and everybody else is a distant second," Murray said.

"Until she realizes what ultimately happened is that Daddy went to prison for killing Mommy," the second officer said.

"Say that again," Murray said.

"You just said, 'Daddy and Mommy are way up

here' and it's gonna bother her because Mommy and Daddy are way up here. When she gets to be what you just said, for some reason, you were convicted of this crime," the second officer said.

"Oh," Murray said, "and then she learned that."

"Five years old. 'Where's my mommy?' She's dead. Where's your daddy? Oh. He's in prison for killing Mommy," the second officer said.

"Of course," Murray said, "that would be devastating to any child. How do I respond to that?"

"That's a possibility in your life," the second officer said.

"And then I would have to spend the next how many years of my life telling Helen that that's not true and Daddy's here by mistake. The system sometimes doesn't work and Daddy's in jail for a crime he didn't commit. And then it would be up to her to believe it or not. Frankly, I don't know what the point of a question like how will Helen deal with this would be, the effect of this on Helen, but what's the point of a question like that? To make me feel horrible?" Murray asked.

"No," the second officer said. "I just think these are things you need to start thinking about. I would, as a parent."

49

Most English-speaking commentators assert that Shakespeare was the world's greatest writer, but a strong segment say "nay" and claim Dostoyevsky's contemporary, the Russian aristocrat Leo Tolstoy, was the world's greatest writer.

Count Leo Tolstoy was the author of the tome most often said to be the world's greatest novel, *War and Peace*. After *War and Peace* was published Tolstoy wrote *Anna Karenina*, which he said was his first novel, in the strict definition of a novel. That is another book that many claim is the world's greatest. As he approached the end of his life, taking the better part of four years, from 1886 to 1889, Tolstoy wrote a short story that at least one critic thought should rank as his greatest story—"The Kreutzer Sonata or How a Husband Killed His Wife." It is a fiction crime story similar in its elements to the verity story told in this book. A successful, educated man ceases to pay attention to his wife, she has an affair, and he later stabs her to death. As Tolstoy himself described the story, it is about a man who "must feel that he had driven her to it [the affair] himself, that he had killed her before he had grown to hate her, that he was merely looking for an excuse [to stab her]."

Tolstoy's killer describes the murder: "I struck her

with all my might with the dagger. When people say they don't remember what they do in a fit of fury, it is rubbish, falsehood. I remembered everything and did not for a moment lose consciousness of what I was doing. The more frenzied I became the more brightly the light of consciousness burnt in me, so that I could not help knowing everything I did. I knew what I was doing every second.

"For a long time afterwards, in prison . . . I thought of that moment, recalled what I could of it, and considered it."

The story was not published for two years because the emperor of Russia, Alexander III, refused permission. The story was too shocking. It was only after Tolstoy's wife, Countess Tolstoy, was granted a personal audience with the emperor of all the Russias that he was persuaded to grant permission to publish.

In 1891 the story was published and did create a furor across Russia and in many places around the world. It was and is considered a great work of art, but the horror described caused discussion in literary salons around the world. Could such a thing really happen? Could a man use his pretty wife only for sex and as a social ornament, then suddenly withhold sex from her and drive her away, and then so coldly murder her when she does the inevitable and is with another man? Could an otherwise proper, educated, well-spoken and well-mannered man be so evil?

50

Interview Room #2

"Right now, I am faced with the decision of how to tell her [Helen] Mommy's not here anymore. That's my prime concern. Other things are bridges that may or may not be crossed in the future," Murray said. "Go ahead. I know it's your job not to believe me. It's your job to doubt me at everything. I understand that and you're good at it. I think you bring a particular set of biases or prejudices to situations like this. I think you have been trained to doubt whenever something seems like it shouldn't add up. Suddenly, in your mind, it doesn't add up. I am not sure that a jury will have that same preconception. I would hope the voir dire process rids such people from the jury. But I don't know. Once I get into this system I don't have a lot of choices what to go with. So I will go with it and make the best of what I can. I have to tell you, both of you, you have seen this again and again. And I believe that you have no reason to lie to me, but I have a hard time believing that somebody like me, and I know me better than anybody, somebody like me could do the crime that you're suggesting I did and not think about some of these things in advance. I just can't believe it."

"Tom," Woods said, "you are dealing with emotions. You are dealing with passion. You are dealing with things that you don't think with a clear head, okay?"

"But my love for my daughter is emotion and a passion, too," Murray said.

"It don't matter," the second officer said. "It all goes out the window when you get to that point. When you get to where you are dealing with this passion and this, all these feelings, you know. We have all been there."

"I guess what I am saying is," Murray said, "I haven't been there. I haven't reached my break point yet. You sat there and you said you were in a situation with your wife where you were actually or wishing or something that she was dead. I think your exact words were, 'I could have killed her.' I have never had that thought, not once. I never wanted Carmin dead. I wanted her reasonable. I wanted her to see it from my point of view."

"She wasn't reasonable at all lately, was she?" the second officer asked.

"I wanted her—no, don't turn around what I am saying," Murray said.

"I'm not turning around what you are saying. I am just stating a fact. She was not reasonable," the second officer said.

"I was trying to get her to realize that she did not have some proprietary claim on our daughter," Murray said.

"Right," the second officer said. "And you didn't want her [Helen] around Larry. You didn't want her around some nut that's talking about astrology and whatever else we are talking about."

"What I did want, what I said to many people, is, 'As long as I am in Helen's life, about half the time, I think I can balance out the weirdness,'" Murray said.

"That was about to end," the second officer said.

"You don't know that," Murray said. "With my conservativeness—"

"No," the second officer said, "*you* don't."

"Because you don't know how the custody battle would have gone," Murray said.

"You're right, I don't," the second officer said. "But I know how a lot of them go. And I know which direction she was going in and what she was going to push, okay. All the buttons she was going to push."

"And I didn't know any of that," Murray said. "But it would have been a bridge I would have to cross. When I came to it, seems to me if I had known all of that, it would strengthen your case against me. But I didn't know it. I had no idea. You are telling me for the first time." Murray paused briefly, then said, "I will give you an even better one. You can look at the whole forty-seven years of my life and I don't have any skeletons in my closet."

"That we know of," the second officer said.

"I am telling you, there are none," Murray said.

"I am just saying, you can tell me that, but I can't prove that right now, that you have no skeletons," the second officer said.

"When Carmin and I lived in central Ohio, we attended a Wesleyan church because that was her faith at the time. If you know anything about Wesleyan churches, they are very conservative and kind of fundamentalist. I sat down with my pastor because I come from a Congregationalist background, more liberal. And I said, 'Dave, all this business about getting saved and confessing your sins,' I said, 'I don't know what I would confess. I mean, I have had a very boring life. I haven't done this. I haven't done that.' And he said, 'Yeah, well, I have basically the same kind of life.' That's who I am. I haven't done anything wrong in my life. I have always led a clean-cut life. I was the original Boy Scout. I am telling you, don't believe me, people who know me know that's true. I mean, you mentioned Carmin's dad had said, 'Well, you better talk to Tom.' He once made fun of me for being so meek and mild-mannered," Murray said.

"No," Woods said. "You come up here like you said, on your own. You have been cooperative."

"You let us look in your car," the second officer said.

"And my home," Murray said. "Have you been to my home yet?"

"Get one thing straight," Woods said sternly. "I don't care how intelligent you are, Tom. All that doesn't matter once things happen."

"Let's talk about intelligence for a minute," Murray said. "If I were going to commit a crime, I would do a thinking man's crime. I would embezzle money or something."

"This crime is not a thinking man's crime?" Woods asked. "It is a crime of passion and rage. It is not embezzling money from the university. It is a crime of passion and rage. That is all there is to it."

"Okay. All right. But I am telling you—" Murray started to say.

"You are coming up with some idea that you wouldn't commit this type of crime. That crime has nothing to do with the situation you are in. There is a problem with your ex-wife and your child custody— that right there fits the mold of a crime of passion or a crime of rage," Woods said.

"But I have told you that I have not reached the point where I feel full of rage," Murray said. "I think I would possibly feel rage when the judge says, 'Yes, Ms. Murray, Ms. Ross, you get eighty percent custody. Go leave, Mr. Murray. You'll see your daughter a week of Christmas, a week in the spring, all but three weeks over the summer.' "

"That's about what it would have been, probably,

if she would have moved to California," the second officer said.

"Well, again, I think I would have prevailed in a custody hearing," Murray said.

"But if you didn't?" the second officer asked.

"If I didn't, then it would be that, yes, or something close," Murray said.

"So there's always a little bit of doubt in your mind?" the second officer asked.

"Although, and again, this is something that Carmin said and you're going to say, 'Oh, but Carmin's not trustworthy.' But she told me this, she said, 'It didn't have to be that way.' That she would try to make sure that Helen and I saw one another frequently. We have the video, what do you call it, teleconferencing, the computer thing that you can see one another," Murray said.

"Yeah," Woods said, "I know what you're talking about."

"Which is not substitute for physical, you know, hugging and stuff, but you see the person. It wouldn't be perfect, but at least it would be something. But, yes, at that point, maybe I would feel rage. But I don't see that point being right around the corner. I am not in rage," Murray said.

"Was there ever any point in your mind that you might lose? You were always one hundred percent convinced?" Woods asked.

"No," Murray said. "Because then I would have filed for full custody a long time ago."

"Now, once the ball is rolling again. With your mediation, you said it was basically a power struggle. According to Nancy, and a new guy's moving to town, you're hoping, 'Hey, there's a light at the end of the tunnel. This new guy's moving to town. They're going to buy a house and live in Lawrence.' And then she tells you it's just temporary," Woods said.

"No," Murray said, "I hoped that they would stay in Lawrence. But I told someone this morning, a colleague, that I thought a custody battle was probably looming."

"And Carmin thought the same thing," Woods said. "Earlier, Tom, you couldn't believe that she had been talking to a lawyer about a custody battle."

"You're right," Murray said.

"Now you're saying you just talked to a colleague and that's what you were expecting," Woods said.

"Yes," Murray said, "I was expecting it. Eventually, we would be in court. I am not saying tomorrow. We both have to be clear that the mediation process has failed."

"Do you think that if Carmin never would have met Larry, and she would have approached you about you and her getting back together, that you would have?" Woods asked.

"No," Murray said.

"I mean, would you have considered it?" Woods asked.

"Give me a date. When?" Murray asked.

"Let's say recently," Woods said.

"After the divorce, you mean?" Murray asked.

"Right, after the divorce," Woods said.

"And she comes to me and says, 'I've made a mistake. I would like to get back together.' And there's no Larry in the background?" Murray asked.

"Larry's not even in the picture. You think you would have considered doing that?" Woods asked.

"I don't know," Murray said.

"And you are trying to keep the family together. You know, obviously, you guys loved each other at one time. And it sounds like you still thought an awful lot of her. I don't know. Did you still love her?" Woods asked.

"I said, I think she still loved me," Murray said.

"She still loved you," Woods said.

"What she told Nancy, 'I still have feelings for Tom.' And I couldn't say that. I am the one who wanted a clear-cut business relationship," Murray said.

"I mean, from everything you say about her, it sounds like she was a great person," Woods said.

"She was a great person," Murray said.

"I was at the house," Woods said. "I saw some pictures of her. She looked beautiful. She looked like a beautiful woman in the pictures that I saw. It just came to my mind, this whole thing with Larry hadn't of happened, you guys could have kept going."

"I had my doubts," Murray said. "But I don't know for sure. No. Because she, well, it comes back to things that she said. No, because all the New Age stuff was getting to be too weird. I tried to follow her. To a point, I read all the books, but then I had to pull back and say, 'I just can't go there.' So, in her language, 'we were on different spiritual paths.' So, you know, it wouldn't have worked."

"How did she get into that?" Woods asked. "What got her interested? Piqued her to go look into that stuff?"

"It was a long processing of reading and studying and philosophizing, but the bottom line is I don't really know," Murray said.

"Basically, they totally go off the deep end, become this spiritual healer, and talking to the angels and dead relatives," the second officer said.

"It doesn't happen overnight," Murray said. "We bought some books together and read those."

"Is there something that you remember? Were you guys at the bookstore and picked up a book and, 'Oh, this kind of looks interesting?' " Woods asked.

"She eventually came to me and said that she didn't like the term 'New Age,' first of all, because it's so pejorative and 'out there.' But she eventually came to me and said that she really believed this all of her life and just hadn't realized it. But she was never comfortable with a traditional Christian faith," Murray said.

"So what religious denomination would she consider herself? I mean, was she into witchcraft, voodoo, anything like that?" Woods asked.

"I think she would say that organized religion is about control," Murray said. "I think she started to attend—and this is something I thought was underhanded—I think she recently started to attend a church in Lawrence. I think the only reason she began to do that was so that if we got into a custody battle, and I said, 'Look, I have Helen going to a church here in Manhattan,' she could say, 'We're going to a church here in Lawrence, too.' But I have every confidence that if she were to prevail in a custody battle that she would stop going to that church. She was not about organized religion. She was about spirituality or spiritualism."

"I just wondered at what point in y'all's life is that," Woods asked.

"I can't pinpoint," Murray said.

"Nothing sticks out?" Woods asked. "We shouldn't have gone to the bookstore on this day or something?"

"No," Murray said.

"Or the library? Or run into this person on the street? What was her thoughts on her spirit after death?" Woods asked.

"Do you know anything about Buddhism or Hinduism?" Murray asked.

"Not a lot," Woods answered.

"She believed in reincarnation. But she also adopted the Hindu term, I think it is moksha, which means that your spirit has attained its perfect form and you no longer have to come back into a human body to learn your lessons. But you can come back if you want to. She thought that she was moksha and was going to be coming back to help other people learn their lessons," Murray said.

"Wow," Woods said.

"It's all very bizarre, depending on where you are coming from," Murray said.

51

Interview Room #2

"Tom, is there anything that you can think of that you want to say while we are still here together?" Woods asked.

"Which I haven't already said?" Murray asked.

"Yeah," Woods answered.

"I am not sure that you ever answered the question that I asked about two rounds ago. What this is, you go away then you come back in again. Is there anything that I could say that would convince you that I am innocent here? Maybe the answer's 'no,' but I didn't hear you say that," Murray said.

"I don't think I am saying that," Woods said.

"But isn't everything going to lead to me? I am the most likely person. I don't know about Carmin's life. I don't know whether she had anybody else in it that she was having this kind of contentious relationship with," Murray said.

"You know for sure that we are going to be checking out all of that," Woods said.

"I hope you check every possible thing you can. I have every confidence that you are going to do your job as thoroughly as you can," Murray said.

"We will," Woods said. "And we're not going to give up on it."

"The same time that you are interviewing me, aren't you pursuing other directions, or do you have all your eggs in one basket, so to speak?" Murray asked.

"We are looking at a lot of things, but there comes a point when you need to just do some prioritizing. You know that," Woods said.

"Of course," Murray said.

"And not stay up all night in Manhattan, Kansas," Woods said. "You would be staying up all night someplace else."

"Let me ask you this," Murray said. "If you are really convinced that I did this horrible thing, why would you let me go? Why would I not represent a flight risk?"

"Maybe you do," Woods said.

"Maybe I do, Doug," Murray said. "So my question is, if you—"

Woods interrupted. "It's a gamble. Coming and talking to you was a gamble. Sitting here talking to you like this is a gamble."

"Why is it a gamble?" Murray asked. "You are looking for the truth."

"You could have told me, 'I don't wanna talk to you,'" Woods said. "You could have got up at any time, every time we came in here. You could have got up and left this room."

"But," Murray said, "I don't have anything to hide."

"I understand," Woods said. "But you still had the opportunity to leave. That's a gamble. Having you sitting here, you were very cooperative. But at any time you could have said, 'I am tired of sitting in this room and I am going home.'"

"Except," Murray said, "the other is, besides trying

to be honest with you, if I just get up and say, 'I have had it. I am done.' I think that casts another shadow of doubt."

"It very well could have," Woods said. "You know, it's just all a gamble. It's a gamble with you. You have agreed to sit in here and talk to us. I have told you numerous times, you are free to go. You didn't have to let us look in your car and all that other stuff. We gambled and went with it. You know, we're playing the odds here. No better way of explaining it."

There was a pause while Murray and Woods looked at each other.

"You didn't ask me about an attorney, did you?" Woods asked.

"Yes. I said, 'If you were me . . . ,'" Murray said.

"Oh," Woods said, remembering. " 'Would I sign that piece of paper.' "

"Didn't I ask you if you would, 'If you were me, would you have had an attorney come in?' " Murray asked. "If you don't have anything to hide, why would you do that? I don't want to do anything that's going to cast more doubt on myself."

"Well, Tom," Woods said, "I don't know. We'll see what you accomplished."

"I am sorry," Murray said.

"We will see what you accomplished," Woods said.

"What I accomplished," Murray said.

"You said you didn't want to cast any more doubt," Woods said.

"Yes," Murray said.

"And some of these things that you talked about and told us, and reasons why blood is here, there, and everywhere else. We'll just have to see how it plays out, if you did, or didn't, cast more doubt," Woods said.

"You already told me you found blood in my house,

but you told me you haven't been to my house yet,"
Murray said.

"I didn't tell you we found blood in your house,"
Woods said. "You told us there was going to be blood
in your house. Nobody has been in your house."

"I beg your pardon. I thought you told me that,"
Murray said.

"You told us that we would find Carmin's blood in
your house, and then you said we would also find your
blood in Carmin's house," Woods said.

"Right," Murray said, "but you did tell me that you
found blood in my car."

"You told us that we would find blood in the car,"
Woods said.

"Yes. You confirmed that is true," Murray said.

"No. We didn't confirm that," Woods said.

"Will you confirm that?" Murray asked.

"Not right now, no," Woods said.

"Why? What's the secret?" Murray asked.

"I don't have to confirm it, Tom, with you,"
Woods said.

"Of course you don't, Doug. I am asking, will you
do it?" Murray said.

"No. I am not the one working on your car. I don't
know all what they've done down there. I am not
gonna tell you one thing or another. One, I can't confirm it till (A) it goes to a laboratory—" Woods said.

Murray interrupted. "Okay," he said.

"You told us there was gonna be blood in your car.
I have every reason to believe then that we're gonna
find some blood in your car," Woods said.

"Yes," Murray said, "unless Carmin managed to
wipe it away. Whatever she used cleared it up. Then
you're going to find something there. You'll probably
find some of Helen's blood in the car, too. She's had
nosebleeds in it. You will probably find some of my

blood there. Can you give me some idea of a time line here, what I am looking at, anything?"

"No," Woods said.

"Nothing?" Murray asked. "Ballpark? Come on! You guys have done this, how many times?"

"Tom, you know all we can tell you now is we are just going to keep going until we get to the end," Woods said.

"Can you tell me when you get the results back from the various tests? Is it a day? A week?" Murray asked.

"No," Woods said. "We've got a crime scene crew that's gonna be going through things for a while. They'll cover every little inch of that place. And they have to do an autopsy on Carmin. Tons of other interviews very similar to what we have already been doing. It's just hard for us to answer you in time frames. What's going to happen next, and that kind of thing."

"Her dad really said, 'You better look at Tom, first'?" Murray asked.

"Tom," Woods said, "there's been a whole bunch of people we've talked to. A lot of people we've talked to that have told us things, we can't, you've got to understand and respect this, we can't go and tell you, 'Hey, so-and-so told us this and that.' Some things we can. We asked that question and they said, there are a lot of people saying we need to look at you."

"But you specifically mentioned—" Murray said.

Woods interrupted, "No, I did not mention him. I said there are a lot of people specifically saying look at you. I never specifically said Carmin's dad."

"I think you did," Murray said.

"Are you gonna call and talk to them?" Woods asked.

"That's why I asked," Murray said. "If they hadn't been notified by authorities, I was going to tell them."

"Do you want to tell them?" Woods asked.

"Now you are suggesting they don't know yet," Murray said.

"I am getting an idea from you if you feel comfortable talking to them," Woods said.

"Sure, sure," Murray said. "Although I don't know how I would do it. It would be very difficult to do. Maybe I shouldn't be so quick to say 'sure.' But I think it would be easier on them coming from somebody they consider a son than coming from a complete stranger."

"You think it would be easier on them over the phone or in person?" Woods asked.

"It would be easier in person, but I am not going to fly out there just to tell them," Murray said.

52

Interview Room #2

There was a pause, and then Woods asked, "Anything else, Tom?"

Murray turned to the second officer and asked if he had anything else to say or ask.

"No," the second officer said, "I don't think so. Unless you've got any other questions or anything."

"So, at this point, you don't have compelling evidence?" Murray asked.

"You are not going to get us to sit here and tell you about our case," Woods said.

"I don't want you to tell me about the case, but I am concluding that, because if you had compelling evidence, wouldn't you go ahead and arrest me? I don't know how this works," Murray said.

"Maybe the right test hasn't been done on the right evidence yet," Woods said.

"Okay," Murray said, "so now I am supposed to go on and resume my life with my daughter."

"Who knows if you can call it that, Tom," Woods said. "Resuming your life. Things are going to be tough around there for a while with you and her."

"For longer than a while, I'd say," Murray said.

There was a pause.

"I get the feeling that you want to talk more about this," Woods said to Murray.

"I don't have anything new to say," Murray said. "I am just not looking forward to going home. What am I going to do? The house is empty. I am not going to be able to sleep. When Helen comes over, she is going to have a million questions, or is going to want to play, and I don't have any energy. When I look at that compared to this, I am more comfortable sitting right here."

"Would you feel better about it, and I am not saying this is what is happening, because at this point it's not, we've already told you that, but would you feel better if you were headed to jail instead of home?" Woods asked.

"No," Murray said. "Heavens, no. I am just wondering how I—"

The second officer interrupted. "You are just wondering how you are going to deal with all this."

"Yes," Murray said. "I am going to have to go over to Angela and Rob. They know I have been detained here all night long. How do I know what they are thinking? Maybe they are thinking they don't want their daughter to play with my daughter anymore." There was a pause. "What I think is, you are a very skilled interviewer. You have been very well trained. I mean, you are good at what you guys do—"

The second officer interrupted again. "I am sorry, Tom, I interrupted you."

"And you keep sitting here," Murray said. "And the same way I am telling you the same thing, you're telling me the same thing, and your intention is to convince me to tell you that I did this thing. But I can't do that because I didn't do it. If you could believe that, you could put manpower in other directions."

That concluded the interview. Tom was told that

they were finished with his car, and just after six o'clock A.M. he departed the interview room. For nearly ten hours, Tom Murray and Doug Woods had been in dialogue about the death of Carmin Ross. Tom understood the situation perfectly and stated it: the police wanted him to confess to the murder. Tom Murray denied responsibility then and continues to deny responsibility to this day. Doug Woods felt he had almost persuaded Murray to confess, and to this day Woods believes Tom Murray is someday going to confess, possibly to him.

ACT III

The only CSI *script Murray had anything to do with is this real one.*

> —Prosecutor Angela Wilson, Closing argument,
> *Kansas v. Murray*

53

As election day approached the question remained: Was Christine Kenney someone who tried the hard cases? Her opponent said she was not. Just weeks after Carmin's murder Kenney's staff had all the evidence they were ever going to have—Murray's interrogation, his statement "All I can see is the blood, all the blood," his computer searches. And when he was told Carmin had died, he didn't ask, "What happened?" He didn't ask how Carmin died. He said he didn't want to know. Nearly a year had passed, but there was no arrest.

Carmin's family had turned from being Murray's defender to wanting him arrested. The change in their perception of Tom started after Carmin's memorial when he blurted out, "How could this have happened to me?" They were angry that Helen remained with Tom. They felt that was abominable—her mother's murderer raising Helen.

The prosecution had repeatedly tried new avenues of obtaining evidence and been thwarted at each turn. They were hopeful of a report of a carpet fiber match, but about a month before election day, that proved to be one more disappointment. Nevertheless, Douglas County district attorney Christine Kenney made her decision. Tom Murray was to be arrested and prosecuted for first-degree murder. They would try a case based on circumstantial evidence.

Again, Detectives Doug Woods and Brad Schlerf conferred on how to proceed in the Murray case. Doug Woods decided to tell Carmin's parents, Danny and Judi, that Tom was going to be arrested. They came from Indianapolis to care for Helen. Woods would not be present at the arrest because he would be standing by near the Ross family to help with processing Helen's custody. The Riley County officers would make the arrest and process Tom Murray.

The teams of police officers from Douglas County and Riley County met at 7:00 A.M. on Monday, October 4, 2004. The Riley County Police ERU team was also assembled and a plan was formulated.

At 8:42 A.M., after Murray had dropped the now almost six-year-old Helen off at Bergman Elementary School, 3430 West Lombard Drive, he drove around the corner. Once he was out of sight of the school he was pulled over by a marked police car. Murray stopped on Gary Avenue near Newbury Street, two blocks west of Seth Child Road. This was about three miles from the police station. A uniformed officer in a marked Riley County police car approached as if it were a routine traffic stop. Murray was driving his maroon Saturn, license tag Kansas RGH 252. The officer approached and asked Tom Murray to get out of his car. There were several other vehicles with officers present, but all were still standing off. The ERU team was present but was standing off.

The officer asked Murray to walk back and sit in the back of the patrol car. Murray complied. He was not handcuffed.

Now the other officers came forward. Riley County detective Brad Schlerf stepped to the patrol car window and told Murray that he had a warrant for his arrest on the charge of the first-degree murder of Carmin Ross. Schlerf read Murray his Miranda rights.

Murray acknowledged and asked that Angela Hayes take care of Helen. Murray said that Angela had a durable power of attorney for Helen's care.

Murray and Schlerf went to the Riley County police station, where Brad Schlerf booked him. Schlerf was the arresting officer of record.

While this was taking place other officers took Helen from school. The proceedings were managed by the Department of Community Corrections, Department of Juvenile Intake and Assessment Service. Because of the police affidavit that Helen's mother had been murdered and her father had been arrested for the murder, she was judged to be a child in need of care. By the afternoon, all the paperwork was completed to transfer Helen's custody to her grandparents, Danny and Judi.

In the meantime, Tom Murray was transferred to the Douglas County Courthouse for his first appearance before Judge Robert Fairchild. Murray called his attorneys, Bob Eye and Pedro Irigonegaray of Topeka, and he was represented by counsel.

In court, Murray's legs were shackled, but he was permitted to wear street clothes and his wrists were not handcuffed. On the basis of the evidence presented, Judge Fairchild ordered a $1 million bond. Murray's attorney Pedro Irigonegaray protested that the amount was excessive and asked that the bond be reduced to $100,000. Judge Fairchild kept the bond at $1 million and ordered a bond hearing in three days.

Afterward, the Douglas County district attorney briefly discussed the case. The *Lawrence Journal World* newspaper reported, "She said one reason it took nearly a year to file charges was that investigators were waiting for forensic lab results." Doug Woods told the author that just before the district attorney approved Murray's arrest, they had a negative report on carpet fibers. The newspaper also reported that "Kenney said her office filed charges once it was clear the investigation had 'exhausted all of its potential.' " They had never obtained the laboratory evidence of the smoking gun, and it looked like they never would, so if they were going to prosecute, they had to go with the evidence that they had had almost from the beginning and proceed with a case based on circumstantial evidence.

As soon as possible all of Tom Murray's students were interviewed. Most were interviewed at the Riley County police station. Many were interviewed in interview room #2. The students who said they remembered said that Tom Murray graded their midterm papers as they were turned in. He should not have had any papers to grade on Thursday morning.

All of Tom Murray's English department colleagues were interviewed.

Three days later there was a bond hearing. Because of Murray's search for countries that did not extradite to the United States, the prosecution convinced the judge that Murray was a flight risk. The judge kept the $1 million bond. Murray could have paid the bond; he had the resources, but he refused to pay. He remained in state custody.

In November Christine Kenney lost her reelection bid to Charles Branson, but Branson ordered the prosecution to proceed.

54

In Kansas law, a preliminary hearing has the same function as a grand jury proceeding, but there are differences. A preliminary hearing is public while a grand jury is secret; in a preliminary hearing the accused is aware of the charges faced while in a grand jury the accused is unaware of the inquiry, and defense attorneys may cross-examine the witnesses in a preliminary hearing, while only the prosecution is present in a grand jury. Tom Murray's preliminary started on Monday, December 6, 2004. It was covered by the news media and well attended.

The first witness was Larry Lima. His direct testimony was a straightforward recitation of facts, times, dates, etc. But his cross-examination by Murray's attorneys was filled with innuendo and led to a flurry of objections by the prosecution. For example, when Lima described consegrity as a spiritual healing process to help people connect with God, Murray's attorney Pedro Irigonegaray immediately asked, "Which God?" This led to an objection by Angela Wilson, which was overruled by Judge Fairchild. Irigonegaray's repeated questioning of Lima about his having sex with Carmin led to a series of objections by Wilson. This hearing and the subsequent trial would be as hard fought as any, with Murray's attorneys putting the government to its proof on each point.

Tuesday had a number of witnesses, including several of Murray's students who established that he was grading papers in class as they were being handed in.

Wednesday, Judge Fairchild heard testimony from Gay Lynn Crossley-Brubaker, including her statement that he had told her, "All I can see is the blood, all the blood."

But much of Wednesday and the first part of Thursday consisted of Brad Schlerf's testimony about Murray's body language. Schlerf's direct examination by Angela Wilson, and cross-examination by Murray attorney Bob Eye, filled one hundred pages of transcript. Murray's attorneys objected to Schlerf's testimony and asked that it be stricken from the record. Bob Eye told Judge Fairchild that he doubted kinesics met the *Frye* standard or the *Daubert* standard and also raised questions of Brad Schlerf's certifications and credentials.

Schlerf testified that Agent Glenn Virden from the KBI and Detectives Ryan Runyan and Rich Lewis from the Riley County Police Department agreed with his interpretation of Murray's body language during the interview.

Judge Fairchild decided that they would take these issues up in a separate evidentiary hearing before the evidence was presented to a jury.

Most of the day Thursday and the beginning of Friday was spent with Judge Fairchild and the public watching the interrogation that had been recorded in Riley County interview room #2 on November 13–14, 2003.

Judge Fairchild concluded that the evidence provided "probable cause" to believe that Tom Murray had murdered Carmin Ross, and he ordered the case set for jury trial.

Judge Fairchild was the man who taught the "Not in My Court" program. He would give every legal benefit to the accused. At the evidentiary hearing before the jury trial, Judge Fairchild excluded Detective Schlerf's testimony about his interpretation of Murray's body language during the interview.

That was a setback, but, the judge also decided that the jury would see the video in open court and have it available to review in the jury room. The jurors could decide the meaning of Murray's body language for themselves.

55

The prosecution had put together a color-coded calendar that showed the only time that Tom Murray and Carmin Ross had had unstructured time alone for the foreseeable future had been the morning of Thursday, November 13, 2003. After that date, Carmin was going to be either traveling or with Helen or with, presumably, her new husband. Woods and Wilson and the other members of the prosecution team put together a detailed summary of the evidence. They were convinced of Murray's guilt, but there was no guarantee a jury would agree.

In fact, prosecutor Angela Wilson told the author that just before trial, "*Everyone* told me that I'd lose this case." This was a criminal prosecution using indirect, circumstantial evidence. It was a hard case.

But they prosecuted the case because everyone on the prosecution team believed that Tom Murray was guilty of murdering Carmin Ross. The prosecutors included not only lead prosecutor Angela Wilson but also attorneys Amy McGowan and Tom Bath.

There was some difference of interpretation of the evidence by the police and the prosecutors. Prosecutor Angela Wilson concluded that Carmin Ross let Tom Murray into her house. That was what she told the jury and that was also what she told the news media.

In contrast, Detectives Doug Woods and Brad Schlerf told the author that they concluded Tom Murray entered Carmin's house through her unlocked back door. All agreed that there was no evidence of forced entry. They also agreed that however he entered the house, the prosecution's theory of the case was that Tom Murray planned to murder Carmin Ross, had the time, motive, and opportunity to murder Carmin Ross, and had a confrontation with Carmin in her living room that was followed by Tom Murray murdering Carmin Ross. Murray's defense was that someone else did it, while the prosecution claimed Tom Murray murdered Carmin Ross.

Tom Murray maintained his innocence. The prosecution's theory was that Tom Murray premeditatedly murdered Carmin Ross. They concluded that Murray's computer searches, shifting explanations for his whereabouts on the day of the murder, the blood spatter and DNA found at the crime scene and in Murray's car, and his ten-hour interview with the police were evidence of Murray's guilt and his attempt to cover up his guilt. Murray's defense was that some other dude did it because at the time Carmin was murdered Murray was either grading papers or driving between Paxico and Manhattan on Interstate 70. Based on the prosecution's theory of the case, which was based on the evidence, it was speculated that the following was what occurred at 1860 East 1150 Road, Douglas County, Kansas, about 10 A.M., Central Standard Time, Thursday, November 13, 2003, with some annotations and comments—

Tom Murray drove his Saturn sedan to Carmin's home and parked in her driveway north of the house. As with the arrogant killer Raskolnikov in Dostoyevsky's *Crime and Punishment*, just before committing murder Murray was nonplussed. He was not angry. He was cold-blooded, determined, and methodical.

When he exited his vehicle he was calm. He strode around the house to the east to the steps leading up to the back door of Carmin's home.

The back door was unlocked and he entered. He walked through the mudroom, through the kitchen, and into the living room, where he encountered Carmin, who was carrying a basket of clothes.

On the police tape at 9:05:20 P.M., Tom said that in his last conversation with her, Carmin had asked, "Did you get my e-mail?" Although they may have exchanged other dialogue, Tom Murray said something to Carmin that caused her to ask him that question. At this point, Carmin is in conversation with Tom, she is not fleeing. She may be concerned, puzzled, she may be afraid, but she is not running away.

Joslyn Dugas said that "Carmin was very psychically attuned." Joslyn thought that if Carmin had seen Tom drive up, she would have sensed danger and called for help. Carmin must not have had any hint that her life was in danger. Nothing happened that caused her to be alarmed.

Tom removed the club concealed under his winter clothes. Using the club, Tom struck her as hard as he could on the crown of her skull. He was probably surprised that Carmin stood there and did not collapse unconscious. Tom must have used some type of club because the coroner testified that blunt-force trauma caused the wounds to her head that laid her scalp open, and that these wounds were not done by a knife.

Based on the report of someone who survived blows to the head in a similar attack, Carmin's brain may have interpreted the first blow to her skull as two different events. One was personal, feeling as if she'd bumped her head on something hard, a common experience, and that she was hurt. But, secondly, her brain may have interpreted the strike from Tom Murray as something external to her; she may have the sense-impression that something hit the roof of her house, as if a bomb exploded on the roof. She may have thought the roof of the old house had started to fall in and that was what caused the pain to her skull. She may have put her hands on her head and looked up at the ceiling. She would be hurt and confused, her brain struggling to interpret the sensations.

As Tom continued to strike Carmin on her skull, Carmin realized at some point that Tom was striking her. She may also have continued to be confused by the bombing on the roof coinciding with the blows to her skull.

Internally, Carmin's body reacted automatically.

Carmin's hypothalamus, in her brain, released the hormone CRF, which moved through blood vessels a short distance into her pituitary gland.

Carmin's pituitary gland released the hormone ACTH into her bloodstream.

When the ACTH reached her adrenal gland, glucocorticoids were released into her bloodstream and were transmitted all over her body, changing glycogen into glucose, so that her muscles would be able to react strongly and immediately. Adrenaline surged into her bloodstream. Her heart raced. A very biochemically complex series of events began to occur to begin the process of blood coagulation, to prevent any more blood from leaving Carmin's body through the wounds being inflicted on her that were tearing her skin and causing bleeding. These autonomic events are part of the body's "fight or flight" mechanism.

Carmin tried to flee.

But Tom's attack continued coming and coming.

Carmin crawled into the living room. Blood spatter analysis concluded that after the first blow Carmin was never more than twenty-three inches above the floor. Tom followed her, beating her on her head, beating her hard.

Carmin's hair was a poor cushion for the blows to her head. Her skin over her skull tore with each strike. Blood was flowing and matting in her hair as platelets caused her blood to coagulate. Her body was trying to keep her alive as the murderous attack continued. There were no less than eleven blunt-force trauma blows to her head.

She crawled under the coffee table, seeking respite from Tom's attack.

Tom threw the coffee table over. He saw blood on the coffee table and the Spiegel catalog.

Carmin, now on her back, tried to fend off the blows with her arms. Tom swung the club and, aiming at her head, intending to kill her with blows to her skull, struck her forearms. Carmin's forearms bled inside. Her internal bleeding would coagulate and cause visible bruising of her forearms.

Carmin rolled over and crawled toward the front door, seeking escape. Seeking, one might imagine, to survive, to protect not only herself but also her daughter.

She almost reached the door, but finally, from the continuing violent blows to her head, as Tom followed her, beating her as she crawled, she became unconscious and collapsed facedown on the carpet. Blood pooled around her.

Carmin was still alive, though for a moment Tom may have thought she was dead.

But Carmin's skull was not shattered. A close examination would show she was still breathing. Her heart was still beating. She was alive. She might live. She might live to testify against him and put him in prison. She might live to marry Larry Lima. She might live to take Tom's daughter and live in California with Larry Lima.

Tom Murray deliberated on the situation. He deliberated on the means to commit murder. He had tried to murder her with his club, but he had failed. He might have thought about beating Carmin until her skull was crushed, but he had been striking her and striking her and he had just learned that it was hard to make Carmin unconscious by beating on her skull. It was harder to crush a skull than he had realized.

So Tom Murray decided to cut Carmin until she bled to death. He might stab her in the heart.

Murray walked into the kitchen and deliberated some more. He picked through the knives in Carmin's Wolfgang Puck knife set. More than one was taken from the butcher block. He selected a sharp boning knife. He walked back into the living room.

He knelt down and, with his right hand, stabbed downward, stabbed Carmin hard in the back, aiming at her heart. But the English professor, the master of language, was not a master of human anatomy. He hit Carmin in solid bone, the scapula, the shoulder blade. The sudden stop of the knife unexpectedly caused his hand to continue down and he cut the pinky finger of his right hand.

Ouch.

That wasn't going to work.

He grabbed Carmin's body and dragged it away from the door, away from the eyes of anyone who might happen by. The drag marks left a bloody trail.

He rolled her over onto her back.

With his left hand he raised her shoulder to expose her neck.

He stabbed her in her throat . . . the blood platelets rushed to stop the bleeding . . . he stabbed her again, slicing her larynx, her voice box . . . the coagulants could not keep up with the widening wound . . . he stabbed her a third time, severing a major blood vessel . . . the blood started down her throat, Carmin started inhaling blood into her lungs . . . again he stabbed, cutting her larynx more . . . she would never talk again, could never talk again . . . and again, obliterating her larynx . . . and again, severing more vessels and tissue . . . and again a seventh time, the knife cutting into and then pulling out of her throat, the sweep of Tom Murray's arm throwing blood up and back . . . but he was not finished . . . an eighth time he stabbed Carmin in the throat, turning her throat to hamburger . . . then a ninth time . . . and a tenth . . . and an eleventh . . . and a twelfth . . . and finally a thirteenth time.

"Thirteen times!" prosecutor Angela Wilson thundered in her closing argument to the jury. "Thirteen times, ladies and gentlemen. Thirteen times, as hard as he could, he plunged the knife into Carmin's neck, his wrists hitting Carmin's chest, bruising her chest and his wrists. Carmin was alive when that happened because the coroner testified that dead people don't bruise."

Her wounds were incompatible with life, though for a time her heart continued to beat, her blood continued to circulate, and she continued to breathe. As the blood loss became so great that the amount of oxygen transmitted to vital organs was too low to keep her alive, Carmin Ross started to die. Her brain died in about ten minutes. Her other organs died more slowly.

Meantime, Tom Murray went to clean up.

Tom Murray put his foot up on the edge of the sink to wipe away blood, leaving a mark that would be debated at trial. A single drop of his blood from the cut on his pinky finger, mingled with Carmin's blood, dropped on the bathroom baseboard.

Carmin's organs were still dying when Tom Murray prepared to leave.

Tom Murray left the door as it was when he arrived, unlocked.

Carmin was dead, murdered.

Tom left Carmin's home, sat in his Saturn sedan, and set in motion his plan to create a "fake reality," the illusion that he did not kill.

56

Jury selection started on Monday, Valentine's Day, February 14, 2005. Each of the 108 members of the jury pool had received a thirteen-page questionnaire. Jury selection was swift, and the trial started on February 17.

Court TV wanted to broadcast the proceedings live, but Judge Fairchild decided not to permit that. However, he did permit CBS *48 Hours* to record the proceedings. That led to two one-hour television programs about the Murray case, one by CBS *48 Hours* and one by Court TV's *The Investigators*, and a segment in a later Discovery–National Geographic special "The Science of Interrogation."

A well-educated, intelligent jury was selected, which both sides wanted. In his opening statement to this jury, Murray defense attorney Bob Eye declared: "So, who killed Carmin Ross? You're not going to know at the end of this trial. Because of these gaps in the evidence. The investigators that had Tom at the Riley County Police Department for all those hours, and asked all those questions, probed, prodded, cajoled, and still could not find enough to arrest him. They let him go. Because, after all those questions and all those hours, all they had was a hunch, and a hunch is all they have today. Hunches aren't proof. They do raise questions. If at the end of this trial, your questions about the investigation, and the information it yielded, are not answered in a satisfactory way, for each and every one of you, your duty will be to find Thomas Murray not guilty."

The jury received a lot of evidence in the form of testimony and exhibits, but there was a lot they did not hear. The judge decided some information was unfairly prejudicial or otherwise excluded by law. The prosecution decided not to offer some information. For example, the prosecution decided that Julie Schwarting did see a maroon Saturn in Carmin's driveway—but on Tuesday, not Thursday.

During the trial the jury heard most of the recorded police conversations with Tom Murray. They saw the video of Murray in interview room #2. They saw his body language. They heard testimony about DNA and consegrity and Tom's controlling behavior. They heard testimony of neighbors and friends and colleagues.

But they did not hear Tom Murray take the stand in his own defense. Murray read books throughout the trial, as if the court proceedings were a bore and he could better pass the time by reading.

In his closing argument, Murray defense attorney Pedro Irigonegaray argued in part: "Let's go back to the crime scene. There's none of his blood there, none of his fingerprints, none of his footprints, no one sees his car there. No one, nor any scientific test, can put Tom Murray in that house on the thirteenth.

"And then Tom left on the early morning of the fifteenth around six A.M. or so, left the police station in Manhattan. And then they followed him to his house and searched it. What did the law enforcement people tell you? They had nothing on him. That's why he wasn't arrested. Because the injuries could have occurred the way Tom said.

"We can speculate all we want, but there's no scientific evidence to show you that what Tom said about nicking his hand in the gutters—and you saw the gutters—and cutting himself when slicing the pineapple. It's not evidence of murder. The Internet activity. Tom was looking at Internet activity that makes it look bad. I see those things and I think, 'My gosh! What luck.' But ask yourselves, 'Is it possible, that what the head of the department said about the fantasy of an English prof may be true?' Is it possible? Is it reasonable, that maybe Tom thought, 'If I have to move to California, maybe this is a way I can do something: a *CSI*-type episode.' Why not? Certainly, you will find nothing in those Web pages that even comes *close* [Pedro shouted the word "close"] to the way in which this murder occurred. Those Web searches are the demonstration of [Pedro points to his head] a mind, looking at real interesting strange twists, like odorless gases and poisoned fish and things, that related to a *CSI* episode, not this crime."

In prosecutor Angela Wilson's closing argument, she said Murray murdered Carmin in anger. And she said, "The only *CSI* script Murray had anything to do with is this real one."

The author, and writers who were consulted and agreed to offer an opinion, thought that under the circumstances, since he could go to prison for life if he was not believed, if Tom Murray *was* writing a crime story, he would have had no hesitation in sharing its plot, characters, Storyworld, theme, and summarizing for the authorities and the jury what was in Act I, in Act II, and in Act III. Writers hesitate to share such details only when they are bound by contract or they want to wait until the story is "polished" (copyedited, line-edited, etc.). But not before his trial, not at his trial, nor at any time since has Tom Murray apparently told anyone the crime story he claimed to be writing. Nothing other than generalities—a story where poison might be used in a homicide—was mentioned at trial. The author wrote to Tom Murray, his lawyers, most of his colleagues, and some former colleagues, asking for the plot or any other details about the crime story he claimed to be writing. Those few colleagues who replied said that Tom Murray never mentioned anything about it to them.

The jury instructions gave the jurors only one option. There was no lesser-included offense, no option for second-degree murder, or voluntary or involuntary manslaughter. As Murray said in interview room #2, either he planned it out or it just happened. The judge and lawyers agreed that either Murray planned it out and he was guilty of first-degree murder or he was innocent and the jurors should not be given other options. His defense lawyers did not argue for the jury to be instructed in lesser offenses.

On Monday, March 14, 2005, after closing arguments in the afternoon, the jury assembled to deliberate for an hour until 5:00 P.M.

On Tuesday, March 15, taking an hour break for lunch, they deliberated from 9:00 A.M. to 5:00 P.M.

On Wednesday, March 16, they did the same thing.

During those seventeen hours of deliberation the jurors again watched the admitted portion of the video of Murray's time in Riley County Police interview room #2 and discussed it. They looked at Murray's Internet searches again. They discussed DNA. They listened to the answering machine messages that betrayed increasing concern by Larry Lima and Angela Hayes and Joslyn Dugas. They heard Carmin's mother's message not to forget to call her father for his birthday. They discussed Tom Murray's shifting explanations for where he was Thursday morning: he was home grading papers, absolutely; then, no, he remembered he also went toward Paxico on I-70, then he went home. He said Carmin had a nosebleed when she went to pick up Pedialyte at Walgreens, but his attorneys stipulated that he signed the Walgreens credit card receipt for Pedialyte on that date. They discussed how Murray's injuries reflected the injuries inflicted on Carmin. They went over every piece of evidence that had been introduced at trial. They discussed the jury instructions. They voted.

On Thursday morning, March 17, they announced their unanimous verdict: guilty.

When Carmin's family heard the guilty verdict they started crying.

Murray, in contrast, looked up from the book about language that he was reading, titled *In Other Words*, to take note of his conviction. He did not display any outward reaction to the news, though he appeared to be the only person in the courtroom without a visible reaction.

57

Two months later, at sentencing, several members of Carmin's family told Tom Murray how much they despised him for his betrayal, for taking Carmin away from them and from her daughter, Helen. Carmin was a rare jewel who should have lived a long life. The looks his ex-wife's family gave him were withering, but Murray all but smirked. Afterward, Carmin's dad told CBS *48 Hours* that he once said to him, "Tom, you're too good to be true."

Typically at sentencing, family and friends plead for mercy for the convict. In interview room #2 Murray claimed that Carmin's New Age beliefs had alienated her family and friends, but Murray lied. It was Tom Murray who had alienated his family and friends. No one appeared at the sentencing to speak for Tom Murray.

When asked if he had anything to say before sentencing, convict Tom Murray said, "I do have statements, Your Honor."

He continued. "I believe it's customary at these proceedings for the person about to be sentenced to offer to the victim, or, as in this case, surviving friends and relatives, an apology. An explanation, perhaps, some kind of atonement. In any case, language swaddled in humility and intended to afford some semblance of greater psychological closure. With all due respect to the Court and to the many other parties involved, I cannot do that.

"I remain nonplussed that the jury believed the prosecution's fairy tale of my involvement in Carmin Ross's death. A fairy tale based on several pieces of circumstantial evidence loosely woven together with half truths, distortions of evidentiary facts, and in some cases outright lies.

"There is good reason why none of the forensic or other physical evidence of this crime implicates me. A good reason why, on a perfectly clear day, no one saw me or my car anywhere in the vicinity of Carmin's house. I have never raised my hand in anger against anyone. Not ever. Much less against the woman with whom I created a child. But that point now seems to be moot. A jury has found me guilty beyond a so-called reasonable doubt. And as a result, I have lost or am in the process of losing nearly everything in my life, my freedom, my daughter, my standard, standing in the community, my job and profession, my home and all my possessions.

"Of course, except in the context of your system of justice, the jury's pronouncement of guilty means nothing. People tend to believe, perhaps have a deep-seated need to believe in the infallibility of that system, in infallibility of juries particularly to weigh evidence and render decisions that are good, and right and true. I am reminded just now that as recently as six hundred years ago much of Europe's population, after weighing the evidence, rendered a decision that it too believed was good and right and true, that the Earth was flat. If there is a lesson here, surely it is that perception is indeed a trick, I think.

"Although we had our disagreements and differences of opinion, and although I did not understand the person she eventually became, I quite agree with

anyone who opines that Carmin was singularly wonderful, loving, and generous, with much to live for.
Not least to participate in the raising of our daughter.
Certainly, she was much too young and full of life to
die. And, for whatever it may now be worth, I don't
believe anyone should have to die in the manner in
which she apparently did.

"The responsibility for that death has been neatly
packaged and laid on my doorstep. I do not mean to
be ill-spirited or disrespectful in the least, but I cannot
accept delivery. I cannot and will not assume responsibility for that which I did not do.

"And my final remarks are in the form of a brief
letter. Dated May 6, 2005. Dear Helen: It's been a
long time since I have seen you, so I thought I would
write you a letter. I want you to know that I am okay
and that I love you very much. It makes me sad that
we can't be together right now, and I know it makes
you sad, too.

"Sweetie, it's not my choice for us to be apart, and
I know it's not your choice either. It's just the way
things are. Since I can't be with you I am very glad
you're able to live with people who love you so much.

"Are you having fun in kindergarten? I bet you are.
And I know you will like first grade, too. I am so
proud of you. Do you remember Johanna and Kenny?
Well, Johanna had another baby. It's a boy, too, just
like Andrew. Johanna wrote me a letter and said to
tell you she loves you. I also got a letter from Ray
and Judy in Wisconsin. Do you remember that we
visited them last summer and rode their boat around
the lake and caught fish? Ray still has a big tummy,
and Judy still has pretty hair. They both said to tell
you that they love you, too. The last time I saw you,
you were letting your hair grow long. Have you cut
it yet?

"My hair is longer now than when you last saw it,

but, otherwise, I am pretty much the same. Tall, blue eyes and strong arms. If you want to, you can write me a letter back sometime, but you don't have to. That's your choice. Sweetie, I miss you every day. I miss hugging you and sitting on the couch and reading you books and making you chocolate chip pancakes and hot grain cereal and going to Java for chai and cookies, and all the things we used to do together.

"Even though you can't hear me, I still talk to you a lot, and I always include you in my prayers.

"Thank you so much for being my daughter. I love you to the Moon and back one thousand fifty-three times.

"Love, Daddy."

No one else had anything to say, so Judge Fairchild proceeded immediately to his order.

"Okay," Judge Fairchild began, "for the offense of murder in the first degree, I sentence the defendant to life in prison. He is eligible for parole after twenty-five years in confinement, and he has ten days from today's date in which to appeal any part of the trial which he believes constitutes error.

"Execution of sentence is ordered, and the defendant is remanded to custody."

The proceedings were concluded.

The bailiff called, "All rise."

Judge Fairchild exited.

Then Tom Murray, wearing his red prison jumpsuit, was ordered by guards to stand and put his hands behind his head. He was shackled wrists, waist, and ankles, then shuffled out of the courtroom and away to prison.

Tom Murray had written his statement and read it aloud. He was a careful writer, a linguist near the top of his profession, precise in language and word meanings, and therefore he said *precisely* what he meant to say, no more and no less. He said he never raised his hand in anger (he wasn't angry when he murdered Carmin), he said he was nonplussed (just as Raskolnikov was nonplussed), he did not say he wasn't there when Carmin was murdered, he said he wasn't responsible for her murder (she was responsible for her own death, it be on her head). As he wrote on page 49 in *Surreptitious Recordings*, Tom Murray "believed in abandoning moral rules in favor of following whatever course of action would lead to the best possible consequences"—what he thought would be best for him.

58

By law, Tom Murray's parental rights were terminated.

Helen was adopted by her aunt Heather and her last name legally changed. Judge Fairchild presided at the adoption.

Brad Schlerf won a bet with Doug Woods. Schlerf had bet that he'd win a conviction in his Opal Trumpp case before Woods won a conviction in his Carmin Ross case. Jerry Gavin was sentenced for murdering Opal Trumpp on September 7, 2004, nearly a month before Murray was arrested for murdering Carmin.

In a January 2006 public ceremony, Doug Woods received the applause of local elected officials and of his comrades when he was awarded the Douglas County Criminal Investigation Commendation for his extraordinary work on this case. Doug was promoted to lieutenant.

When the author asked Doug's dad, Jim Woods, what he thought of Doug's work in this case, he answered that he thought Doug showed common sense and he was proud of him. Doug and his dad enjoy watching Doug's son play on the junior high football team. A big fellow like his dad and his grandpa, Doug's son plays in the line.

Judge Fairchild was considered for appointment to

the Kansas Supreme Court, but that went to Judge Johnson. Judge Fairchild may yet be appointed to the high court. Meanwhile, he continues to preside over cases in Douglas County.

Brad Schlerf's primary assignment with investigations is now computer crimes, Internet crimes, and intelligence and forensic work. He does the type of computer detective work that Dean Brown did on the Murray case. At his own expense he went to New Orleans for advanced computer voice stress analysis training.

Angela Wilson handled a number of cases involving children and has toys in her office, including, the author observed, a large Yoda doll from *Star Wars*. Wilson explained that she and her son are *Star Wars* fans and she'd found the *Star Wars* theme useful.

Tom Murray will be eligible for parole in 2029.

That, for a time, was the end of the story.

But most stories, including this one, have an epilogue.

59

In June 2007, two years and a month after he was
sentenced, Tom Murray filed an appeal in the Kansas
Supreme Court. On Thursday morning, September 6,
2007, the justices of the Kansas Supreme Court heard
oral arguments in the case of *Kansas v. Thomas E.
Murray*. The reader can listen to these oral arguments by visiting the Kansas Supreme Court Web
site, kscourts.org, and searching the archived oral arguments.

The room where the oral arguments take place is
large. Its east side has four rows of public seating in
eighty comfortable cushioned chairs. The chair colors
alternate in bright green, purple, blue, and red. By the
time the Murray oral argument began, most of these
chairs were occupied.

The carpet is of blue and alternating light and dark
green colors in a flower-petal swirl pattern. A heavy
blue fabric backing on the walls around the public
area muffles sound. The walls behind and around the
court area consist of seventeen brown wood-grain col-
umned panels. Overhead, twenty-five fluted lights lit
the court area, with thirty-two fluorescent lights over
the public area. The fans blowing the filtered air provide a soft but audible background sound. In the court
area there are tables for the legal adversaries, two

chairs each, no water containers, just brown wooden tables. The blond-wood podium has a digital clock with bright red lights that count down the twenty minutes each side is allowed. The podium has wings for any extra papers or books the advocates might carry.

The west side of the room has the elevated bench where the seven justices preside. An American flag and the flag of the State of Kansas are to the left and right of the bench. The great seal of the State of Kansas, in bronze, is on the center of the west wall.

Tom Murray's attorney, the young Sarah Ellen Johnson, arrived first. She was short, maybe five feet tall, and petite. She wore a dark pantsuit and dark high heels. She wore a lace-embroidered light-colored blouse, very low cut, and much of her sternum was visible, which was in fashion. She had long dark black hair that was curly and appeared crinkled.

Prosecutor Angela Wilson wore a long skirt that went to her ankles, with a long slit in its back. She wore dark flat shoes. She had short dark straight hair. She wore a purple blouse that was buttoned to her neck, revealing nothing, covered with a dark suit top that matched her skirt.

They were professional women, and were polite and proper, but they were also gladiators about to enter legal combat. The American legal system is an adversarial system based on Aristotelian mutually exclusive disjunctive logic, either/or: in each case someone wins and someone loses. It is the system Carmin Ross left in favor of the problem-solving methodology of mediation. It is ironic that justice in her case rests on the system she rejected.

There were other lawyers present for cases to be argued before and after the Murray case. They carried briefcases and briefs in manila folders. Only Angela Wilson was different. She carried a black backpack. It held her papers, a three-ring binder, and her laptop computer.

Before the proceedings began, the clerk of the court, Carol Green, stood to review the rules and procedures. She cautioned the lawyers that if they wished to reserve time for rebuttal, they needed to ask permission at the very beginning of their case. The lawyers were bound to the clock, but the justices were not. The time taken in your case is as long as the court members continue to ask questions, she explained.

Carol Green said that because of media interest, she was mentioning that the earliest the court would reach a decision in any of these cases would be October 26. She could not say that they would have a decision on that date, but that would be the first date they would announce any decisions.

The Murray case had generated the media interest. Present were a true-crime-book author, reporters for six local and regional news media outlets, and a television crew for a pool feed to the television stations.

At the west wall a hidden door opened. A big security guard who wore a western suit stepped up and surveyed the room. He looked like a quarterback surveying the opponent's defense. When satisfied that it appeared safe, he stepped back. The chief justice entered first. She is a strong-looking Kansas woman, no-nonsense, dark hair, seventy-two years old. Then in strode the other six justices, four men and two women, entering in order of seniority, wearing somber dark robes. They alternated directions: when one turned to the left, the next turned to the right. They went to each chair and stood behind it. They then sat in the same order they entered, the chief justice first, then the others, each waiting until the more senior justices were seated before he or she sat. It was choreographed and enhanced the drama.

For a moment it appeared that each person in the room was absorbed in his or her own thoughts and feelings, their own inner struggles with the great and consequential issues about to be addressed.

When the Murray case was called, Sarah Ellen Johnson spoke first. It was her client who brought the appeal. The burden of persuasion was on her. She asked to reserve three minutes for rebuttal and the court granted her request.

She immediately launched into her strongest argument and attacked co-prosecutor Tom Bath's statement in his closing argument that "his best friend thinks he's a murderer." Johnson pointed out that Gay Lynn Crossley-Brubaker never said that she thought Tom Murray was a murderer. She specifically said she could not answer that question. True, Gay Lynn voluntarily contacted the sheriff's department and told them of Tom Murray's apparently incriminating statements ("All I can see is the blood, all the blood"). But to have prosecutor Tom Bath misrepresent this fact in closing argument, she argued, was such a grievous legal error that it rose to the level of depriving a citizen of a fair trial. This court should order a new trial.

Most of the time Ms. Johnson kept her hands solidly on the podium, raising them occasionally to make points.

While Johnson was interacting with the court, Angela Wilson was busy with her laptop, presumably reading the exact transcript of Tom Bath's remarks and the context in which he made them.

When Angela Wilson had her turn, she was a Jedi warrior. Her hands almost never touched the podium. She was waving them about, steepling her fingers, holding her hands as if praying, then moving them left right up down as if casting spells. She spread her hands as if giving blessing to the points she was making so that the court would adopt them. She was varying the cadence and pitch of her voice, using every technique of body language and verbal persuasion available to her. It was a performance.

Mostly, though, she used the facts and the law. She did acknowledge that Tom Bath said "his best friend thinks he's a murderer." That was because Gay Lynn had become suspicious. She went to the sheriff to report her suspicions. When Murray's attorney Pedro Irigonegaray asked Gay Lynn if she thought Tom Murray murdered Carmin, she answered: "I can't answer that yes or no."

The Kansas Supreme Court has overturned a murder case conviction for prosecutorial misconduct in closing argument and that case had to be retried. In that case, the court set standards for overturning convictions because of unconstitutional closing arguments. Angela Wilson argued that this case did not rise to the standard for overturning criminal convictions articulated by this court. The jury understood that arguments are not evidence. Judge Fairchild told them in open court, and they each had their printed copy of the jury instructions.

But then another matter was raised. One point that Sarah Lee Johnson had raised in her legal brief but had not addressed in her oral argument. It was commonly accepted to be one of the weaker arguments, but during Wilson's argument Justice Lee Johnson interrupted and asked if it was proved that Murray's DNA had been found at the crime scene, as was asserted in the closing argument. Justice Johnson appeared to think the evidence was more ambiguous. The expert witness testified that the analysis showed that the blood found was "consistent" with being Murray's blood. It was definitely a human man's blood. It was commingled with Carmin's blood. It was important evidence that could have persuaded a jury.

In the heat of determined legal advocacy Angela Wilson interrupted Justice Johnson and talked over his remarks.

Defense attorneys are fond of pointing out that DNA is statistical. It can logically exclude an individual, but it cannot prove to a logical certainty that the blood matches an individual, only to a high degree of probability.

Wilson asserted that it was a question of interpretation as to whether being "consistent" with Murray's DNA is the same as being identified as Murray's blood. The statement was made in closing argument, not during the evidence introduction. By their demeanors it appeared that Justice Johnson and prosecutor Wilson did not agree on this point. Their give-and-take went beyond Wilson's scheduled time. When it appeared that the justices had concluded asking questions, Wilson asked if there were any more questions. There was silence, so she thanked the justices and sat down.

Sarah Johnson waived her rebuttal. She had reserved three minutes but did not use them. The event was over.

The chief justice declared a ten-minute recess. The justices exited in the order they had entered, the chief justice first, then the associate justices. Then the crowd exited.

60

The Kansas Supreme Court did not rule until late January 2008. They unanimously affirmed Murray's conviction.

Murray began his interview with the police by pretending to be an ally, wanting to help the detectives solve the case, when in truth he was their opponent. He thought he had devised a solid alibi, one that explained, for example, why they would find murder research on his computer. But the brilliant academic was either ignorant of basic commercial storytelling or colossally incompetent at it. Had Murray studied, for example, commercial writing instructor Michael Hauge's famous lectures in *The Hero's 2 Journeys* or *Screenwriting for Hollywood*, and had he then followed Hauge's advice to create even the most elementary draft of a fictional crime story outline, he might have raised reasonable doubt in the mind of a juror. But to this day there is no evidence that Murray had taken any steps to outline or write a commercial crime script for *CSI* or any other crime program. Prosecutor Angela Wilson was correct in her closing argument that "the only *CSI* script Murray had anything to do with was this real one."

Thomas E. Murray, Ph.D., the professional linguist, was supposed to be a world-renowned expert in communication, but he knew only words and was ignorant of the importance of body language in human communication. His words claimed he was innocent; his body shouted that he was guilty.

In the end, on the matters that counted, Murray's opponents were better educated than he was.

In the end, Murray's opponents were smarter than he was.

Now questions have come up as to what Murray will do for the rest of his life in prison. Persons experienced with the Kansas Department of Corrections have said it is possible Murray will be assigned to teach English to other inmates.

On hearing that, one father said, "If a man murders my daughter, I don't think it's punishment to see him sentenced to a life of teaching English."

To express views about Murray's punishment being teaching English, the Kansas governor may be contacted at:

Office of the Governor
Capitol, 300 SW 10th Ave., Ste. 212S
Topeka, KS 66612-1590

Or via the governor's Web site at http://www.governor.ks.gov/contact.htm.

Appendix—Jury Instructions

IN THE DISTRICT COURT OF DOUGLAS COUNTY, KANSAS

Seventh Judicial District

State of Kansas,   Plaintiff,

Vs.   Case No. 04CR1543
                             Div. No. 1

Thomas E. Murray,   Defendant.

INSTRUCTIONS

It is my duty to instruct you in the law that applies to this case, and it is your duty to follow all of the instructions. You must decide the case by applying these instructions to the facts as you find them.

In your fact finding you should consider and weigh everything admitted into evidence. This includes testimony of witnesses, admissions or stipulations of the parties, and any admitted exhibits. You must disregard any testimony or exhibit which I did not admit into evidence.

At times during the trial, I have ruled upon the

admissibility of evidence. You must not concern yourself with the reasons for these rulings. I have not meant to indicate any opinion as to what your verdict should be by any ruling that I have made or anything that I have said or done.

Statements, arguments, and remarks of counsel are intended to help you in understanding the evidence and in applying the law, but they are not evidence. If any statements are made that are not supported by evidence, they should be disregarded.

Your only concern in this case is determining if the defendant is guilty or not guilty. The disposition of the case thereafter is a matter for determination by the court.

INSTRUCTION NO. 1

The State has the burden to prove the defendant is guilty. The defendant is not required to prove he is not guilty. You must presume that he is not guilty unless you are convinced from the evidence that he is guilty.

The test you must use in determining whether the defendant is guilty or not guilty is this: If you have a reasonable doubt as to the truth of any of the claims required to be proved by the State, you must find the defendant not guilty. If you have no reasonable doubt as to the truth of any of the claims required to be proved by the State, you should find the defendant guilty.

INSTRUCTION NO. 2

It is for you to determine the weight and credit to be given the testimony of each witness. You have a right to use common knowledge and experience in regard to the matter about which a witness has testified.

INSTRUCTION NO. 3

In order for the defendant to be guilty of the crimes charged, the State must prove that his conduct was intentional. Intentional means willful and purposeful and not accidental.

Intent or lack of intent is to be determined or inferred from all of the evidence in the case.

INSTRUCTION NO. 4

Ordinarily, a person intends all of the usual consequences of his voluntary acts. This inference may be considered by you along with all the other evidence in this case. You may accept or reject it in determining whether the State has met its burden to prove the required criminal intent of the defendant. This burden never shifts to the defendant.

INSTRUCTION NO. 5

The following facts have been agreed to by the parties and are to be considered by you as true:

1. The shoes collected from the defendant were intact when collected, but the soles were separated from the uppers during processing by the K.B.I.
2. There were no restrictions on the defendant's travel from 11/15/03 to 10/4/04 either within or outside the United States.

INSTRUCTION NO. 5A

You must consider this case without favoritism or sympathy for or against either party. Neither sympathy nor prejudice should influence you.

INSTRUCTION NO. 6

You may not find an element of a crime from an inference that is based solely upon an inference.

However, you may draw reasonable inferences from facts established in the evidence.

INSTRUCTION NO. 7

A finding of guilty for the crime of murder may not be based solely upon evidence of motive. Rather each element of the crime must be proved beyond reasonable doubt.

INSTRUCTION NO. 8

The defendant is charged with the crime of murder in the first degree. The defendant pleads not guilty.

To establish this charge, each of the following claims must be proved:

1. That the defendant intentionally killed Carmin Ross-Murray;
2. That such killing was done with premeditation; and
3. That this act occurred on or about the 13th day of November 2003 in Douglas County, Kansas.

INSTRUCTION NO. 8A

Premeditation means to have thought the matter over beforehand, in other words, to have formed the design or intent to kill before the act. Although there is no specific time period required for premeditation, the concept of premeditation requires more than the instantaneous, intentional act of taking another's life.

INSTRUCTION NO. 9

A defendant in a criminal trial has a constitutional right not to be compelled to testify. You must not draw any inference of guilt from the fact that the defendant did not testify, and you must not consider this fact in arriving at your verdict.

INSTRUCTION NO. 10

When you retire to the jury room you will first select one of your members as presiding juror. The person selected will preside over your deliberations, will speak for the jury in Court, and will sign the verdict upon which you agree.

Your verdict must be founded entirely upon the evidence admitted and the law as given in these instructions.

Your agreement upon a verdict must be unanimous.

[signed] Robert W. Fairchild
Robert W. Fairchild
District Judge, Division One

Acknowledgments

I acknowledge the influence Jon Franklin and his work had on my writing. On August 11–12, 1981, I read Franklin's nonfiction novel *Shocktrauma*. It had such an impact that I know exactly when I read it, in a single session. In 1988, I read Franklin's book *Writing for Story*.

I acknowledge the example that author Gay Talese provided with his April 1966 *Esquire* magazine feature article "Frank Sinatra Has a Cold." When Sinatra was the biggest-name entertainer in the world, Talese was promised an interview. But when Talese arrived at the appointed time and place (a tavern), he was told Sinatra had a cold and would not give the interview. Talese was permitted to stay in the tavern, observe, and interview others. He wrote what he could and the piece was successful. When people broke their promises to give me an interview, or I was denied courtesies and access afforded other writers, I persevered with Talese's example in mind. This was not only a hard case to try; it was a hard book to write.

I learned of Talese's feature through reading Tom Wolfe's *The New Journalism*, a book I acknowledge and recommend.

A big thank-you to my literary agent, Jake Elwell. Jake is now with Harold Ober Associates and was formerly of Wieser & Elwell. Jake kept gently turning away my dozens of book ideas until I came to him with this one. Bravo. Jake knows a good story when he sees it.

And thank you to my editor, Kristen Weber, who saw the potential in this story and stuck with this book through its delays and difficulties. *Ad Astra per Aspera*.

Thank you, Felisa Osburn of Kansas State University's Hale Library.

Thank you, Cheryl Collins of the Riley County Historical Museum.

Thank you, Marolyn Caldwell of the Great Manhattan Mystery Conclave.

Thank you, to psychologist Annette Gnagy Hampton, an expert in human factors analysis, who read and commented on the manuscript.

Patricia Carter, who operates the Wichita chapter of Sisters-in-Crime, a true-crime-readers' book club, and her daughter Sharon Huggins read the book and made key comments and suggestions.

Glen Sharp, former editor of the Wichita State University student newspaper the *Sunflower*, and author with Rip Gooch of *Black Horizons: One Aviator's Experience in the Post-Tuskegee Era*, made valuable comments on the book proposal and book.

I thank Joslyn Dugas for two long interviews at her office; Judge Robert Fairchild for an hour interview in his chambers; court reporter Tammy Hogsett for her transcript; District Attorney Charles Branson for a meeting in his office; and prosecutor Angela Wilson for her phone calls, e-mails, an interview in her office, and an audio recording of her closing argument at trial (wherever I wrote "she shouted" it's because she can be heard *shouting*).

Angela Wilson has left the Douglas County District Attorney's Office. She is now deputy attorney general for the Division of Consumer Protection and Antitrust in the Office of the Kansas Attorney General.

A big thank-you to Lieutenant Doug Woods and his dad, retired Kansas Bureau of Investigation agent Jim Woods, for their help, interviews, and comments.

A great big thank-you to Detective Brad Schlerf of the Riley County Police Department. Brad was kind enough to spend hours with me reviewing the video of Murray's interrogation in interview room #2, discussing body language, and answering many questions. Brad also provided relevant portions of the transcript from Murray's preliminary hearing.

Carlton Smith, a longtime successful crime reporter and best-selling author of dozens of true-crime books, was generous with his advice. Carlton Smith is a gentleman in the best sense of the word and a journalist-author par excellence.

Stephen Singular, also a longtime successful nonfiction author of many valuable books, true crime and other genres, was very kind and supportive.

Author Gregory Allen Howard, who wrote *Remember the Titans*, *Ali*, and *Factor X*, shared several writing "secrets" that he'd learned during his blockbuster career of writing feature films and television series. Thank you, Greg.

Tom Towler, a modest man but a longtime successful author of scripts for television series, including *Police Story*, *JAG*, and made-for-television crime movies, including *The Hunt for the BTK Killer*, was very helpful, supportive, and thoughtful. He read the manuscript and was encouraging. Martie Cook, whose book on writing for television I consulted, was Tom's assistant when they were both at Universal.

I thank author and writing teacher Michael Hauge (*Writing Screenplays That Sell*), mentioned in the body of this book, for his inspiration, good work teaching, and a wry comment that brought me a big laugh when I needed one.

Paul Fecteau's undergraduate faculty advisor and college English teacher was Tom Murray, the killer in this book. Paul, a true-crime writer and author of *Never So Cold: Spectacle and Loss in Wichita's Infamous Butterworth Trial*, was forthright about his experience with Tom Murray and helped to copyedit this book.

While some writers and authors are selfish and combative, paranoid that some other author might seize a perceived advantage (and I had run-ins with several such writers and prospective authors while writing this book), the authors acknowledged here were generous with their support and gallant in their actions. As Stephen Singular said to me, "There's plenty of work to go around and no reason for authors to make things harder for each other."

The closest I have to an older brother is my friend Charles Liles. Charles and his wife, Sherri, provided important feedback on the book proposal and manuscript. Charles is a retired police lieutenant, so admired that he received a medallion from the Wichita Police Department after BTK was captured, and a skeptic. He questions everything. After reading this manuscript he said, "There's no proof he did it, but there's no doubt he did it."

My longtime friend Steven Vincent Reinert, former computer systems manager for the University of Kansas Physics Department and a Lawrence, Kansas, resident, was instrumental in helping me with many things, including obtaining photographs.

For most of his thirty-three-year career in information technology at the University of Kansas, Richard Kershenbaum was manager of information services for academic computing. He is also active in historic preservation in Lawrence and helped with obtaining photos and other information and material for this book.

Carol and Roger Stewart read the proposal and manuscript and made valuable comments. Carol gave me a copy of Lisa Gardner's 2003 fiction crime novel *The Killing Hour*, in which the murderer is a linguist.

Thank you to Brenda Williams, longtime Manhattan, Kansas, resident and Kansas State University graduate (Phi Beta Kappa), who attends football games and participates in the "Wildcat Growl," for providing local color and comments about the place she calls "Manhappiness."

K-State graduate Mark Hughes lives in San Diego, California, but thirty-four years ago we were roommates in the men's dormitory at Hutchinson Community Junior College in Kansas. Mark is a successful author of published literary short stories. More often than not, on Sunday evenings in 2007 we spent a wonderful hour on the phone discussing our writing.

Thank you to retired Wichita police chief Floyd B. Hannon Jr. and retired Wichita Police Department deputy chief Jack Bruce for their insights into police practices.

Paul Joseph Gulino's masterful book *Screenwriting: The Sequence Approach*, which I read in March 2007, opened my eyes to a new way of seeing how stories can be written. Bravo, Paul. Although his book addresses writing screenplays, I recommend it for anyone writing a book-length manuscript that tells a story.

While writing this book I reread Christopher Vogler's *The Writer's Journey*, which I recommend.

Bela Kiralyfalvi was one of my undergraduate college professors at Wichita State University. He assigned me to read Lajos Egri and taught me to write a dramatic stage play.

In my final semester of law school, Professor John Christensen taught my computer law seminar. I've never worked harder writing anything than my paper for that class. I worked so hard on this book that I've had flashbacks to that intense writing experience.

A big thank-you to my wife, Mary Ann Beattie, M.D., for her tolerance and support while I wrote this book.

Thank you to my son, Jacob, who read and commented on the book proposal.

Bruce Cowdrey, my ninth-grade English teacher (1970–71) at Allison Junior High in Wichita, and Katie McGroarty, my tenth-grade English teacher (1971–72) at Wichita High School West, enthusiastically encouraged me to write for publication, which resulted in the *Wichita Beacon* evening newspaper paying me to write a "Teen Talk" column when I was age seventeen (in 1974). Although there have been intervals when I was not published, I've never stopped writing. In stark contrast to the English teacher featured in this book, these two were warm, wonderful, supportive English teachers and their students loved them. This book is dedicated to Bruce Cowdrey and Katie McGroarty, wherever they are.

TRUE CRIME AT ITS BEST

MY LIFE IN THE NYPD
    by James Wagner with Patrick Picciarell

James "Jimmy the Wags" Wagner takes readers behind
the badge and into the daily drama of working New
York City's toughest job in New York City's toughest
precinct. It's the NYPD as no one has ever seen it
before—from a street cop who walked the walk
through the turbulent 1960s, the violent 1970s, and the
drug-fueled 1980s.

FATAL VISION
    by Joe McGinniss

The writer Joe McGinniss went to visit Dr. Jeffery
MacDonald, with the intent of writing a book that
would help clear his name. But after extensive
interviews and painstaking research, a very different
picture emerged. This is the electrifying story of a
Princeton-educated Green Beret convicted of slaying
his wife and children.

"A haunting story told in detail." –*Newsweek*

About the Author

Robert Beattie is the author of the *New York Times* and *USA Today* nonfiction best seller *Nightmare in Wichita: The Hunt for the BTK Strangler.* After Dennis Rader was captured, he told the news media that he resurfaced as BTK out of jealousy of Beattie and his book. The board of the Wichita Retired Police Officer's Association voted Beattie an associate member of their organization and their "2005 Distinguished Associate Member Award." Beattie was awarded the 2005 *Sons of the American Revolution*, Washington Chapter (Kansas), "Law Enforcement Commendation Medal." Robert Beattie became a paid writer in 1974 when he wrote a "Teen Talk" column for *The Wichita Beacon* newspaper. In 1989 his stage play *Fire Escape* won third prize in the International Physicians for Prevention of Nuclear War "Cease Fire" contest. He wrote the feature article "The Best Books of the 20th Century" for the Mensa *BULLETIN* millennium edition. He wrote peer-reviewed papers on emergencies in spacecraft that were published in the *Case for Mars* technical series. Beattie worked as a firefighter-medic for many years and received a commendation for resuscitating a drowned child. He earned degrees with majors in Natural Sciences and Mathematics, Human Resources Management, and Law. He currently serves on the Wichita Airport Advisory Board and is writing a novel. He lives in Wichita, Kansas, with his wife, a pediatrician, and has three children, and four grandchildren.